MVFOL

D1177065

Tender Power

Tender Power

A Revolutionary Approach to Work and Intimacy

Sherry Suib Cohen

Addison-Wesley Publishing Company, Inc.
Reading, Massachusetts • Menlo Park, California • New York
Don Mills, Ontario • Wokingham, England • Amsterdam • Bonn
Sydney • Singapore • Tokyo • Madrid • San Juan

The lines from "Natural Resources" from *The Dream of a Common Language, Poems 1974–1977* by Adrienne Rich, are reprinted by permission of the author and W. W. Norton & Company, Inc. Copyright © 1978 by W.W. Norton & Company, Inc.

Library of Congress Cataloging-in-Publication Data

Cohen, Sherry Suib.
   Tender power.

   1. Women executives. 2. Sex role in the work place. 3. Power (Social sciences) 4. Tenderness (Psychology) I. Title.
   HD6054.3.C64   1989   658.4'094'088042   88–7481
   ISBN 0–201–09242–5

Cover design by Linda Kosarin
Text design by Janis Capone
Set in 10-point Palatino by Neil W. Kelley, Georgetown, MA

ABCDEFGHIJ-MA-898
First printing, December 1988

For Larry, again, always.
Most tender power.

Contents

Acknowledgments

I owe much to the generosity of many women who, with passion, fed me the springs of their passion, their power and their tenderness. In particular, these women have been inspirations:

Cese MacDonald, Lois Nathan, Betsy Nolan, Kathy Lewis, Marjorie Austrian, Rose Scotch, Gloria DiGennaro, Bonnie Ann Black, Eleanor Donnenfeld, Lois Cogen, Trudy Wiener, and Barbara Sunden.

Thanks are also due to:

Patricia A. Gibbons and Meryl Hechtman of the incredible Howard J. Rubenstein Associates Public Relations Firm, who led me to the American Woman's Economic Development Corporation (AWED) and the Committee of 200: many important contacts came from this kindness. Juliet Goldsmith of New York Hospital, Cornell University, Jayne Tear, and Dr. Michael DiGennaro were also very supportive. Special thanks are due to Joanne Krieger, Manager of Public Relations, and Barbara Beasely, Senior Vice President of Marketing of Mary Kay Cosmetics, who read several drafts of the manuscript and offered suggestions for which I am most grateful.

Dick Bartlett, President and Chief Operating Officer of Mary Kay, has been, from the start, a determined defender of the concept of Tender Power.

Perhaps, most of all, the visions, the victories, and the frustrations of those who agreed to be interviewed for this book will stand as testament to the new definition of strength that relies on cooperation and affiliation instead of bullying and isolation: to those who spoke on the record and to those who preferred anonymity, I am profoundly grateful.

To Doe Coover, of the Doe Coover Literary Agency in Medford, Massachusetts, I offer warm appreciation and admiration.

To my own agent, Connie Clausen of Connie Clausen Associates in New York, I give, once again, loving thanks for her impeccable judgment, transcendent talent, irrepressible humor, and majestic faith in me. I cherish her.

To an original thinker, Diane Reverand, Senior Editor, Villard Books/ Random House, I am indebted for the very title—Tender Power.

The finest perks in the world of writing and publishing are the rare people I meet and make part of my life. One of the rarest, most brilliant and sensitive, is my editor at Addison-Wesley Publishing Company, Jane Isay. She has been the moving force behind Tender Power and a dear new friend, putting to rest the old macho myth that the workplace is no place for affectionate, nurturing intimacy.

To Norman Birnbach, Diana Gibney, Laura Noorda, Janis Capone, Debra Hudak, Lori Foley, and Christopher Caldwell of Addison-Wesley and Bonnie Ann Black, my gratitude for the mechanics involved in bringing Tender Power to life.

Finally, my family—Larry, Leah, Adam, Jennifer, my son-in-law Steve who is ever vigilant with the spotting of research possibilities, my mother Jane who is my mentor, and my father David who is my ally—is the heart of my work and my vigor.

Prologue

Thus far women have been the mere echoes of men. Our laws and constitutions, our creeds and codes, and the customs of social life are all of masculine origin.

The true woman is as yet a dream of the future.

Elizabeth Cady Stanton, at the age of 72,
speaking to the International Council of Women, 1888

And so we leave home, we leave the apron and . . . put on . . . tailored executive suits. . . . And now we take ourselves in hand, tailoring ourselves to the specifications of this world we are so eager to enter. We strip our bodies of flesh, our hearts of the overflow of feeling, our language of exuberant and dramatic imprecisions. We cut back the flight of our fancy, make our thoughts rigorous and subject it (this marvelous rushing intuitive leaping capacity of ours) to measures of demonstration and proof, trying not to talk with our hands, trying hard to subdue our voices, getting our bursts of laughter under control.

Kim Chernin, *The Hungry Self*

Two women, one yearning for power, the other for tender; separated by a century but connecting with the same thought: Women, echoing men, cannot speak in whole, authentic voices.

We *will* have our power and we *will* have our tender, but until we have both, the true woman is indeed a dream of the future.

It is the instinctive knowledge of warmth, empathy, nurture, connection to others, intuition, and cooperation that has been women's special strength throughout the ages. These are the tender traits.

It is the intellectual and economic freedom, the clout to lead, make money, make decisions, say no, say yes, change the world, rouse the government that have been women's proud attainments throughout the last two decades. These are the power moves.

Together they are glorious.

As women entered the marketplace, its turbulence and jagged edges wore down the tender traits until women's power was rechanneled as a rough, tough thing. And, although women succeeded to a great extent, many harbored secret doubts about how good the new, cold power really felt. Many began to share their secrets, in the old connecting ways, and spoke of exhaustion, frustrations, and the growing knowledge that a dog-eat-dog business life and a harried, self-sacrificing personal life was very far from the dream they dreamed. Intimacy was out and armor was in.

Still, who would give up the foothold onto the marketplace and economic independence? Who could even afford to give up the gains? Not one.

So many of us begin to ask—is there another way? Can we succeed in business on our terms? Can the male turf be turned into a more humanistic turf? Maybe, just maybe.

Can both men and women reshape a male-designed marketplace so that nurturing is allowed to fuse with advancement and empowering others becomes an alternative to power over people? Maybe.

Working as allies, can men and women learn how to inject caring values into harried homes and unfeeling workplaces? Can we more equally share the responsibilities for family? Can we, in short, tag tender onto power? Just maybe.

If we succeed, we'll be at the cusp of an historical revolution. If we succeed we will reinvent ourselves.

If we fail, the shattering and dangerous growth of cutthroat competitive practices and stand-alone self-massage will throttle American spirit, American progress, and the American sense of fun.

Tender Power is a celebration of Elizabeth Cady Stanton's "true woman" who is not a dream of the future, but a presence of now. *Tender Power* is a reformation for men, for women, and for children who will not settle for tender or power but want both.

1

Borrowed Voices

She stands before one-hundred-seventy-nine aggressive male colleagues, the only woman in the bunch. Because she's sold more than any of them, she has won the right to address the convention.

She's very excited. They're somewhat less than excited.

This is her dilemma: Unbelievably, she has two separate speeches prepared. Until this moment she does not know which one she'll offer to her expectant colleagues.

One of them is the usual locker-room macho filled with "when the going gets tough, tough guys get going" bromides. It is designed to assert control, establish her credentials as one of the guys, show everyone the guts, the spunk, the dauntless nerve that got her where she is. It has humor and it will inspire, much in the manner of the fabled locker-room coach. It is the speech every man in the audience anticipates. It is the speech most would present.

It is the speech that gives her moxie.

The other speech gives her away. It discloses her sometimes anxieties. It reveals how many times she was desperate to confide in someone but didn't for fear of being thought weak. It exposes her disgust with the dog-eat-dog competition, the lack of cooperation that sometimes made her furious. It divulges her worry that the fast track doesn't often make room for the human need to play with family and friends. The other speech gives the spotlight to those few who nurtured and empowered her. The other speech is designed to explore another way. The other speech makes her vulnerable. It also has wit and panache but she knows it will be judged a "woman's" speech.

Like the man who had to choose between the lady and the tiger, she makes her difficult choice. She grins and starts to talk.

The Feminist Mystique

Throughout history, feminists have fought for equal status with men. The newest wave of feminists, inspired a quarter of a century ago by Betty Friedan's ground-breaking book, taught us to discredit the so-called Feminine Mystique that for years had so insidiously suggested that women deserved less than men. Now it appears that for many there is a *"Feminist Mystique,"* one that presents its own set of problems when it suggests that, to be powerful, we must act, talk, and do like men. More and more of us are dismayed that qualities of caring, nurturing, and commitment to the welfare of others are being sacrificed in the name of progress.

As women first began to knock on the CEO office door with an eye to occupation, other women began to cheer. And as they laid claim to his chair, his pinstriped suit and his foulard tie, his bluffness of manner, his insulation, his dollars, and his status, we continued to cheer. Never mind if many of us, while reveling in the gains and the power, suffered a vague sense of discontent. It was as if we were part of a masquerade. We were not wholly ourselves. The power and the glory were a firm fit, all right. It was the male manner that hung awkwardly.

But never mind. We'd manage. We'd deal with that when we had time. We had big fish to fry and we couldn't lose the momentum.

It's time to make time. It's time to reclaim our different voices.

It's an irony. As we thrive in the workplace, our sense of satisfaction which should be soaring, is waning. Too many women are saying, writing, thinking that there's something missing. These women, our daughters, our friends, our sisters are impossible to ignore.

On our way to power in the marketplace, in our brave and womanly march to equality, women seem to have stomped on *tender*. As a direct result, many of us have begun to display, then be uncomfortable with, new male stereotypical behavior. We're trying to do it all, have it all at once, and by following men's rules. By negating the parts of ourselves that are special and feminine in the truest sense of femininity, we throw away our tools as we cling to the toolbox.

It is understandable that we stomped on tender for a while. In climbing the ladder to power, it was necessary to demand, pull rank, insist, act like tough guys, and on occasion be very, very loud. In general, to act pretty much like men. Every liberating movement needs its macho manners; stridency, megaphones, and tough-guy talk become de rigueur. Selfishness and commando tactics are not unheard of. As the old joke goes, you have to bop each donkey over the head before you can teach it to dance. "First," explains the trainer, "you have to get their attention."

Having gotten men's attention, many of us are beginning to question the heavy price we pay. We are paying for victories that are not yet even won. We are taking on the very characteristics we condemn in men, and we see our best women friends acting like men we would never date today, let alone marry. We have called the men who would keep us out of the marketplace combative, selfish, spoiled, hard-nosed, unhearing, unsharing, controlling—and we try to ape them. Early feminists told us to reject domineering, vengefully competitive attitudes. Today we are under pressure, not to reject, but to adopt these traits commonly associated with male behavior.

But, say some powerful feminists, tenderness is a human and not an exclusively female trait. I believe that. But, I also believe that although women don't own warmth, cooperation, gentleness, and empowering of others, it has been women who have most eloquently expressed these traits. Perhaps women, oppressed by society for so long, discovered that tenderness was all there was for them.

Carol Gilligan, Harvard social psychologist and author of the groundbreaking work *In a Different Voice*, says that women have known from the beginning about intimacy, nurturing, and the power of relationships because they were expected to know these things. Their different concepts of morality and self-esteem come largely from teachers past and present. These teachers are responsible for planting the roots of tenderness. The first teachers in the first years are traditionally mothers. Because, say many experts, females tend to identify more strongly with children of their own sex, it is predominately the little girls who get the benefit and the lesson of empathy, one deep-growing root of tenderness.

Little girls in this Freudian society are not asked to separate from their mothers in the same way that little boys are; therefore, an appreciation of connection is more intensely instilled in girls than in boys. Connection then is surely another deeply planted tenderness root.

As boys and girls grow, they learn different modes of game playing from male and female role models. Studies have shown that little boys tend to play competitive team-type games, far more than little girls. Furthermore, they learn from role models to compete with friends and play with enemies in ways that preordain the model for corporate success. Little girls, on the other hand, tend to veer toward turn-taking games like hopscotch and jump rope, rather than toward competitive sports like football and basketball. Thus, turn-taking, a more cooperative way to play (as opposed to cutthroat competition), is demonstrated most readily by girls.

Even fairy tales are subtle teachers. Little girls learn that the kindness and caring of Snow White and Cinderella win the day, while little boys identify with the princes who conquer the world by destroying the enemy. The folklore teaches girls to be passive and servile, and much has been written about how insidious and destructive this message is. Nonetheless, there is also the message that tenderness in woman is romantic and good, and this has always been clear in the emerging female consciousness. The helping professions, nursing and teaching, have traditionally been practiced by women, thus planting the tender root of empowering others at yet another stage of life.

To complete the cycle, as little girls and boys grow up to become parents it is the little-girls-turned-women who pass on the fruit of the tender roots of connectedness and caring to their female offspring far more passionately than they pass them on to male children. There are thus many reasons why women got very good at the adoption and expression of tenderness—got better at it than their brothers.

To say it never happened, that women are no better at connection, empowering, and nurturing than men, is like saying the emperor has new clothes, when in fact he is naked.

All women don't express their femininity in affiliating ways, but more do than do not. More women are drawn to nurturing than are not. More women allow themselves to disclose secrets and show vulnerability than do not. More women practice cooperation than do not.

Make no mistake. Those women who are not enamored of the tender arts aren't aberrations or even unfeminine; they are simply practicing their own, unique brand of femininity. Still, they number fewer than those who have become skilled at empathy and emotional expressiveness—qualities identified with feminine culture.

When the world changed, women began to look hard at the intriguing possibilities economic power held for them. Instead of buttering up their husbands for higher household allowances, why couldn't they begin to bring home the bread themselves? Why indeed? There was only one problem. To others, and even to themselves, their voices seemed too low and gentle to command the proper authority.

In order to finally seize a fair share of power in a male-dominated business world, many women have felt impelled to speak in borrowed voices. Many of us have smothered cooperation as we adopted the male mode of competition. The tough talk, the sacrifice of nurture, the business suit and tie, the looking out for Number One, have become a way of life. Tenderness has been trivialized, shunted off, regarded as disempowering.

The result? Many women today feel devalued, devoiced, and deprived, because they feel they must operate only with power and little tenderness. The male wardrobe is a poor fit, and it makes us feel ungainly, awkward—*inauthentic.*

When was the last time you looked, really looked, at the new career strategy books for women? They urge guerilla warfare, battleground strategies, killer techniques. In her 1987 book *Women vs. Women: The Uncivil Business War*, Tara Roth Madden holds that women are doing each other in in the marketplace. While the seventies were distinguished, says Madden, by a period of feminine networking and making connections, a "let's-pull-together" ethic, today is marked by a cutthroat mentality. Women on the top rung reach out to grab whatever they need to stay in place, often oblivious of the women on the lower rungs of the corporate ladder. Many in low-level positions are jealous and angry as they see their sisters leaving them far behind without so much as a backward glance. Middle-level women, trying to maintain new authority and life-styles, trust no one and empower few. Generational clashes between young hopefuls and older achieving women are sending the young ones to analysts and the older ones to plastic surgeons. Competition is the new watchword. Because of limited room at the top, the new macho woman is forgetting her networking and cooperative skills. Instead she pushes her way to the head of the line, leaving a wake of casualties.

It isn't just in their careers that women have lost sight of tender and are regretting it. When was the last time you took a look at mothering? I don't mean the apple pie-baking mom who still exists, maybe, in Menasha, Wisconsin; that mom who had all the time in the world to teach her sons about courage and her daughters about morals. I mean today's mom who is torn between work and home and who is always nervous about one place when she's in the other. That kind of mother has a whole lot going for her, but what she generally doesn't have is the absolute certainty that she's doing the right thing by her kids. That kind of mother labors under too much stress and uncertainty and a passion to be wonderful at everything. I don't believe there's a working mother on the face of the earth who doesn't feel some guilt as she raises her children. We know this, and we share our *angst*. It makes us feel better but it doesn't make it go away.

Few working mothers have enough time not only for their families but also for reaffirming their values. They strive for the strength to cope with multiple roles and the blurring of moral boundaries that seem to accompany their fast-paced world. One young mother I know in Chicago who is a highly intelligent and moral woman told me that she would pull any string, break any rule, lie any lie, just to get her daughter into the nursery school of her choice. She was embarrassed to confess it, and she hated herself for such machinations, but since that child was to be alone so much, she had to be in a wonderful place.

I listened, no stranger to her discomfort. Many of my friends, in the wake of the women's movement, taught their kids to be cute and clever and to have a trenchant, biting wit even at age seven, just so they could get into the best class and have the best teacher. All through school they taught them less about working and playing well with others and more about achieving, more about being president of the class. Watch Jane run. Watch Jane *push*. Watch Jane teach Jennifer to decimate Jimmy in the blocks corner—and, incidentally, to stay away from the doll corner.

I know whereof I speak. I spent many years being Jane, shoving my own Jennifer. I loved Jennifer and I hugged her a lot. But I also taught her killing combat play, instead of tenderness and cooperation. My friends were doing the same with their kids, and I wanted her to have and to be everything.

I stopped, finally, when my daughter, wiser and truer to her essential self, said *no more*. At least I knew enough to take her seriously. For her, rebellion was self-preservation. At the time I thought her "ungrateful"; now I am grateful for her affirmation of a gentler self.

Make no mistake, I celebrate the women's movement. It freed me, along with thousands of other women caught in the trap of society's expectations. It was the women's movement that taught me that I didn't have to limit my life to mothering and teaching if I heard the call to something else. I could be the corporation head, the senator, even, my dream of dreams, the writer. I could do it all.

In a way, that was true. But, in other significant ways, it was not true at all. The women's movement, exquisite as it is, doesn't yet speak for every woman. There are many who feel confused and strained.

Reclaiming Tenderness

I have listened hard to the muted voices of my generation, my daughter's generation, and the very newest generation. Many express a yearning for a new philosophy and approach to business and personal life for both men and women, one that would allow us to use the traits traditionally associated with women without giving up any of the hard-won victories. The voices do not dishonor the pioneers who first fought the battle for woman power; it's not difficult to understand why the first generation of businesswomen had to adopt inflexible male stances. But now, with far more than a foot in the door, it's time to reemphasize our human birthright to cooperation, sensitivity, and empowering of others.

Women and men alike stand to gain if businesspeople and businesses adopt a tender strategy. Practically speaking, to infuse humanistic values in business increases the profit margin. Customers who are emphathized with, listened to, and connected with are more loyal customers.

The traits that bring internal strength to both managerial and worker levels are also a matter of simple, caring gestures. Respect for individual quirks, attention paid to friends on the job, nurturing of psyches, and a general lightening of the business morale make people want to achieve, make them want to stay connected to the corporation. A boss who massages her workers' egos by sending notes of commendation for jobs well done, a co-worker who offers to take a Saturday shift because he knows how important it is for his pal to cheer on the Los Angeles Lakers make for long-appreciated memories.

The art of parenting also needs an infusion of practical tenderness. In recent years parenting has undergone some profound changes. A generation of working mothers felt that self-esteem and professional success were joined at the hip. Today, the family priorities that were reordered are being reordered once again—to accommodate the growing legions of men and women who say they are merely visitors in their children's lives and they simply need more time for their families. This "homecoming" movement is a sure trend, says Faith Popcorn, chairman of Brainreserve, a New York concern specializing in trends. It is both a power and a tender choice for those who adamantly refuse to choose between work and family and instead want both. Homecoming, says Popcorn, is not antifeminist, "it's a way of living life to the fullest. It's a move that protects their marriages. It gives a couple time to strategize, time to get things done and time for sex."

Even the state of the nation demands we reclaim power from machismo operation. With the rights of children and mothers ignored in so many workplaces, with political processes and candidates in serious moral disarray, with child and wife abuse proliferating, and with health and educational systems suffering from corrosion, it's high time for women to infuse the male ethos with tenderness.

The voices who lately yearn for such a new approach don't speak to make it easier for society to swallow the idea of competent and powerful women. Women don't ask for a more sensitive approach as an apology for advancement or as a massage for slighted male egos. Women yearn to express authentic feelings of tenderness because they know it's the only hope for a world bogged down in a posturing angry stance. We yearn to teach those men who don't yet know about the kind of relief that comes with dropping macho manners. We yearn to add empower to power in the vocabulary of the next decade. We yearn to create a more caring partnership society with our men because we know that if we continue to try to "do it all" our own feminist revolution is doomed.

We live in an increasingly splendid world of opportunities for women, but more and more of us are becoming sensitive to prejudice against connectedness, nurturing, and compassion. When we tentatively express concern for others, it's misunderstood as weakness. When we let up on the battle for the tough-guy image, we are censured by many of our own sisters. When we try to bring eons of feminine tradition into the male bastions, we're cut off, or put down. When we ask that men share our tenderness, they either ignore it or express it clumsily. Some male atavistic memory decrees that tenderness weakens power bases; except for the wisest, tenderness is devalued by too many businessmen.

The most direct way to infuse these tender values into a workplace—and thus increase its capacity for power—is to recognize that there are differences between the way that most men and women do things. Dr. Carol Gilligan calls for "a recognition of the differences in women's experiences and understanding." It is these differences, large and small, that are so apparent to anyone who cares to see beyond dogma.

Dr. Jean Baker Miller, author of *Towards a New Psychology of Women*, sees the differences.

Women have a greater and more refined ability to "encompass others' needs," she says. They can recognize others' needs and respond to them without feeling a diminution of identity. This is a tool of great power. (The only trouble comes, says Dr. Miller, when women are forced to serve others' needs or are expected to do so.)

Women, says the famed researcher, seem to better understand the nature of cooperation. They participate in the "lesser task," she says sardonically, of helping other humans to develop while men do the "important" work. They are also more well skilled than men in emotional relatedness. These are all tools of great power if used in the pursuit of business.

In fact, says Dr. Miller, "An abundance of women's psychological strengths exist but cannot flourish or come forward fully in a world that sorely needs precisely these kinds of strengths."

Unless we invite them to come forward. Unless we cherish them. Unless men and women who argue for tender business practices are the most accomplished managers and workers in the corporation.

It is, in short, the tender differences in women that, valued by women and adopted by men, can change the course of presently dehumanized business and social policies.

The studies get reported, the experts agree and dissent, and all the while, Tender Power—the most extraordinary force—lies there for the taking.

Tender Power

What is Tender Power and why is it different from plain old power?

Plain old power, the way it is usually practiced in the traditionally male-dominated environment, is the stuff of old boyism.

- *It's directive.* "Do this—I don't really care about your problems at home . . ."

- *It's self-advancement at all costs.* "C'mon—it's a dog-eat-dog world and bleeding hearts don't get to be CEOs."

- *It's keeping space between you and others, not connecting.* "Let them get too close, let them know what makes you hurt, and you're dead."

- *It's always valuing the bottom line over caring.* "I don't care what the compassionate thing to do is—I care about the *cost effective* thing to do."

- *It's always about facts—never feelings.* "Give me rational argument—don't bother me with intuition!"

Tender Power, on the other hand, is a quite revolutionary approach to potency, equally available to men and women who don't fear trying something different. To understand it, look at the way thirty very different men and women have individually defined the words *tender* and *power*. These are some of the meanings given *tender*:

vulnerable	loving	passionate
soft	gentle	generous
empathic	considerate	kind
sensitive	merciful	

These are some of the meanings given for *power*:

vigor	ability to influence
potency	ability to lead
strength	muscle
pressure	force
energy	brawn

At first glance, the definitions for tender and those for power look like diametric opposites. Look closer. In combination, most of them are wonderfully sensible.

Loving Potency or Sensitive Strength or Generous Brawn or Empathic Leadership . . .

This then, is what Tender Power is all about:

It's about a brand new definition of power and strength, one that relies on cooperation instead of bullying or impersonal directives.

It's about the *heart* of government—a government that gives value to its youngest, its oldest, and its poorest citizens.

It's about partnerships. The war of the sexes is neither celestially nor biologically ordained. Instead of the old "Me Tarzan, You Jane" model, men and women can learn to develop hands-on and equal responsibility for home, family, and work. The new heroes and heroines of our society want to be committed to work and home, but not enslaved by either. They understand people are not automatons, able to cut off one part of themselves as they concentrate on another.

It's about empowering others, about a generosity of spirit that passes knowledge on down to those on the lower rungs of the ladder.

It's about empathy, the human ability to put one's self in another's shoes and so much identify with that person as to truly understand her feelings.

Tender Power is about a softer silhouette for women who feel less than themselves in hard and arrogant postures.

Tender Power is about not blaming yourself for the failure of love or the problems of others; it is about taking control of your life, and rejoicing in positive differences.

Tender Power is about true choice. It's about respecting an individual pull to nurture, to career, or both. Tender Power never stands in judgment about what is worthy enough for another to cherish.

Tender Power is about personal growth, not "Superwoman" goals. Superwoman was never a woman's invention—only a comic lady.

It's about appreciating mothers and not blaming them for everything. The overrated Freudian theory of the evils of momism ring false as a generation of children raised in single-parent households learn the hard way how heroic a mom can be.

Finally, Tender Power is about *not* imitating men. Tender Power doesn't drag race or even peel rubber. It doesn't only come in suits and swagger. It doesn't limit locker room talk to hostile takeovers. It encourages sharing, disclosure of pain as well as joy, and, when appropriate, conversations about babies, health, Kafka, and percentage points. Tender Power is doing it not the male, but the most human way. Tender Power is ancient female wisdom.

A Revolutionary Act

Too much of a good thing, of course, can be crippling, and it is this that gets feminists nervous when we talk about feminine traits. One writer, Carol Becker, referred to women's need for connection as "the tyranny of niceness." Her thesis is that because women became such superb caretakers, because they learned to intuit others' needs before they were even expressed, others tended to take advantage of such perception, expecting women to perpetually fulfill their needs. From such tyranny, oppression was born. No one denies that.

Still, women's capacity to respond to unspoken needs is a magical trait. Why in the world should we disclaim it? Why, instead, don't we help to train others to be more sensitive?

It is this training to which poet Adrienne Rich refers in her wonderful lines:

> *A woman turns a doorknob, but so slowly*
> *so quietly, that no one wakes*
>
> *and it is she alone who gazes*
> *into the dark of bedrooms, ascertains*
>
> *how they sleep, who needs her touch*
> *what window blows the ice of February*
>
> *into the room and who must be protected:*
> *It is only she who sees; who was trained to see.*

If indeed the tender traits can be taught to all, it is essential that we celebrate them loudly, insistently, joyfully. We must really tell our families, our men, our government that power combined with tenderness accentuates the power. It doesn't diminish it.

But first we must tell ourselves that if connectedness, nurturing, kindness, and helping others is the fuel that makes our wheels turn, we must claim the right to display these tender traits in business as well as at home. Because we have been concentrating so hard on getting the power, keeping the tender is turning out to be nothing less than a revolutionary act.

Achieving women now must begin to convince other achieving women to forego obvious masculine behavior. An historical voice tells us to respond to decency and tactics *not* formed on battlefields with battlefield mentality. We can enter any fray; better though to turn frays into mutual attainments, to form partnerships with men instead of playing the old adversarial games. The only way to do it is to act, dress, and work in ways most comfortable to us. The majority of us, women and men, would rather talk than fight. The fight may have been necessary in the beginning of the liberation movement (as many of us believe it was), but now it's time to achieve by our own rules and standards.

We mustn't blame ourselves for feeling confused. In many ways, we send ourselves double messages every day. Self-help books proclaim that we must stay warm, receptive, and sensually alive, yet we must attack in the male mode. High-profile personalities inform us that macho is passé, while high-profile career dress shops tell us that we've got to don that corporate uniform.

Just when we thought it would be safe to emerge in the workplace with clenched fists and clutched briefcases, the pundits tell us the divorce rate is booming because women are not spending enough time with their mates. They have always placed the blame on women's shoulders. This time we will not accept that blame. The guilt belongs to a macho-mannered society, not to us.

If, in the beginning, we felt impelled to shunt aside our mates, homes, and feelings of compassion and responsibility for others, we need no longer do so. These are not just facile words. In the pages that follow, you will see how powerful women feel about reasserting their unique voices.

If you are a woman, indeed if you are a man, who is tired of combat strategies, tired of cutthroat economics, tired of seizing power at the expense of someone else, tired of priming three-year-old Johnnie to grab the competitive edge in his nursery school interview, tired of being blamed for the failure of relationships, a better way is possible.

But how did we misplace tender?

Misplacing Tender

When the Feminine Mystique was born, a new generation of women warriors determined to prove themselves independent and strong rose from the ashes of the home hearth. In droves, women entered the workplace and the political arena, first in a trickle, then in a stream. They knew in their heart of hearts they could be as powerful as men, but they had to prove it. They started out by trying to look, talk, and act like their sons, brothers, and fathers. It seemed to have some effect. There came a veneer of hardness and vengefulness, even murder in the eyes of women who wanted to be the corporate whip, not the corporate wife.

It worked. Traditional wives and mothers gave way to the hordes of women who sought to win, then wave, the power wand. In reassuring numbers, women became doctors, lawyers, politicians, judges, editors, executives, heads of state, even policemen—or rather, policepeople. To the surprise of no woman, they were great at their work.

Whether from excited choice or from reluctant necessity, more and more women began to work outside the home, until, in 1987, a full sixty-two percent of all women were employed. Experts predict that by 1995 only about one in seven women younger than age forty-five will be a full-time homemaker. In 1988, the New York Stock Exchange reported that fifty-seven percent of all their new investors were women. Women were buying four out of ten new cars. Twenty-five percent of the people in medical schools and a third of the law students were women. The number of female managers has doubled since 1972! Suicide rates in the female population were down by more than half from the rates in the seventies. Power was paying off. Who needed Tender?

Out came the management experts, the adult education specialists, the business writers, all determined to teach women how to succeed even more brilliantly in the male marketplace. Beat them at their own game was the message. Act tougher than tough, tougher even than those men. Swallow tenderness. Lean and mean. Baby, you've come a long way.

We're no dummies; we women learned the new lessons very well. Women on fast-track career patterns naturally began to suffer the same stresses that afflicted their men in high places. Ulcers, headaches, nerves, high divorce rates became increasingly familiar. We even invented a few stress-related complaints of our own, like endometriosis. It was exhilarating, it was enticing, and many families' money problems were lessened; still, the toll on women who were doing things the male way became increasingly heavy.

What we didn't bargain for was the double dose of stress we were getting —double that of men's stress. Not only were we dealing with life's problems in the same rarified atmosphere of men with the same problems, we were denying an essential part of the values with which we were raised, just to fit in the new world. Men at least were trained in cutthroat competition. We weren't. Anything that read cooperation, bonding, nurturing, or self-disclosure we were taught to disdain. They took away our tools. With one hand tied behind our backs, it's a miracle that we did so well. Imagine how well we could have done if we marched into the marketplace with our new skills *and* the powerful human technology we already owned, intact.

To reach for male power, we thought we had to become men. It's no wonder our stomachs began hurting.

It's only a matter of time till you grow the emotional calluses you need, they reassured us. Harden your hearts. Don't allow for vulnerability. Woman is tough. We proved that. But woman is also tender. That part, we forgot.

The emotional calluses grow. They feel unnatural.

A Better Vision

What we've gotten is good—but it's not enough, because we had to give up too much for the getting.

Reports filtering down from the mental health field tell us that women seem fearful of losing their identities in a workplace that is more dehumanized than human. Many young women, once resentful of losing careers to wife and motherhood, now greatly resent losing wife and motherhood to the workplace. The "helpless" woman is now but a crisp neutered version of herself, who inside still feels panic as each new statistic tells her again and again that she may really have to do without family if she chooses the fast track. She always knew she was never really helpless, but she becomes increasingly frustrated by the sterility of each new option being offered to her.

Men are not untouched by women's turmoil. It shows up across the kitchen table and in the bedroom. The self-help manuals have taught women, quite rightfully, how to claim responsibility for their own sexual pleasure or lack of it; what they haven't taught quite so well is the expression of tenderness in the midst of all this seizure of control. Men and women, lately conditioned to believe that the sole difference between them is anatomical, learn to relate in only physical ways—the result is a stupendous failure of communication.

Looking out for Number One, accepting responsibility for one's own pleasure and economic success, has its virtues. Many researchers feel however that the "me generation" is so absorbed in itself that it has little time for others, even at the breakfast table. Tender takes time, and it appears that individuals lose the thread of connection when they're too busy to find time to communicate. Relationships lose clout.

Society also loses when tender disappears. Anthropologists have found indisputable evidence—in the form of unearthed Neolithic statues and stories carved in stone—of more peaceful times when men and women worked together in easy equal partnership. These people, our ancestors, harvested their crops, hunted their bison, and told stories around the hearth. Consideration and cooperation reigned. The unearthed art was stunning in what it did *not* show—and it did not show any evidence of cruelty or violence-based power. No rape, no rampages, no cutthroat competition.

So what happened? When Western civilization, male-dominant and distinctly nontender, became the norm, war, competitive undercutting, ulcers, high divorce rates, and that cutthroat competition also became the norm. Patience and relatedness flew out the window, and without tender, power didn't even seem to have true authority.

Now, it's now. Our mentors, our religious leaders, our feminist sisters, even our bosses, teach us to be assertive when we see wrong and seek right. Many of us feel just plain uncomfortable in a world that seems to stress narcissism and doesn't cherish connectedness.

We look for new answers, assertively.

The answers don't seem to lie in the spate of self-help books all called *Women Who Love Too Much Who Leave Men Who Are Peter Pans* and versions thereof; nor do they lie in business manuals for women called *Guerilla Warfare*—and versions thereof.

Where *are* the answers?

Try this:

There's a better vision. It calls for tenderizing. It bestows a new strength to both men and women.

Dimples of Steel

I think of Diane, an extraordinarily successful businesswoman. She's a compassionate, caring boss to her employees, a wonderful human being. What's more, she has dimples—soft, endearing dimples that warm her smile.

"Dimples of steel," says one business associate who has dealt with her fair but hard-line business practices. "Watch out for those dimples of steel."

Diane is well loved in business. Her associates would die for her. She never forgets a condolence card, a thank-you note, a warm touch that expresses her desire to connect with those who work for her. She stresses cooperation, not individual competitive battles. Yet she is absolutely firm and persuasive in her business dealings. She's earned the respect of her competitors. She's knowledgeable. She is as powerful as anyone I know.

Dimples of steel. Tender Power.

If women can reclaim warmth and womanliness, they can better share these things with men. They can renounce being honorary men to be honored women. The new vision calls for a more tender workplace, a new method of managing, a more sensitive health and child care system, and a sounder family structure. Past divisiveness between the sexes can be written off. A society that recognizes and respects differences while emphasizing human similarities can be reconstructed. This is *not* an impossible goal.

Not only is it a possible goal, it is a logical goal as well. Change is in the air, and important demographic trends point to the resurgence of a more connecting family life. Even romance and courtship are coming back into favor. The businesses that will fare best, say experts, are those that are patterned after the widely successful Japanese model where loyalty, familylike closeness, and the empowering of others spur the bottom dollar. "A new traditionalism centered on family life is in the offing," said the *New York Times* in late 1988. "Those businesses that prepare themselves for this will fare the best in the 1990s and beyond."

We listen. We listen to the voices all around.

As I began to research *Tender Power* I sought out real women whose powerful voices would describe to me in words their tender needs.

2

Powerful Voices, Tender Needs

I'm not a social scientist, or even a licensed poll taker; thus there are no scientific absolutes in *Tender Power*. I cannot measure, nor even come close to measuring, the uneasy feeling in many women that has come along with the extraordinary gains of the decade. Even if I knew how, to measure it would be difficult, because it is such a very quiet groundswell; this need to reclaim an authenticity of voice born of women's unique experience is only just beginning.

If I am not a scientist, I am a terrific listener, kind of an unofficial observer of trends. From years of journalistic digging, I can spot a trend when it's there, and, make no mistake, it's there. Women are recognizing the differences in their experiences and acknowledging their great human value.

As I conducted my interviews, I was stunned by the numbers of women in high and modest life positions who needed to talk, who passionately wanted to be heard. On all sorts of tracks, fast, slow, and muddied, women paused with eagerness to share ideas and to say yes, yes, yes, I *have* felt that! Often they would pause for sometimes very disquieting moments—to question a power structure that makes them indistinguishable from men; a power structure that has them acting and speaking in uncomfortable macho stereotypes. Here were women comfortable with power and success, but uncomfortable with the rules and behavior they had to accept.

It was, in fact, quite something to listen to these women who had begun to realize that they can add to and humanize today's personal and financial culture, adding a powerfully feminine dimension to the segregated male society of the past.

I wanted to set the stage for *Tender Power* with the living voices of women who feel less than themselves because they missed expressing the values and traits of their woman-heritage. I also wanted to share the living voices of women who are doubly successful because they cherish and display the tender aspects of feminine culture along with new gains of power. To that end I decided to conduct a focus group—an informal one, I grant you—but enough like those used by advertising and market research firms to pinpoint the problems and successes of various products. In those focus groups people sit around and talk about why they like a certain product and why they don't—how it disappoints, and why it works. They try to be specific about how it makes their lives better or worse. They focus in on a given situation.

For our focus group I was after women's opinions (both good and bad) about how power and tender operated in their lives. It wasn't as scientific an expression as real focus groups can be; in fact, it felt a good deal like the old encounter groups that were so satisfying and popular at the inception of the women's movement. They worked because they used a technique that had been women's for centuries—sharing. Whether you call it a coffee klatch, networking, or a focus group, when people are honest about fears, failures, and strengths, good is sustained by all in the connecting.

These, then, are some of the thoughts of the women who came to my living room one blustery autumn evening; women who were strangers to each other, but who were prepared to talk about Tender Power—or the lack of it—in their business and personal lives.

Marjorie is my oldest friend from college. We were both good girls and listened to our mothers. Marjorie studied for a "safe" career in speech therapy, got married, and had children, following the family script that was written for her. When she was forty-three, and very sad, Marjorie said, enough!—and opted out of an emotionally dry marriage to become what she had always wanted to be—an actress.

"I think that I want to talk about nurturing," she said to the rest of the group. "I don't feel that I nurtured my children as well as I could have and I haven't been the kind of mother I wanted to be. Apparently, for a long time, I also wasn't the kind of mother my children wanted me to be.

"Once, just before I left my husband, my son said to me, 'You're not like a real mother.'

"My heart broke. 'Why not?' I asked him.

" 'A real mother,' he said, 'stays home and cooks and takes you places when you need to go and doesn't go out and *act*!'

"I felt so guilty, I was in tears all night. 'Please make me a real mother,' I begged God. 'Oh, I want to be a real mother.'

"That was the low point in my life. Now, I feel differently. I know a real mother doesn't hide the things she wants and feels. A real mother acts like a woman—whatever form her womanness takes.

"Finally," said Marjorie, "I did what I had to do. Ironically, although I left my husband and dented the family structure, nurturing myself allowed me to become the mother of my dreams to my children. When I liked myself and liked how I lived and worked, the mother in me became surer and warmer. I no longer resented my life and I was able to give so much more to my kids without feeling guilty."

What did it take? More courage than Marjorie knew she possessed. She said no to a loveless marriage, renounced economic stability and a career she never liked, and began again to learn to be an independent woman.

"I can even take care of my own mother now," says Marjorie. "She's coming to live with me next week. A few years ago, I would have greatly resented having to do that. So, for me, it has been a question of gaining the power of self-affirmation. When I was powerful in that sense, I could express my deepest, most tender self.

"I must tell you that I really didn't always value the part of me that yearned to be an actress. It was immature, I was made to feel. It wasn't serious like speech therapy. Now I know how important it is to be able to make personal choices," said Marjorie, her doe-brown eyes thoughtful.

"Choice and respect for self. Look—one kid gives you grief because you're not home baking cookies; another makes you feel guilty you're not out there competing in the office like his friends' mothers. I was one of those who really needed the women's movement."

Trudy, a blonde, attractive, and husky-voiced woman in her early fifties, listened grimly to Margie. Recently widowed, she spoke of her bitterness toward the women's movement.

"I was one of those whom the movement made cringe," she said. "I felt guilty and lacking when all those magazine articles began to come out—lacking—when once I was so sure-footed! The militant feminists made me cringe because I stayed home to nurture. My children, my husband, my sisters, my parents, and my dear friends were my heart and the strength of my life, but when asked by other women what I did, I became ashamed to say 'I'm a housewife—I don't do anything.' Even when lots of women in my position started picking up the word 'homemaker', it didn't make much difference. 'Well, I'm a homemaker' didn't cut it either. I knew I moved *mountains*, but I squelched pride in that and resented women in a position of power because I felt I embarrassed them. I resented the whole women's movement—I didn't even like reading about it—because I felt they looked down on me.

"Then my husband died. I went out in the world to work. You know what? My experience as a nurturer held me in fine stead. All the time I thought I was doing nothing, I'd been networking—learning how to interact with others, learning how to work both ends. What I had was pure gold, and others had been making me feel it was worthless. My whole life, it turned out, wasn't superficial after all.

"Today, I work for the largest human services agency in the country. It's caring work, empowering of others, my kind of work. I'm good at it, baby! All that nurturing paid off and turned out to be big business for me. I wasted too much time putting my life down," Trudy concluded triumphantly.

We all felt like cheering—all except, perhaps, Diana. Living in suburbia, she was the perfect wife, mother, community volunteer. She was also the president of the PTA, active in the League of Women Voters, and baked the best brownies. It made me, then an intellectual snob, nervous when I moved, kicking and screaming with two young children, to her community. When I conquered my snobbery (because I needed to learn about casseroles, gardens, and butchers) I came to see Diana's power and profound intelligence. When her children were grown, she went back to school, earned a Master's degree in Business Administration—and has *not* lived happily ever after as a middle manager in the corporate world. It seems the skills that Diana perfected—nurturing, giving others strength, sharing—count for little in the corporation.

"I'm going to give you all a fact of life," said Diana. "There is no nurture in really big business. I'm a middle manager at AT&T. All the things I learned to trust—like cooperation, caring, being concerned with the welfare of your peers—all that's dead in the corporation. The Harvard MBAs run big business with competition. Period. They may get ahead personally, but I have news for them; the corporation itself would prosper tenfold if different values were injected.

"I just found out that three of us went into therapy from the stress imposed on us by our own Harvard MBA boss. The ironic part of it is that none of us knew the others were suffering. The atmosphere at work consisted of never sharing with anyone else for fear of confidences betrayed. My boss's method of operation was, in one word, divisive. He reasoned that if he made all of us compete with each other for the sake of the client, we'd scratch and fight and come up with great results.

"Some reasoning," Diana grimaced in the recollection, "all we did was hide in our own little corners, blocking out cooperation. But, despite that, the MBA boss went on to get promoted. If the company only knew how much better we'd produce if we weren't scratching at each other—they'd have demoted him.

"Trust, caring—all the traits I'd valued in my very busy life before business, flew out the window in the business world. It's made me feel very bitter and deprived.

"I know that cooperation and connecting with people is the only way to run a life and business, but I'm not allowed to express that. I feel frustrated in that I have no power to control the way I'd like to run my business life. What is power anyway? Control over your life," finished Diana.

As in every gathering of women, some are vocal and some are more quietly contemplative. In this last category was Ellen, a gentle, sensitive, high school teacher in her forties, with an unexpectedly impish bent. She has two sons and has recently separated from her physician husband. It has been an excruciatingly difficult time for her, but her profession buoys her spirit. In a way, she is the bearer of the flame, the educator who can change the world as she molds young opinion. Now, it was her turn to speak about nurturing. We leaned forward to listen to her quiet voice.

"I'm very impressed by what Diana just said about power meaning control over one's own life," Ellen said.

"I often felt powerless and out of control as I went about nurturing others in a nurtureless marriage. And now, embittered and toughened by the grimness of that failed marriage, I'm trying hard to retain the tenderness and compassion that is in my soul. I have to tell you—it's hard to nurture, be nice and fair—and still retain control over your decisions."

The group nodded in assent. And then, Eleanor began to speak. Eleanor is the classic volunteer. In her early sixties, she is regarded by all who know her as an effective woman, and yet, since the early days of her marriage, she has never taken a paying job. As the president of the National Council of Women, she organized, networked, politicked—and all without accepting a dime. She is never still; when she's not volunteering for an organization, she's volunteering at the museum, or she's baby-sitting for her very small granddaughter. Friends constantly say to her, "Grown-ups get paid for their work. You could be leading a giant corporation with your talents. Why devalue your work by *giving* it away?" She doesn't see it that way. Also, she looks at nurturing from an interesting perspective—her husband is one of the most famous gynecologists in New York.

"I have to laugh when you talk about control and nurturing in the same breath," she says, "and how nurturing has traditionally been woman's skill. It turns out that there's a new phenomenon out there—the new man. This man is well meaning, but in the end he can't seem to stop himself from trying to control even woman's quintessential experience—childbirth—and he asks women to view this ultimate act of nurturing in the male 'victory' mode. The new man, in his excitement at being a potential dad, often misunderstands the birth experience and tries to have it happen his way.

"I mentioned that my husband is a gynecologist," Eleanor tells the group with a twinkle. "Well, according to him, some of these 'nurturing' prospective dads are a big pain to their wives. They'll do everything they can to transform childbirth into a competition.

"My husband says that today hardly any woman comes to the doctor without her husband, or support person, or whatever you want to call him. He has to know, what's this, what's that thing, and what's happening? These guys think they're pregnant and they want control. The awful news is that their requirements of doing it *right*, doing it *best*, are driving their wives up a wall.

"Sometimes, my husband tells me, the women get to a point in their labor where they need some help, some anesthesia, but the New Husbands are in there cheerleading—'No, no, we can do it! We can do it! No painkillers! Natural all the way!' *Their* rules—not only in the work room, but in the delivery room!

"We're crazy to listen. We're letting them do it to us," said Eleanor.

The vision of the male cheerleaders made every woman in the group smile. We had all had experience with some men, and lately even women, who read weakness into an admission that help is needed. These people represent the stiff-upper-lip contingent who see work, play, and even birth as a time to display unflinching toughness. It seems to me that all this invincibility most men and many women now feel they must project comes from a weakening of close ties. The art of connectedness has always been a female skill. Was it in danger of becoming a lost art?

Betsy had something to say about that. In her early forties, she is an entrepreneur, president of a successful public relations and literary agency. She's imaginative, funny, forceful, independent, and usually looking for love in all the wrong places. Recently, she moved her offices to a huge loft where she both lives and works. On the one hand, she has created a nurturing little nest with her employees—"We make lunch together, we gossip, it's snug and tidy and pretty." On the other hand, she is often intellectually wary of using her feminine traits in a business world where her training and experience has dictated different behavior.

"I was always very independent and separate, not connecting," she tells the group. "I moved to a new place every six months and I thought that was very glamorous. Frankly, for a long time, I rejected women as friends. I thought they were pretty catty. I hung out with guys and I didn't even like to hire women in my public relations business, because I found their lives really intruded into their work time. With men you just didn't get suckered into whether so and so's husband is a jerk and what her mother was doing to drive her crazy.

"Lately, I've been following my instincts, doing things differently. Actually, I've been doing all the things my professional magazines tell me to avoid. For instance—it's clear, even to me, that I'm nesting in.

"I've bought a loft and I live and work in the same place—and I love it! I have lunch with the people who work for me—one of us cooks, the others straighten up in between clients. I'm connecting in other than business ways. In a sense, I've even turned my employees into my family, which is good, but what happens when one wants to leave? I may throw myself off the balcony—isn't that what mothers do?

"I've also discovered that not having women friends has been a great loss in my life. Now my closest friends are women. I look at the lives of my well-married pals and, I have to admit, that I miss that too, more than I thought I would. Succeeding at work was my goal. I've done it. I want the other thing too, it appears.

"I stick to things. I've learned how to persevere because I'm afraid of failing. If I fail, who am I? In a sense, I've done well at business because I've learned how to make human attachments. My friends are the most important things in my life. Can I say it—I've done well because I'm a *nice* person, also. Right?" asked Betsy.

Right!—she *was* a nice person. Niceness had a lot to do with what we were talking about that evening. It seemed to me, I said to the group, that being connected felt nice and the new macho manners many women had been developing somehow had little room for niceness. Perhaps, I also mused aloud, women instinctively valued the joining of people because of their experience with the most elemental connection of all—the birth connection we had just mentioned.

Eleanor was bursting with a story she wanted to share with the group. "Can I tell you about the greatest day of my life?" she asked. We settled in to listen.

"My daughter was pregnant, about to give birth, and we were spending the afternoon together.

"The day that Gail's water broke," remembers Eleanor, "the baby's dad was filming a commercial in the middle of Long Island Sound. I may be a real know-nothing doctor's wife, but I knew the birth was imminent and I wasn't leaving her side. We both got over to the birthing center as fast as we could move.

" 'She needs a coach,' said the midwife. 'Where's the father?'

" 'I'll be her coach,' I said. I'm usually very talkative and I was nervous I'd make a big nuisance of myself, but I didn't. I felt calm, I felt great, I felt happy, I felt right. I was going to help my child birth my grandchild.

"I sat on—it was like a little milking stool—and Gail sat in my lap, and she sat with her back to me and I had my arms around her. She pushed and I pushed, and we grunted together and we had a great time. We pushed that baby almost out.

"Then she said, 'Mom, I think I'd like to get on the bed now,' And she did, and the midwife said, 'Hold her feet now, Eleanor.' So I held her feet. Gail said, 'I'm going to focus in now. You just give me bulletins, Ma.' So I did.

" 'You're opening,' I said. 'You're closing. My God—you're not closing—this is it!' And the moment was here, and the baby's head presented and I saw such a lot of hair and I said, 'Gail, whatever it is has such a lot of hair! Push! I want to see what variety we have here.'

"And out she came. I didn't even realize it was a girl at first, because I saw the cord and to tell the truth, I didn't know if it was a cord or a penis. Then, I figured even *my* grandson couldn't have a penis that long, so I said, 'Oh my, Gail, we have a girl. . . .'

"And she said, 'Beatrice is here.'

"Beatrice was my mother. So I felt that my mother and daughter and my daughter's daughter were all there together giving birth to each other. Connecting. I'll never forget it," said Eleanor.

For a long moment, every woman in the room was silent, savoring Eleanor's story. You didn't have to be a mother, but it was helpful to be a woman in order to fully empathize with the feeling of intergenerational connectedness that her granddaughter's birth inspired. It wasn't that caring men couldn't understand the poignancy of the moment; just that their experiences, different from women, must lead them to view birth differently. Differences in the male and female experience do exist. It serves no one well to pretend they don't.

Christine, a vocal member of the focus group, agreed. She is a certified legal assistant in a small law firm, and in her early thirties, she's chosen not to marry. The oldest of a warm, hugging family of eight children and on a modest salary, she finds herself financially and actually responsible for her alcoholic brother, her divorced sister, and her sister's children. She does this, not with a martyr's resignation, but with a wry kind of black humor. She touches onto many things, calligraphy, art, theater, Talmud study, but still she feels that she's failed to live up to her intellectual potential.

"We've got to respect differences," said Christine. "I have two small nephews growing up with women as heads of the family and we bought them dolls to play with—and they don't want the dolls. We were morally opposed to giving them guns, so what do they do? They pick up sticks and make guns with them. I'm constantly going around to my nieces and nephews saying 'Girls can be doctors, boys can be nurses' and yet, the differences always show. The only thing we can do is hold tight to our womanness and share the wealth of nice woman traits with men—just as we pick up the good stuff that's in men. But act like them? Ignore differences? No way."

Gloria agreed emphatically. She was born the youngest of seven Chinese sisters and brings a rich heritage of intellect and courage, and a warm mix of mother-manager/self-achiever, to family dynamics. After seeing her two children into elementary school, she entered law school in her early thirties. She has just begun to practice. Her husband, an English professor, is a willing half of a total-partnership marriage. He cares for the children, cleans, cooks (although not nearly with Gloria's marvelous skill), and in doing so is so manly he makes proponents of male dominance look silly.

"I, for one," Gloria said, "do not believe you have to be like men to be respected in business. I feel if you stand up for your principles, if you display caring along with authority—men may say 'come on, come on'—but they ease up, make no mistake about it. And soon, they start to use some of your techniques because it's obvious they work. You do not have to compromise your values to get to where you think you should be. My immediate boss is male, the other vice presidents, save one, and all of the CEOs of the large hospital where I'm an attorney are men, and I absolutely do not end up talking tough-guy, macho stuff to gain power. In fact, you know what? I have a double-edged sword. If I support my decisions with data, I can also use my feminine wiles to make a point. Wiles are perfectly legitimate and wonderful tools. You fall into awful traps if you don't insist upon using your woman strengths, but, I caution—you have to come up with the hard facts as well as the tenderness."

"I hate that word—*wiles*—" said Christine. "It has such a negative connotation. If you say wiles, you're going to be misunderstood. Words are powerful. They can stereotype you."

"Would you be happier if I said 'feminine ways'?" asked Gloria.

"Not really," said Christine.

"Why do we have such trouble claiming woman tools?" asked Gloria.

"It's not the tools," Christine answered, "it's the semantics. I hate to be thought of as, well—girlish! That's what 'feminine wiles' brings to mind to me."

Quietly, softly, Ellen stepped into the discussion. "I think that what we're searching for is a *feminine sensibility* that works in men as well as in women," she said. "I have two sons and they're both very different and I love them both for their differences. But, one of the reasons I so admire my youngest son is that he has a feminine sensibility. I know what it is, but I can't explain it and I wish I could say I instilled it, but I'm not sure of that, at all."

The conversation turned to empowerment of others—an ancient female trait. Ever since Eve, women have been empowering their children, their husbands, their friends. They've been sharing the wealth, the things they know and the things they newly learn. It is women who have always taught others how to gain authority. It is women who have always freely bequeathed their strength to friends and family without too much fear of hostile takeovers. Empowering others has been viewed, however, as a negligible asset in the male-structured business world.

Then someone very special to me spoke up. She is Kathy and we go back a long way. At twelve she was my student in the first class I ever taught. She was a Brownie, uniform and all, but she didn't look like the prototype Brownie with pigtails, a dazzling smile, and jump rope. Kathy had the pigtails and the smile, all right, but she was massively handicapped with cerebral palsy and had to forego the jump rope. She just barely managed walking. The principal of the school told me not to invest too much time in Kathy—she'd just end up in a sheltered workshop, if she was lucky, doing busy work. More than anything else, Kathy wanted to be "a mommy." Twenty years later, here she sat at my house, still massively handicapped, but having managed to make it through college, get married (to a similarly handicapped young man), and give birth to two beautiful, quite physically normal, daughters—who adore and admire their mom. Now, in my living room, leaning forward in the effort of making her words intelligible, Kathy spoke to the gathered women.

"I hear you talk about empowerment," Kathy said. "Well, that's *all* I ever do. Cerebral palsy tends to limit your choices. My marriage is not perfect, but I hold it together. If we split, where would I go? Where would he go? Eddie's a good man, but sometimes he gets terribly frustrated.

"So daily, I try to give him strength. I wake myself up at 2:00 A.M. to wake him, so he can get to his work. If I didn't get up, he wouldn't get to work. I listen to him endlessly. I bear his angers and his sense of hopelessness. By giving myself to him, I think I do make him a sweeter man. He only has me to make him whole."

She paused to swallow and draw breath. You could hear a pin drop.

"I empower my children daily," she continued laboriously. "It isn't always easy for them. Sometimes my husband and I embarrass them. It's hard to have your parents come to Open School Day, when they talk and walk funny. So the kids have to explain us to their friends. But, I think that I've given them strength and courage to do that. I think I've given them pride.

"There are times though when I turn to Eddie, usually at night when everyone else is asleep, and I ask him—'When is it my turn to *get*? Who is going to give me courage when something bad happens?'

"He's usually asleep and doesn't answer."

In the silence that followed, someone asked, "All that empowering you do, Kathy—doesn't it take too much time from doing what *you* want?"

Kathy reflected for a moment, then answered.

"I don't think so. Face it. I don't have too many choices. The movement has not done much for the disabled. I'm fighting just to be considered human. Look—I'm a trained social worker. No one would hire me. I couldn't find work anywhere. Once, in desperation, I tried to sell cosmetics door-to-door. Women wouldn't open their doors to me because they thought I was drunk.

"So, if I follow my instincts and spend all my time giving to my family— well, to me, it's a miracle I have them. And, you get back—don't worry. When you give strength to others, you get back. My daughters will do all I couldn't because I've given them power and caring values."

She stopped to rest. Talking is not easy—especially when you have to make a point.

"This is hard for me to tell," she stumbled along, "but I was an abused child. Now—my dad has Alzheimer's. He lives next door to me, with my mom. It's not in me to pay him back, in kind. So I go over daily to help my mother diaper him. My little girls have watched me do that, for a couple of years. Now, they insist upon doing the same.

"The first time I saw them do it," said Kathy, "I was horrified. 'You don't have to touch him,' I said, 'it's not your responsibility,' I told them. 'I'd never expect you to do that for Daddy or me.'

" 'But we will,' said my little one. 'He's our grandfather, we want to do it,' said my eldest."

Kathy paused. "What's that worth?" she asked, "in a world where others routinely shove the disabled and the aged in institutions or nursing homes?"

It was worth a lot, we agreed. More than we could say.

"Could we spend a minute on juggling?" I asked the assembled group. "I'd like to find out how women can manage to retain qualities of compassion, affiliation, and caring when they are being challenged to do something men never had to do—and that is to do it all."

Barbara is a National Sales Director for Mary Kay Cosmetics. In her thirties, she says she is "not one bit domesticated"; but she loves working for and with women because, she says, "it's women who put the cookies in everybody else's cookie jars." Barbara said she was qualified to speak about juggling because she raised two children, "one hand bouncing the baby and the other holding the business phone."

"The answer lies in balance," Barbara said. "Maybe women, and men, have to lower their expectations at certain points in their lives so they won't feel they missed out, later on. For me, the balance lies in working at home when my kids are small. You *can* do it all—if you do it in sequences, rather than all at once. My children think a telephone grows out of every woman's ear because I chose to conduct my business from my home; as they grow, I can spend more time away.

"Every woman needs to work out temporary compromises, if she wants it all eventually, and partnership agreements with her partner, if she has one," said Barbara.

"In a way, I see the new corporate cycle for women as being as straight-jacketed and governed by men as the old marketplace that didn't include women. I think women are definitely rebelling against exchanging the stereotype of home, hearth, and kids for yet another stereotype of income, status, and power. One's as restrictive as the other."

Trudy broke in. "I'm scared for my daughters," she said. " 'Please, please, don't try to do it all,' I tell them. 'You don't have to do it all. Don't listen to pie-in-the-sky magazine articles. If you try to do it all, something important will suffer—like you.' "

"We hear so much today about how healthy children must 'separate' from their parents," said Eleanor. "And about how everyone's responsibility is to herself. Let me tell you, I don't buy it. What I buy is loyalty and connecting. I went to Florida once with my newly divorced sister, and I hated it. All the senior citizens sat around talking about what used to be and how wonderful things were when the family was together. I came home, and my kids were all at the house to greet me and I lined them up and I said 'What do you see?'

" 'You Mom—we see you,' they said, mystified.

" 'Wrong,' I said. 'You see your Burden. Me. If, when the time comes, you think you're going to put me away on some shelf in Florida, or in a home, think again. I'm your Burden. Me. Your mother. Don't forget that.'

"They all laughed," remembers Eleanor, "but the message sunk in, and I wasn't kidding. All this today talk—me, me, me—I have no time, my mother is such a pain. What happened to human values of responsibility, connection, duty? They sound dated? That's what's wrong with both men and women in today's workplace. Power doesn't feel good when you're a rat. The whole system needs revamping, if you ask me."

Lois is the youngest of four daughters. "The women's movement passed me by," she said, "and I never really ventured out except for some volunteer work and art courses." Was she satisfied with her choice? Not really. "When I was away from my home, I wanted to be there where my family was, and where it was safe. When I was home, I wanted to be somewhere else." It is only recently, now that her children have grown, that Lois has begun to paint—and sell! She feels stronger and happier than ever. The night of our meeting she wanted to talk about showing vulnerability.

"Most men I know would like to be more open, I feel sure of that. In their heads, they can appreciate what a show of vulnerability can do for one's psyche. But, let the walls down to the world? No way. I think that little has changed. Men don't open up any more now than they used to, despite all the books that say how good it is to share secrets. And, I'll tell you something else," Lois said, "I just read an astounding statistic that said one of every three adults in this country is in therapy. Is that the result of the walls we put up? How come women haven't managed to teach men what we know?—that sharing intimacies feels good."

"Because it's the hardest thing in the world," Trudy said. "I'm a widowed person," she volunteered. "I have to admit I never use the word widow—it makes me cry—so I say single. But, I feel such comfort with all of you tonight, I use it now. I'm a widowed person. My husband was a sensitive man. But, when he used to cry, he felt he had to hide it—he pretended he was coughing. That always made me infinitely sad."

"My husband is sixty-three," said Eleanor, "and sometimes, something sad he's watching on television takes him completely by surprise and he gets all choked up. Then, he looks around furtively as if to say, 'I hope nobody saw me.' You can't expect a sixty-three-year-old, or a sixteen-year-old, who's been taught to shelter his emotions, suddenly to share them. You want to teach men to be comfortable with intimacy and to allow vulnerability? Start when they're eight! If we managed to teach women to be successful in the marketplace, why can't we now teach men, and their sons, how to bond, how to express emotion?"

This focus group was alive. Women who were strangers were connecting. Laughter was easy and spontaneous. Gripes were plentiful. Solutions were even more plentiful. We could have gone on all night. The focus group lasted late, much later than I expected. For the women who met in my home, it was another bonding experience, something our generation is forgetting how to do. Many of the women called to ask for telephone numbers of others. They seemed to want to keep the conversation alive, keep the connection strong.

Conversations like this go on in a dozen, in a hundred, in a thousand small impromptu groups across the country. There's a need for the old strengths.

It comes to this: Gratefully celebrating the gains of the past decades, many women now feel strong enough to make their revolution come full circle by championing yet another revolution—one that would have as its aim the emergence of a more connecting, compassionate, balanced society for themselves and for their men, children, partners, and friends. Many of us see a deterioration of vital affiliations—with our infants, our aged, our working partners, our government, our families. Our connecting links are rusting. It's not that women love too much, but that we've lately been loving in a too detached way.

The women of the focus group expressed many mutual concerns. Many of them were struggling with or knew someone who was fearful of seeming weak if they acted warm and compassionate in predominantly male workplaces. Most of the women expressed unreserved admiration for the ambitions and achievements of the women's movement. Not one of the women was anti-male. Although some felt unfairly manipulated by some men, no one expressed unreasoned indiscriminate grievances against men, even though many assertive women have been accused of anti-male hostility in an attempt to discredit feminists.

Most of the women hadn't given a great deal of thought to the idea that they had to suppress much of what was feminine and humanistic at work, but the more they talked the more they remembered uncomfortable pressure to conform to macho mannerisms.

Some women expressed dismay at what seemed to be a change in women's relationships with each other. "Rivalry makes me uncomfortable," said Margie. "I hate to scurry for approval at someone else's expense. I used to feel a kind of frivolous intimacy with women—that's gone now. Everyone's looking over her shoulder to see who's gaining."

Many of the women at the focus group expressed dissatisfaction with love relationships; men, they said, appeared to find it very difficult to open up these days, and even worse, there seemed to be less time available to work on these tenuous relationships.

Sure, we've made it into the working ranks, and the air there is fresh and stimulating and we belong and we're great at it, but the truth? There's something missing. For many of us, an aching gap with the persistent pain of a toothache represents the part of ourselves we gouged out in pursuit of power. For many of us, young and older, a personal or work life that leans toward a devaluation of intimacy, family, and consideration of others is proving as dissatisfying as it has been for most men. Even worse, we're not succeeding as well as men because they, at least, don't have the history of tenderness, as we do.

And therein lies the first step: building new histories of tenderness and of power.

There are many places for that first starting step—in the home, at work, or within the context of personal relationships. Probably the stage that most dramatically spotlights women's unique qualities is the workplace. There, invisible biases against kindness, connecting, and nurturing daily handicap women. There also, many women from all walks of life and on varying working levels are fighting the good fight to strengthen power with the diplomatic use of tender.

3

The New Managerial Woman

Dilemmas of the New Mystique

Several years ago, I was a high school literature teacher. It was a good and appealing career because I got to read a lot and talk with young women who thought all they had to do was decide what they were going to be when they grew up.

Almost all their teachers, and I include myself, told them how fortunate they were to be born into a time when they could have it all. They could be caring and cooperative and fabulously successful at work. All they had to do was be diligent and true to their values (and remember their English teacher with admiration).

I hope they don't remember me with anger. What I told them was wrong.

Instead of the Brave New World I promised, they're often discovering a callous, cloddish work world in which they do not neatly fit. The Feminine Mystique has been replaced with a new mystique which, like all mystiques, misses reality. The new mystique hinted that my pupils could Superwoman their way to the top if they simply shut their eyes and ears to the voices inside of them. It doesn't matter if the fit's imperfect, was the lesson they learned; forget about the loss of self you feel; keep your eye on the goal. The goal was success—success defined in the traditional male way. Money and prestige and power are ends unto themselves. The other stuff would wait.

What a dilemma. On the one hand, my students wanted to be themselves, their truly terrific selves. On the other hand, no dummies they, it soon became clear that the workplace required tunnel vision, a no-nonsense, blinders-wearing approach; do your work, claim your prizes, don't bother about anyone else and certainly, don't bother *us* with your personal problems.

My students soon discovered it was easier to adopt the male dress code for success than to redefine success in a womanly mode.

Womanly modes were a little, well, outdated.

Leave those feminine values at home, *please*.

On the other hand, the workplace never demanded that men leave their masculine values at home.

Try working as a neutered person. Try working well and succeeding when everything you've learned about connection, warmth, friendship, and empathy must be shed. In a tough world, where women are pulled apart by their wishes to be themselves and still comply with what the workplace seems to demand, the only logical solution is to be everything that everyone wants you to be. Simple. My students could be the lawyers, the secretaries, the CEOs, the wives, the mothers, the housekeepers—all at once. That's what I told them. Never mind that men never laid such a burden on themselves.

They found out they didn't have to do it without help—this neutering of themselves. There were plenty of books on the subject. The books would show them what was wrong with them, but would not teach them to celebrate their femaleness. If they thought loving too much was a handicap, for instance, they could find therapy sessions for Women Who Love Too Much to find out how to love less.

What a mistake. All that self-blaming, all that earnest trying to do it all, only hindered our work lives and put dents into our personal lives. At work, we sacrificed femininity to build career credits. We tried not to love so much. At home, we tried not to cheat anyone of what we used to provide in the way of nurturing and creature comforts. Lately, we're not feeling greatly successful at either work or home.

Betty Friedan recently wrote that "the *new* mystique is that women can have it all. There's a whole new generation of women today, flogging themselves to compete for success according to the male model—in a work world structured for men with wives to handle the details of life."

It's interesting to note what the few who make it to the top levels feel. According to a profile offered by Korn/Ferry, the world's largest executive search firm, the composite senior woman executive feels that "her greatest obstacle to success was being a woman."

Is it possible that we're attacking this from the wrong angle?

Naturally a woman's greatest obstacle to success is being a woman *if she is trying to be a man*. But what if she isn't? What if she pulls out all the stops, and boldly, gloriously, powerfully, tenderly uses all her woman-strengths—as any woman can do? Consider this statistic: According to the polls, the same composite senior executive woman "takes primary responsibility for the care of her children as well as for household tasks."

And here's the zinger: According to a survey taken by USA TODAY, only one in five women—twenty-one percent—said they wished to give up this responsibility. As most women expand their horizons, they're ambivalent about giving up the thing that has always brought them self-esteem and gratification (along with a lot of anxiety)—and that is the ability to take care of home and family.

This is not to say we want to do it all. In an economy where two out of every three women who work have full-time jobs, women still want and need equal support from spouses and other help sources. But, they still want to do at least a part of it all. For whatever reason they work, few choose to relinquish the joys of family life, as well as the responsibilities that come with the home.

There's no denying the fact that although working women are flooding the marketplace in great numbers (seventy percent of all American women aged twenty-five to fifty-four either work for pay or are trying to find a job), they are a distinct minority, in both middle and certainly senior management. The top tiers still elude us—only two percent of senior executives in this country are women.

Is it possible that this may be even slightly related to the practice of women working as they think males would work? Frank Sinatra does it his way, but women who try to do it "his way" rarely grab the gold ring.

Patricia McBroom, author of *The Third Sex*, disagrees that women can reclaim tenderness and still succeed. She claims that the reality of today's corporate culture dictates that women will not gain the authority they seek unless they learn to simulate masculine job behavior. She does note, however, that the "typical" corporate female executive in 1982 paid a heavy price for the masquerade. More than half of these typical corporate female executives were unmarried and almost two thirds of them were childless. By comparison, only four percent of the male corporate executives were unmarried and only three percent of the male executives had no children.

The irony is apparent: Women are adopting male executive job behavior, but are not adopting male executive family behavior. Women executives give up their authentic behavior and an intimate family life to reach the top. And the men? The men give up nothing.

It's not only in the corporation that women mimic male behavior to their detriment; in countless other occupations all over the country too many women are doing it the male way and losing the game. Take the women in blue, the brave new breed of female police officers. The women's movement, with pressure and politics, cleared the way for women to enter the law enforcement field. Now, too many policewomen think that being policemen best fills the requirements of the job. Janet Henkin, Ph.D., director of the Criminal Justice Institute of Chapman College in Orange, California, calls it the "Jane Wayne Syndrome." Women on patrol, she says, suffer from "role confusion. They act excessively tough, take unnecessary risks, exacerbate volatile situations, and antagonize citizens to prove to their peers and to the citizens that they must be taken seriously. The opposite effect occurs; no one respects them and they look like caricatures of policemen. The challenge," says Dr. Henkin, "is for women officers to become comcomfortable in the largely male environment in which they operate by using human, caring, woman traits. That's going to give them true authority."

Dr. Henkin holds workshops for female police officers in which she shows them how to use humor, sensitivity, and "manipulation—it's not a dirty word" in plying their trade most effectively.

In business the situation can be just as destructive. No longer are women helping other women in the office, lending a sympathetic ear, an understanding nod, or an encouraging tap up the ladder to their female colleagues. In learning to be competitive, many women have lost the art of compassion.

"What about cooperation, networking, mentoring—all that cozy stuff the movement supposedly fostered? Why are we so willing to kick our sisters in the pants?" asks Anne B. Fisher in an article for *Savvy* magazine. It's no good ignoring the fact that the problem exists. Books like *Women vs. Women: The Uncivil Business War* and *Woman to Woman: From Sabotage to Support* are popping up on bookshelves everywhere, to the great dismay of many. It is difficult to find many feminist and prominent female business leaders who will even discuss the problem. They claim that pointing to examples of women backbiting other women only creates an atmosphere of blame.

"If you drag that dead issue out again, it just opens up the old can of worms and underscores the sexist stereotype of cat-clawing women," says one female CEO. "It helps men to say 'women just can't get along with each other.' They can then conveniently dismiss the whole sex as clawing cats."

There's another school of thought on this. Without scapegoating the well-meaning women leaders, denying problems and differences is no way for women to operate. It's not a question of blame, either; who can blame the pioneer feminists for dropping the female values to adopt the male traits? In the early, turbulent days of change it was necessary: First, we had to get their attention, those male business leaders, and they could only hear their own vernacular. But now? It's time for reclamation.

I go into my local bookstore. I see a book for men, written by a man. It is called *Waging Business Warfare* (David Rogers, Scribner's). I look on the next shelf and find *Office Warfare*, written by a woman (Marilyn Moats Kennedy, Scribner's) for women. *Waging Business Warfare* is full of information on men and the business mode in which they've operated for the last millenium, but I see nothing in *Office Warfare* that tells women how to operate with the skills they've been accumulating for centuries. Is it because those skills are not relevant in business? Nonsense.

Mary Cunningham, once executive vice president at both the Bendix and the Seagram corporations, says she truly believes "that there's a beautiful consistency about being human beings and about caring about the bottom line, because both are inextricably linked. In fact, what makes a small business work is the very set of nurturing qualities we're talking about. It means that you say (and earn profound gratitude) 'hey, can I give you a hand tonight?' when a fellow worker has to stay later. It means that if someone's family member is sick and he can't make it to work, you're going to say 'is there something I can do to help you out?' so he doesn't have to worry about getting the pink slip.

"The sense of team, the display of caring and nurture, makes a profitable enterprise, in the end. The most effective businesspeople I know are those who try in a collective way to make something better than it was when they first came on board.

"You do not have to *become* a politics game player in order to understand *how* the game is played. We can become savvy about the games people play in the corporate world without adopting their despicable skills and traits," says Cunningham. "I honestly believe that's very achievable. In other words, you can be a nurturer, be very sensitive to others' feelings and needs, employ cooperative values; all this can stand you in good stead, but you really do have to be sophisticated about what's going on around you. I was so busy not wanting to play the game, that at Bendix, I turned a deaf ear to the game. I never did it again because that guarantees you'll be used in someone else's game—it's being naive."

Yes, says Cunningham, there is room for feminine qualities in the corporation and indeed, it is these qualities that will magnificently support women in their climb to the top levels.

Because many women have felt intimidated about displaying connectiveness, they inadvertently discourage other women from being themselves. Until women stop hiding, defending, or in some way contorting those nurturing traits that are uniquely theirs, they will impede their own progress, says Cunningham.

The Feminine Context

It might be wise for corporations to consider the study of managerial traits in a new context—the feminine context.

The feminine context depends on stirring people to produce their best work because they feel good about the organization and because they feel good about themselves. The feminine context combines firm direction along with the empowerment of others. Cooperation, for instance, as women have developed the art through the ages, is an example of power and empowerment. As we help each other to explore, discover, and ripen, we find new sources of strength within ourselves.

Managing within the feminine context depends on what Robert H. Waterman, Jr., in his book, *The Renewal Factor*, describes as the ability to manage change. The only constant, he says, in today's business is change, and the organizations that best succeed are those that are "continually adapting their bureaucracies, strategies, systems, products, and cultures to survive the shocks and prosper."

It is women who best know how to manage this kind of change, we with our instinct and ability to always hold the changing family structure together, and we with our age-old talent for smoothing over, accommodating, and adapting. It is we who can best teach how to break bad habits, a prerequisite of managing change without breaking the backs of people. How can we do it? We can do it with compassion, curiosity, and cooperation. We can do it through sharing the power and the glory. We've always done it. Now that women are an integral part of business organizations, why should we discard what has always worked in order to adapt to an ethic of blind unaffiliating, cutthroat competition? It doesn't make sense.

"If you want to be a good manager," says Lois Wyse, president of Wyse Advertising in New York, "first be a good mother. All the things a mother provides—comfort, praise, scoldings, motivation, entertainment, teaching, punishment and rewards—are what shape the basic behavior system for corporate interaction. Most of all," says Wyse, "an honest and authentic voice that represents you and the way you really live and believe is what influences others to follow your lead."

It's interesting to note that some successful women, along with the power plays they've learned from men, instinctively bring to the marketplace the very skills that male business experts have long put forth as the solution to lagging corporate performance. When men openly display them, they're called managerial; when women openly display them, however, they're called "manipulative." Ego-massage, networking, the ability to listen well and affiliate with others are within the feminine context far more than the masculine, and yet, an author of a rough, tough business manual would rather choke than characterize the traits as feminine.

Florence Skelly, former president of Yankelovich, Skelly and White, analysts who document trends and life management styles, also believes that female qualities are definitely an asset that should be used in business. One of those qualities, and a significantly effective management tool, is the ability to manage the "here and now" says Skelly. "Men," she notes, "are long-range dreamers. They want to look at the big picture twenty-five years from now. It's women who anchor us to the five year plan and make it happen today. That's because women are so good at shifting and fixing. We learn it early in life; we see it at home. Men make all the big plans—they're bringing home four people for dinner. Then women have to fix and shift—call the butcher. (He's out of veal? What about lamb?) Those female qualities of fixing and shifting—employing the substitute agenda—are why we get it done."

Many powerful business leaders agree. Mark H. McCormack, the author of the best-selling *What They Don't Teach You at Harvard Business School*, suggests that ancient feminine tools like mollifying, empathizing, and accommodating are sound business practices. "Acknowledge the other person's feelings," says McCormack. "This is the oldest psychological technique in the world and works just as well in negotiations as it does in any other form of human relations." Barter and sweeten the deal, find ways to accommodate your adversary's self-interest. Put yourself in the other guy's shoes, the business expert advises. Shifting and rearranging inflexible agendas is good business practice.

"Somehow," says McCormack, "negotiating has been confused with machismo as though the whole point is to outlast your opponent, to make him back down first."

The ability to empathize with another human being and behave accordingly has many benefits. The direct marketer who sells soaps or reproduction furniture from a catalogue will be able to understand his customer's needs and make a far more vivid sales pitch if he is able to visualize the product first in his own, then in the customer's living room. The intelligent manager who remembers how embarrassed and angry and vengeful it made her feel to be criticized publicly will never do the same to her own employees. And although there are legions of warm and sensitive men, it has always been more within the feminine than the male context to be generally more empathic to others. What a pity it would be to forever shelve this trait that would serve so well in business.

The feminine context, interestingly enough, often includes faith in God. In a society where more and more people diffuse stress by seeing a psychiatrist or working out in their gyms, there is still a significant portion of American working women who find relief from business tension in religion.

"My pastor is more than my religious leader," says Mary Elizabeth Cleaver, from Elgin, Illinois. "He's my trusted business advisor as well. When I'm up against a stone wall, my pastor is always good for a novel solution."

Women of diverse faiths today seem to be seeking to satisfy rather than squelch spiritual yearnings within recognized and also very personalized religions. Where some years ago the big-city ethic would look suspiciously at the businesswoman who speaks of finding practical answers in faith, today more and more achieving people talk of finding direction through prayer.

Although certainly there are many women who leave their faiths because they find them irrelevant to modern life, increasingly more are claiming these intangible supports. It's interesting to note that women are far more religious than men; pollster Lou Harris estimates that a substantial forty-six percent of women are regular church attenders, followed by a much lower thirty-three percent of men. Harris also notes that the heaviest churchgoers come from the South, followed closely by the Midwest, then the East, and last the irreverent West. In business environments where morals and ethics seem to carry less sway than the bottom line, perhaps the new spiritual awakening bodes well for humanity.

The Male Ethic and the Economy

The presence, in great numbers, of women in the marketplace compels a reevaluation of the male ethic of business—for humanistic reasons but also because the male ethic is not working so stupendously.

What have been the costs of blind, cutthroat, unaffiliating competition? Lagging productivity, as the import figures reveal, a huge turnover of the best people, distrust and suspicion within the ranks, political infighting and sabotage, workers who expect to be ignored and who expect to fail (and who do exactly these two things). These are the costs the American corporation is paying.

Recently, the entire top echelon of a fine New York advertising agency resigned in protest of harsh business practices to start a new competitive company. Something similar happened to the mergers and acquisitions department of a leading Atlanta investment banking firm and also to one of the city's prime law firms. Stock market analyst Robert Prechter believes that Wall Street is headed for the most severe bear market since the early thirties, as people tend to focus more on moral and spiritual values than on win-at-any-cost as a means to self-fulfillment. Business is dropping in many restaurants, the fashion industry is in a state of angst, and the nation's waning competitive edge in foreign commerce expresses itself in a lack of respect for the environment and for business as a responsible institution. All over America, cynical industry is dumping its waste into our precious waters; they are also polluting the air and the spirit. Something rotten in the state of business management is darkening the national mood.

According to pollster Louis Harris, the United States is "over the hill" economically. Recently, a cross-section of top American businessmen were asked to choose between the United States, Japan, and Western Europe: Which country is best in key economic attributes? The results, says Harris, were "startling."

- On which produces the best-quality products and services, the Japanese won with fifty-eight percent, the U.S. is a distant second at twenty-one percent, and Western Europe only gets seven percent.

- On which has the highest rate of increase in productivity, again Japan won hands down with seventy-five percent, followed by the U.S. at eleven percent, then Western Europe at six percent.

When the American people were asked the same questions, three in every four went along with the business leaders' judgment on productivity. "There is little doubt," says Harris, "that traditional American confidence in the nation's economic prowess and capacity to out-compete the rest of the world has been badly shaken. By the mid-1980s, notes Harris, close to nine in every ten Americans expressed serious concern over competition from Japan."

Certainly there may be all sorts of explanations for this turn of events, but one likely explanation comes from Mary Cunningham, ex-corporate vice president at Bendix and Seagram corporations.

"If you look at what is currently being highlighted as the ultimate managerial style—the secret for management in the late eighties and early nineties—most management seminars will continually put up the Japanese as an example. Japanese managerial style is all about the very skills and qualities that have been traditionally described as feminine. The Japanese are personified motivators. They are into participatory style . . . not into aggressive-dictatorial style, which is typically addressed as masculine. They are listeners. Empathizers. These are all the qualities that have historically been described as feminine. And they also, ironically enough, are what are being described now as Japanese. Heaven forbid they should be described as feminine!" says Cunningham.

The American economy, operating with a colder, more callous mentality than ever before, seems to be dragging its once springy feet. Perhaps if marketers paid closer attention to the tensions and changing expectations of both men and women who find it chilling to Compete and Kill, who feel a somewhat embarrassed nostalgia for the old-time values of generosity, emotional responsiveness, and strong moral fiber, we'd put more bounce in our march to success. There's a lot of talk these days about what's gone wrong with American business ethics: the scandals of insider trading, influence peddling by top political appointees, television evangelists being ousted by their congregations, and even Pentagon bribery. When a moderator recently introduced a speaker on the subject of "Ethics in Advertising," the moderator couldn't help but remark that the speech would no doubt be brief.

As one political hack after another falls, as one business after another folds, is it really too simplistic to suggest that we might actually try a little tenderness, try to reclaim some of that ancient female respect for fairness, cooperation, and sensitivity to others?

Tender Power: A Trickle-Down Effect

Many excellent businesspeople and many feminist leaders point out that there will always be places and situations where those who seek to implement macho manners with tender traits will feel profoundly thwarted. In businesses led by those who misunderstand or are threatened by acts of nurturing, one must go with the flow or leave. It is self-defeating to feel guilt at not succeeding at tenderness when one truly has no choice. A woman—or a man—who wishes to align with a traditionally male-mannered corporation may just have to swim upstream with the rest. In corporations where old habits are irrevocably ingrained, you may just have to tough it out and keep your knowledge of a better way within you. It is interesting to note that one of the most feminine power traits, a heightened intuition, may well give you early messages of when Tender Power is up against too tough a barrier. Some of the most spirited defenders of a different way have learned to reconnoiter and wait for a better day. "When you're part of an all male macho situation," says Linda Kline, president of Kline/McKay, an executive search and human resources consulting firm that services many of America's Fortune 500 companies, "there isn't a thing you can do but respond in kind if you want to get anywhere at all. Florence Nightingale herself couldn't make a dent in some businesses. Women are good at going with the flow and when the cards are really stacked against them they tend to adjust if that is what they have to do."

Still, Kline, co-author of *Career Changing: The Worry-Free Guide*, says that from her vantage point, although it's enormously difficult for women to display traditionally feminine traits in many corporations, there are some very real steps women can take toward the goal. She offers some suggestions:

"It's not useful to be a male clone. The male workplace is scared to death of overly aggressive women who only bring out the worst in overly aggressive men. On the other hand, too much disclosure and warmth scares them off also. These men themselves have been forced into molds which required them to cut all tenderness from their own psyches, so they're sure not going to countenance too many of these traits in women, practically speaking.

"Most large companies are organized along military lines and the thrust is to make the boss look good by getting the job done. Frankly speaking, if you're a middle manager, your boss only cares that he/she looks good, in the end. That's why women who are considered the toughest in business tend to find other outlets for their warmer, nurturing traits, whether it's cats, plants or kids."

It's ironic, says Kline, because women in most large businesses traditionally have been the ones who train the new male trainees in the best management techniques. They are, however, stoically prepared and feel no surprise when those trainees immediately surpass them in position. Most corporations recognize the power in a woman's business touch, but they still keep her out of the executive suite.

The solution, says Kline, is to *nurture down*.

"If it's impossible to nurture up, in the corporation, women can surely gain from nurturing down. The effect trickles throughout the whole organization. If you want to make those below you work their hardest for you, treat them with empathy, and kindness. Empowering others makes them want to follow you anywhere! It will show in their work and will, in turn, make you, and the boss, look good. If strong women make a concerted effort to lead using tenderness with their power, everyone else will get used to it."

Then, says Kline, if and when you get to be top dog, you can do anything you please. "Women who finally do reach the top rung of whatever business is their game," says Kline, "almost always use feminine traits and are visibly conscious of the strength of their womanness. Top-rung women are in the best position of all to nurture down and set precedents of cooperation and caring."

Perhaps one reason why top-rung women don't always nurture down is because they're afraid that those under them will take advantage of their niceness and usurp their power. That fear is unfounded, says Barbara Tober, editor-in-chief of *Bride's Magazine*, and a woman who occupies the top rung of a powerful corporation. "When you give strength to others, you strengthen yourself," she declares. Women, says Tober, traditionally have always acted as teachers to the uninitiated. In the corporate life this really shouldn't change. Competitive jealousy of underlings undercuts the corporation and the leader's strength. "It's a magical thing," says Tober, "to discover that even when you think you're on the top of the ladder there's always a new rung to gain. If you actually teach others to become you, undreamed of new doors open."

How, specifically, does Tober teach people to "become her"? To begin, she has instituted an "Image Day" at work and everyone from entry level on up takes part. Professionals are brought in to teach workers how to get to be the boss, how to winningly present themselves, how to negotiate, how to argue a winning point. Personally Tober nurtures down as well, by encouraging employees to take classes and develop initiative in order to advance within the organization.

Other women executives have come up with other winning ways to nurture down. By so doing they have bettered the emotional and productive tenor of their workplaces. Their methods are described in the following paragraphs.

One small-business executive, following Tober's lead, offers an all-expenses-paid semiannual weekend retreat in a nearby vacation spot for the whole office to air views and plan strategies. Not only is the venture a legitimate tax-deductible expense for her, it is also a superb opportunity to touch base personally with everyone who works for her in a congenial and different atmosphere. Her employees return to work feeling coddled, understood, respected, and invigorated.

Advertiser Lois Gould has a subtle way of nurturing down. She says she never creates "sexual ghettos," and that is an encouraging and spirit-raising policy for her employees. "Most of us women complain loudly," says Gould, "when men put us in neat, little compartments. Now, whenever we can, let's get rid of the stereotypical thinking." Thus Gould gives the Revlon account to the male executive and the Merrill Lynch account to the female executive. She hires male secretaries and female sales managers. There is a feeling of *possibility* in the office that is extraordinary.

One female executive sends monthly suggested-reading lists through the ranks of her female employees—books that encourage them to succeed, express themselves, and have fuller personal lives—even if it takes time away from the corporation. She *never* suggests books that denigrate women by claiming that they love too much, make foolish choices, or ought to learn to tolerate difficult men.

Another female CEO never fails to hand out small, unexpected gifts to employees. These cost her very little but work to massage the egos of her employees with great tenderness. "I make sure to give away apples and other fruit from my garden, for example, to people at work. Even hard men crumble," she says, "when faced with a beefsteak tomato right fresh from the earth. It's a nurturing, loving act, and people not only pay back such personalized consideration, they pick up your act and make it part of their own repertoire, spreading the good!"

One manager, an ex-actress, utilizes role playing in her nurture-down efforts. Regularly, she hires specialists to come in for a *"coping"* session. Everyone, including the very highest chief executive officers, "acts out" various situations the specialist sets up—situations that may represent personal roadblocks or intraoffice failures of communications. The mere acting out of employees pretending to be the boss, and the boss taking the role of underlings, is a device that creates great empathy and sometimes both hilarious and anger-releasing moments. When you role-play the boss, even in front of the boss, you learn how to assume and express power; when you role-play the employee, if you are the boss, you *must* learn, quite graphically, all about the needs of that employee.

The most powerful nurturing down often occurs in female "clubs" or "networks." Personal status is dispelled in an atmosphere of equality as women's best impulses to relate to and nurture others are expressed. Many powerful women feel a strong responsibility to share the secrets of their success, to "give back" some of the advantages and luck that have come their way. Whether we do it from true altruism or from a superstitious feeling of "you've got to give if you want to get" is not important. What is important is that in small and large cities, strong and successful women are lecturing, counseling, and simply supporting women who are not quite as strong, as they nurture down through the ranks.

Barbara Tober, for one, doesn't discount the possibility of nurturing up, even though many working women are pessimistic about being able to do it.

"I just feel like I'm 'brown-nosing' my teacher whenever I'm tempted to show warmth or support or even give a constructive suggestion to my boss," says Nellie Gallant, an insurance sales person from Topeka, Kansas.

"Yes, we have grown up in an age when our peers would criticize us for showing allegiance with a teacher," agrees Tober. "It was always 'her' against 'us' and anyone who warmed up to 'her' was a traitor. Nothing could be more destructive to business and getting ahead than this particular philosophy.

"It *is* true that many executives," says Tober, "are remarkably ungracious to compliments. That may be because many executives are themselves always swimming upstream and feeling that if they pause they'll take a gulp of water and drown. But, it is equally true," declares Tober, "that there are bosses out there who will literally melt from an honestly offered nice word: personal uptouching tends to make managers look harder at workers. Try it, risk it! Go up to the boss even if she's on a gallop down the hall and say something like, 'I loved your last meeting and I thought perhaps we could try this . . .' or write a note and say 'I'm proud to work here and I think I could do even more than I already do.' "

DANA Corporation chairman Gerry Mitchell finds ways to listen to the voices in his corporation and, in so doing, encourages nurturing up as well as nurturing down. Posters of Mitchell hang in the offices of the $3.7 billion manufacturer of auto parts and industrial products: WRITE A LETTER TO YOUR CHAIRMAN is the message under each poster, and attached to the poster are thick pads of tearsheets already stamped and addressed to Mitchell. Every single note received is a note answered and often heeded.

Certainly, every company head is not as eager to solicit warmth and make personal connections with underlings. Furthermore, anyone who attempts nurturing up has to be prepared to receive nothing for her trouble. Not everyone will stop dead in his tracks to acknowledge you. Maybe you *will* be accused by peers of trying to butter up higher-ups. So what? We're all so terrified of that possibility we go full tilt in the opposite direction and ignore the teacher, ignore the boss, and perpetuate a cold, hierarchical business atmosphere.

Both males and females on the top rungs have to be relentless about being role models of empathy if they want to put warmth and cooperation back into the corporation. Women in particular have a precious responsibility to other women to act appreciative of respect and kindness. Most important, they should never devalue or put down decency in the work field. Barbara Tober recalls a young southern woman, transplanted to Philadelphia, who once told Tober that she loved her job but was crushed when her boss said to her one day, "Why don't you try to stop saying 'please' and 'thank you' so much? We just don't do that up north."

4

Corporate Leaders:
The Highest Rungs

Only two percent of all women managers have made it to the highest rungs of the business ladder, and only three Fortune 500 companies are headed by women. Indeed, one would not be accused of wild exaggeration to note that the top rungs continue to be a barely touched frontier for women, despite our vast numbers in the marketplace. We are, however, making some small progress. According to a 1986 Heidrick and Struggles survey of corporate women officers employed by Fortune 1000 companies, four out of five are at the vice presidential level or above—and that's up from one third at this level in 1980. The average annual compensation for these women officers on the highest rungs is $116,810, which is a figure in stark contrast to the beginning of the eighties when fewer than ten percent of the group earned this much. The price women pay to be on this top rung? It's high in personal relationships.

- The majority of these women are childless. Almost a third say their work affected their decision on whether or not to have children.

- More than half of these executives who have not married say that the choice is influenced by their careers.

- 21.3 percent of the corporate leaders are separated or divorced, up from 18.5 percent in 1980.

The cost of achievement is high for several reasons. Once on the fast track, very few ambitious women or men take time off for nurturing. It has always been realistic to assume that time off means losing many of the footholds gained. This often translates into a decision to remain childless. Furthermore, the fast track usually means very late hours, short or no vacations, total attention to career. This cannot help but bode ill for lasting relationships between men and women. It's difficult enough for one person in a relationship to be on the fast track, but when two tread the ladder upward, either the entire fabric of the American family can become threadbare or, with new strategies, new career game plans, and a new business philosophy the family fabric can wear like iron. This is where tender should enter.

This is where power enters as well. Those women at the top have it within their power to make a difference in the way humanistic values are injected into the business world. By their own actions, they can set standards of confidence in a better way to work and live.

It must be admitted that there are genuine limitations to the flexibility of top-rung women who wish to promote cooperation and empathy. For starters, making changes in management style can backfire.

"You really begin to think that you're nothing without your position," says one woman president, "and so you hesitate to make yourself vulnerable by acting warm and empowering instead of hard and directive. Still, some of us are starting to challenge the Pavlov's Dog Syndrome—reacting with the accepted tough confrontational stance to every new challenge. I for one have been pulling out the old feminine techniques that worked well for me at home. Call them tricks if you want, I don't care. It's good management."

If only top management could pull out the old feminine techniques more often. Actually, the woman president who challenges the Pavlovian Syndrome is just the tip of the iceberg. Quietly, more and more powerful women are asserting humanistic tendencies and finding out that acting human strengthens their personal power base.

As I conducted interviews with the top-rung women, I discovered that although many will not overtly claim feminine traits to be prerequisites for the best kind of leadership, their actions belie their hesitancy to be publicly associated with nurturing characteristics. CEOs who understand about compassion still don't want to talk a whole lot about how they spend time doing for others; somehow that smacks too much of the oppressed, servile woman whose image they're trying to elude. The difference between the CEOs and the oppressed women, though, is that the CEOs don't hesitate to advance their own causes at the same time as they empower others. Top-rung women, instinctively aware of the benefits to be gained from niceness, don't attempt to diminish other women, as do managers in the competitive mold. They usually don't dread dealing with emotions—their own and others'. "Still," said the vice president of a large fabric house, "I certainly don't feel confident about discussing my insecurities with anyone else but my husband, and even that happens under cover of closed bedroom doors. I know it sounds naive, but I had no idea, until recently, that anyone else feels the same way about this unspoken prohibition on sharing problems. I've the sensation of being a feelings freak, unable, much longer, to keep up my facade of know-it-all executive."

What will it take to bring humanized work out in the open? What will it take to make the tender traits more universally palatable? The women's movement has mobilized women to fight for equality and human principles, but feminism must move along, beyond mobilization. When women, spurred by passion and skill, finally reach the top rungs, it will certainly take their audible acknowledgment of the tender skills to give them credibility. Certainly humanistic impluses must trickle down to help women who are on their way up.

What follows are the voices of some top-rung corporate women that ring true with caring, even though their owners don't necessarily characterize themselves as tender. Just as women's struggle for economic independence became accepted into the public awareness of the seventies, perhaps in this decade, the acceptance of ancient female traits as being powerful human traits will also become absorbed into American social and business culture.

In the meantime, top-rung women have a clear responsibility to prove Germaine Greer, an early feminist, wrong. "If I have one more executive wardrobe described to me," said Greer, "I will go stark, staring insane. I'm not interested in executives of either sex. As far as I'm concerned they're all male. I don't think it's any hardship not to be able to get a seat on the board of General Motors or Bendix. If you're enough like a man, you'll get one." The following women are not like men and board seats and prominence are already theirs.

Tootsie Roll Chief

You can't get much more prominent than Ellen Gordon, president of the Tootsie Roll Corporation. Gordon seems one of those *happy* presidents, a woman who somehow has managed to do it all in relatively nonfrenzied sequences, rather than all at once. Even if she is not thrilled about admitting she has a different management style from her male counterparts, she does. Plenty of Tender Power at work here. In addition to her top-echelon corporate status, she is the president of the Committee of 200, an international organization of businesswomen who, typically, own businesses with annual sales volumes of at least five million dollars or run corporate divisions with more than twenty million dollars in annual sales. Approximately eighty percent of the members are entrepreneurs. The remaining twenty percent occupy, with Ellen Gordon, the rarified air of the multimillion-dollar corporation.

Gordon's a powerhouse.

More important, she has a sense of humor. Her personal stationery is emblazoned with a mouth-watering picture of a Tootsie Roll on the envelope. That touch of playfulness alone would set her apart from mordantly serious counterparts.

"I was the first pregnant women on the Stock Exchange, and as a matter of fact, they didn't know what to do with me. But I held my ground and I stayed.

"My style is more persuasive and insistent than loud and tough. I'm certainly aggressive, but in a very quiet way. A woman who deals that way is less likely to be shut out from information that circulates along the communications network—information she absolutely needs. I think that women, and men too for that matter, who don't continually try to prove their competence in loud and macho ways, are much more persuasive than tough guys. I've always felt Don Juan probably wasn't much of a man because of the way he was constantly compelled to prove it."

A most difficult problem in current corporate politics has been the issue of child care and just who gets to do it. More and more top-rung women are increasingly dissatisfied with settling for an hour of that infamous "quality" time, let alone the decision to remain childless. When asked about her feelings on the matter, Ellen Gordon said that she's very much aware of large numbers of women who reluctantly decide to postpone or put off having families because career demands are so intense.

"It makes me sad," she says, "to think that those women who would want children under less pressured times, will wake up one morning and be horrified that the opportunity is lost.

"I just want to *deck* women who are so involved with their computers that they cut off other yearnings, until the biological possibilities are almost gone. You can always do most of it somehow, particularly if you have a nurturing partner and the courage to try alternative ways of being with your child. My youngest traveled with me when I was on the road. It meant she had to go to two schools every week, something that would make some child care specialists very nervous. It turned out to be a fascinating experience for her, and one which she took in her stride. One school was a classical New England preparatory school where all the parents were professors at Harvard and MIT. In Chicago, she went to a school that was fifty percent comprised of minority students. She learned different things in each, some of which stood her in fine stead, some of which were contradictory. For example, in one school she was allowed to wear sneakers (there, they were called gym shoes), but no blue jeans. In the other school, where they called a sneaker a sneaker, blue jeans were the accepted mode of dress. Did all this get her crazy? Was I selfish to ask a young girl to accommodate to my work and family needs? I don't think so. My daughter thrived from her varied life."

With a woman as president at Tootsie Roll, are child care arrangements given priority? No.

"I'm sorry to say, it's a big, big problem, here as elsewhere." says Gordon. "If we have a product manager who wants to go on a three-month maternity leave, I'm in trouble. We're a middle-sized company and don't have six other product managers to move in and fill the void. It would be great if things were different, but right now, it wouldn't be realistic to suggest they soon will be. Where entrepreneurial women can be more flexible, corporate women just can't—at least not in today's corporation."

Ellen Gordon is surely a sympathetic president, personally experienced in the problems of taking on the Superwoman myth, but even she has few answers to those women who can't afford to travel with their children or place them in different schools. Even she falls back on talk of "realism" instead of pushing for new realities. She says she looks forward to the day when "gender is a non-issue and when one doesn't think male or female executive, but just plain executive."

Gordon may look forward to the day when gender is a non-issue, but some experts feel it will be a long time coming—and question whether it would even be desirable. Pointing out valuable differences in management style can mean progress for both men and women. For instance, one rule in CEO male politics, says Kathryn Stechert, author of *On Your Own Terms*, is "no holds barred—but keep tactics carefully concealed so no one else, particularly superiors, can discern your activity." When a woman is the focus of the competition, the "gentleman factor" enters the picture. Men are terrified of looking like bullies when they lash into women, and often cut down on the toughness. Dorothy Gregg, an executive vice president of a communications research firm, says "Men can carry on their deadly assassinations of one another without anyone thinking twice about it. With a woman, a man is a little more careful in his behavior than he is competing with another man. He has to be more adroit, more subtle. If he's not, he'll be marked as clumsy, as making a clear attack on the woman—and that's a 'demerit' in the game."

Why not applaud the "gentleman factor" and its mentor the "lady factor"? Why not demonstrate, as do many liberated business leaders, that those who work for ladies and gentlemen, instead of bullies, work harder and commit to the corporation more loyally? Why make a non-issue of gender when it is precisely women's gender differences that will bring American business back on its feet where it belongs?

If the concept of Tender Power became a plus instead of an unknown, if the public consciousness demanded empathy and cooperation instead of "deadly assassination," if the lagging United States production figures are ever traced back to bully tactics as they should be, perhaps then we can make gender a non-issue.

Until that day, we all need powerful, yet non-bullying, role models, who put their values up front with their profits and their money where their mouths are. We need women presidents who will insist upon empowering workers with strong solutions to the human problems of child care, elder care, and lack of personal leisure time. We need to celebrate, not camoufl-age, gender-different leadership if the differences lead us to a kindlier, thus more effective, workplace.

How do you get the public consciousness to demand empathy?

Perhaps a good place to start is with the industry that contours the public consciousness—tells it what to like and what not to like—the advertising industry. Anyone with an eye to trends knows that trends are shaped on Madison Avenue, where many of the nation's most powerful agencies are housed. There we find the typical strong, creative advertising executive, the guy who is perceived as having few scruples as long as he can sell his client's products—the "Madison Avenue man."

Lois Wyse is strong, creative, and powerful, too, but she owns an overload of scruples and sensitivity, and although she's a shaker and a mover in the advertising world, she's definitely not a Madison Avenue man. Her office, as a matter of fact, is on Park Avenue, an equally impressive thoroughfare, and there she wields her power and her tenderness.

With a Name Like Wyse, She's Got to Have Smarts

When Lois Wyse and her first husband went into the advertising business, they worked hard, but mostly piddled around, until a jam company asked them to come up with a snappy and memorable slogan. Lois offered "With A Name Like Smucker's, It's Got To Be Good," and the rest is advertising history. Today, Lois Wyse is president of Wyse Advertising, one of the largest agencies in the country. Besides being the recipient of major advertising awards, including the coveted Clio, Lois has managed to publish many books of fiction and nonfiction. With such a level of production, does she operate with a brusque, single-minded, no-holds-barred aggression?

"Are you kidding? You're looking at someone whose dream was to be safe, loved, popular, and distinctly unradical. I cannot tolerate criticism. I stumbled and fumbled my way to success," says Wyse.

"That's why I love business, this business in particular. In advertising, you're dealing with human behavior at every level, and I know people respond when you show empathy and kindness in the pitch of a product. A gentle but perceptive person doesn't intrude into the client's or the consumer's own protective coloring."

Women, says Wyse, generally have a more sensitive finger on the human pulse. For that reason, she would never suggest any advertising that implied that there are benefits from bullying, violence, or behavior that ignores kindness. In terms of business relationships, Wyse says that women are in general more supportive of each other than their male counterparts are. She suggests that businesswomen feel comfortable with—and will go out of their way for—each other. They still have to deal with that "old dumb thing of men who are critical about women. When I told my partner what a great relationship I immediately struck with a woman who runs a huge company, his visceral response was—'sure, you don't emasculate her.' Tired, tired, tired thinking. If men would only put their dukes down, they wouldn't have to worry so much about being emasculated."

Wyse says she thinks of herself as a walking layout. "The nicest, best-looking part of me, is what I try to sell. If I choose to assume the role of taste maker, and I have, I can't be a slob. Neither can I come on too strong, be offensive and inconsiderate of others. If these are female virtues—sure, I use them. Authenticity is what gives me my authority. I can't look like ten years ago and talk like ten years ago if I'm selling today's taste, and neither do I want to talk and look like someone I'm not—a male.

"Frankly," she says, as she speaks of running a big business, "I think women who are all-woman are a lot less fearful about business than men. They make decisions much more easily. That's because a man, for the most part, *is* his job, and a woman is herself. I'm Susie, chairperson of the ABC Corporation, and I'm also Bob's mother, and I'm this and that—but a man, he's the chairman of ABC Corporation, and the minute he's *not* the chairman of the ABC Corporation, he falls apart and doesn't know *who* he is. When the stock market blew its top, I heard of four male suicides, but I haven't heard of one woman who shot herself because she lost money in the stock market."

And yet in 1985, only 9.2 percent of all working women were executives who might reasonably have had enough invested to even consider jumping out of the window. And therein lies the rub, according to Wyse. Tender Power seems to have its limitations in today's corporate world.

"Realistically, you are just not going to get to be the president of General Motors speaking in an authentic woman's voice, because the men are just not going to let us in. We're going to be able to run service businesses, we're going to be able to run creative businesses, but in my lifetime I will not see a woman be chairman of General Motors, unless some nice guy leaves her enough stock to assume control," says Wyse.

The nature of top-level stewardship cannot be assumed in one generation, says Wyse. Women must first get footholds in smaller businesses, using graciousness and cooperative values. And women, she notes, must then cool down.

"Younger businesswomen are so confused about their roles today. There is too much hysteria, biological clock nervousness, do-it-all frenzy," she comments. "If you're forty, you have a tenth of a chance to get married and if you're twelve, you can get married instantly—that sort of thing. Their fathers are divorcing their mothers and marrying women twenty-five years younger. There's a lot of anger directed toward men and even anger directed toward other women who preceded them, and who, many feel, have trapped them and sold them a Superwoman story. We've really got to go back to affirming those values we always held dear. In the end, it will be cool, unangry, caring heads that stay on the fast track all the way to the top. Eventually, it will happen."

Nurturing is not a household word in the majority of American corporations. Most corporate cultures have been defined and programmed primarily by men. Unless (and it is rare) a woman like Lois Wyse or Ellen Gordon just happens to sit in the boss's chair, women who enter the corporate life on lower rungs of the ladder are almost surely going to meet resistance when they employ traditionally female strengths.

There is, however, a certain level of corporate activity that is headed primarily by women, and that is in the field of women's magazines. Here women who have reached the top can utilize the ethos, the pathos, and the logos of women in their finest management styles. The corporate leaders who head women's magazines, if they're good teachers and articulate about women's intrinsic values, have it in their power to educate whole segments of the American population that read or are influenced by women's magazines—the magazines that reflect our times and shape our opinions. A man whose wife is being challenged by *Lear's*, a brand new magazine geared to the mature woman (the one who wasn't born yesterday, as its logo reads) is a prime target for having his own feminine consciousness raised along with hers. A teenager whose mother is excited by new possibilities offered by a piece in *The Ladies' Home Journal* begins to think about reinterpreting her own possibilities. The printed word is a powerful weapon; corporate women who shape magazine policy can by example and ideology change the way the world thinks and moves. Nurturing, for example, can become a word that equally describes men and women.

And even though "the Cosmo Girl" is better known as an example of the sexually and professionally assertive woman, she too can be a nurturer.

Everyone knows who the first Cosmo Girl was.

That Cosmo Girl

One of the leaders in the corporate publishing world is Helen Gurley Brown, editor-in-chief and the person whose name is almost synonymous with young achieving women who are as secure in their swinging good looks as they are in their sexuality. Although the Cosmo Girl is often criticized as being a rather plasticized version of the flesh-and-blood original, *Cosmo* continues to sell—and sell, and sell. Helen, who has a finger in every *Cosmo* pot, has written of her tentative beginnings, her insecurity as a "mouseburger," and her determination to use every feminine wile she could call on to remake her image into something quite powerful and still quite human.

To a very large extent she has succeeded.

In the publishing industry, she's known as a kind and generous friend. I remember her brand of loyalty from personal experience. Years ago when I was writing a book with the then Cristina Ferrare DeLorean, headlines broke, and the implication was that her husband, John DeLorean, was every bad thing known to man. In Cristina's high-powered world, it was interesting to see how many of her friends and associates turned against her, wouldn't touch her with a ten-foot pole, for fear that some of John DeLorean's infamy would rub off on them. Helen Gurley Brown was one of a very small group of women who didn't sever the Cristina connection, didn't turn a cold shoulder. She was a loyal, good pal.

It comes as no surprise, then, to hear that, despite her reputation for being the stern taskmaster who has kept *Cosmopolitan* magazine virtually on top of the women's magazine market, she operates her business in the capacity of a very caring chief executive officer. One might say that, because the market is women, Helen can afford to use tenderness as a tool of power; one might say it, but one would be wrong. Business is business. Most of *Cosmo's* staff, on both the editorial and the business end, are men. Numbers must add up, whether the business is automotive parts or women's magazines. People must be made to produce. Brown represents the power of tenderness and the way that the combination of tender and power seems to encourage productive enterprise.

"Frankly, ever since I was in my early thirties and in group therapy in Los Angeles, I became convinced that inside, men were just as capable of emotion and vulnerability as women, and I surely saw male executives who are as capable of loyalty and support as female executives. The trouble is, most men show these instincts mainly in therapy; wasn't it Gloria Steinem who always said that men only had to get in touch with their emotional natures, which are there, but just tamped down?"

Is Brown a business nurturer? She says that there's considerable nurturing done at *Cosmo*, and not all of it by her, by any means. In fact, she maintains, the best way to loosen up the logjam is to let emotional life progress naturally, even at the site of big business.

"How can people work when they're in pain? There's no question that in these offices, on certain days, personal discussions take precedence over business discussions. Anger and unhappiness must be exorcised, and I've walked in on many scenes of emotional stress—and walked right out again. If people must take up business time during business hours, I guarantee they'll work on after business hours to finish the job that has to be done. Allowing workers to act human, after all, is effective only as long as it gets the job done. I'll be honest, if I didn't have a success on my hands, I might act a bit more 'Prussian.'"

Precisely how does Brown support her employees? What tools of tenderness produce her success?

Stroking is good. Helen says she's always careful to stroke before she "lowers the boom. One must compliment before she complains, encourage and appreciate before pointing out what should be done differently. I can defend my system because it works. People who are encouraged to have their little vapors also tend to work like beavers once the vapors are dissipated."

Helen Gurley Brown is against "aggressiveness"—that kind of angry hostility and resentment that prods destructive competition—but very much in favor of assertiveness that doesn't allow "any grass to grow under your feet because you're a woman. You're in there pitching for the assignment, the promotion, the salary, the secretary, the corner office—whatever you feel you deserve. Just for the record, I prefer people that pitch overtly, rather than secretly."

And then, she confides, she just hates it when her budget is "closed" and someone pitches for a $5000 raise. Or, when someone mentions that she plans to take a month's vacation, all at one time. Helen admits she doesn't like to *hear* about vacations, let alone raises.

"But can they let me get away with that? Of course not, at least not if they're assertive, and they better be, to survive."

That Woman's Day *Woman*

On perhaps the opposite end of the spectrum from that Cosmo Girl is the *Woman's Day* reader, who is more conservative, more home and cooking oriented, a tad older—although readers of both magazines are out there in the work force in at least equal numbers. Ellen Levine occupies the top rung at *Woman's Day* as editor-in-chief, and her influence on millions can be said to be vast. She is highly regarded by colleagues and by the political world as a brilliant, intuitive, responsible woman. Having served admirably on the President's Commission on Pornography, she got high marks from politically astute observers for her authoritative presence.

I was not surprised, then, when her secretary invited me in, precisely at the moment scheduled for our interview. I have a little theory on this: It seems to me the more powerful the person to be interviewed, the more respectful she or he is of others' time. The lower down the rung a person is, the longer the interviewer has to wait.

Levine is wonderfully glamorous, and her long, silvery hair gives the lie to millions of hairdressers who say white hair makes you look old. The walls of *Woman's Day* are a flattering pink, a true, soft, but strong hue.

When she is asked whether her personal style of leadership is feminine, she immediately replies that feminine can be warm and graceful, and feminine can be rough and tough, depending on the female we're talking about. Then, because she knows what female *I'm* talking about, she owns up to, what sounds to me, the former.

"There are many ways of doing business," she says, "and for a long time this magazine was run in a stand-offish fashion where power came from the top and floated down. I tend to like power to bubble up and down at the same time so people feel a strong sense of control and contribution. I feel that it's to my advantage that people see me as human and vulnerable and even silly sometimes—I'm not above wearing a fabulous mask on Halloween—although that can occasionally backfire."

Women leaders, more than their male counterparts, tend to prefer face-to-face encounters to a "guess-what's-on-my-mind" style, say many experts. How does Levine operate?

"When I first arrived here," she says, "people weren't accustomed to being told what the boss thinks. They'd try to guess or to ferret out information, and they weren't at all sure they liked my way of telling them gently but directly—'this needs work, this is a problem, or this is great.' But, it seems to me that people who work together have to personally connect. I majored in political science, but a degree in psychology would have been helpful in this business. The bottom line is, you have to remain true to your instincts. If a man with whom you're working is 'threatenable,' he will be threatenable on many levels. You can threaten him with the macho-woman thing, you can threaten him because he finds you attractive—so you just can't worry about how not to threaten male peers or male subordinates."

And she offers an example of being true to one's instincts.

"It seems to me, on one level, that many women are uncomfortable being steely tough, and when they have to create the behavior they think is appropriate to their position, it comes out badly. When I don't know how to do a thing, or I feel insecure about it, I generally ask for help. It wasn't always so. Early in my tenure here, I had to fire a few people. Inevitably, I'd get migraines the day before, the day of the firing and the day after. Once, I went to a neurologist and he asked if I was under stress and I immediately answered 'no.' He asked what I'd done the day before, and I told him I fired someone. 'Don't you think your headaches relate to that?' he asked me, and I said, 'Absolutely not.'

"The next time I fired someone the person disappeared right before my eyes in the haze of the migraine.

" 'Okay,' I said, 'this *is* stressful, I don't want to admit it to anyone and consequently I'm postponing my emotions and they're coming out somewhere else. In the effort to get on with it and prove to people that I can do it all by myself, I'm inducing a kind of collapse in myself.'

"*So now*—when I have to fire someone, and it's very rare, first I run around talking to senior people at the office. 'What's the first thing I should say when he comes in my office, should I start immediately with the bad news and follow up with good news?'—stuff like that. We trade opening sentences. No one feels any more comfortable with the situation than I do, I've found. Actually, the one person I met who could fire someone easily was not a person I liked a whole lot, anyhow. The point is—once I followed instincts, asked for help, allowed myself to show nervousness, I banished the migraines. I think, perhaps, a lot of men might feel as I did, but would be too self-conscious to seek help."

Levine believes in being outspoken in "a feminine way."

"I'm persistent and dogged about what I want to say," she offers, "but I guess that I'm softer and gentler in the way I pose questions and make statements. I have no problems with using a balance of sex appeal along with the rest of my legitimate self; men use their sex appeal at work, all the time. It's a question of balance: I wouldn't want to be too sexy, too tough, too soft—but an appropriate mix. I'm a woman, it's what I am, take it or leave it—I won't diffuse it."

Levine is often photographed with her children, her husband. How does she manage the do-it-all trap?

"I didn't work full time when my children were babies. Many women feel strongly that if they can possibly manage it, it's better to be at home during the earliest months. On television, the movies, in all the media, we're portraying the ideal as getting back into the work force as soon as possible. I think it's absolutely outrageous that there should be societal pressure put on the woman who chooses to be home with that baby, that it's, somehow, less than powerful to do so. The ideal, of course, is to work part time, just to keep those fingers in the business. When I had a baby, I talked the editors of the paper where I worked into allowing me a three-day work week. They prorated my salary accordingly. Of course, many women simply can't afford part time—and ideally this society should help them out."

Levine shares a management secret. To me it sounds suspiciously like Tender Power.

"If you know what motivates someone, if you can identify with that person—actually creep into his head and figure out what he's thinking, you can get the best from him. Call it women's intuition, call it manipulation—it works. I know, for example, that women have a need for good workplace relationships—it's a food we crave. Naturally, I'm going to make sure that this workplace offers time for women to bond with each other, and for men to do the same if they can. Intuiting people's needs is my prime management tool."

"I am more nurturing than I ever thought I'd be," she notes. "When you have achieved some status, you can allow yourself more warmth. Just look at women doctors. A few years ago, female doctors were *tough*. I mean, you didn't go to a female doctor because your breasts would be bruised after she finished examining them. Now, female physicians are much softer because they don't have to be road-busters, out there kicking down the barricades. They're much better physicians for it. I'll tell you—the time is ripe for women to show their true colors and what glory there is in those colors. No imitation of them is possible."

If the women's magazines are a corporate arena where strong but compassionate business practices can be introduced, certainly the same is true of periodicals that reach out to a more general population. The content of daily newspapers also shapes the nation's perceptions. There, signs are clear that the nation is becoming more respectful of the place women's concerns have in the lives of all. Indeed, women's concerns, those issues of humanity that used to be relegated to what was once called the "women's pages," are now reaching out to men as well. "Women's pages," have transmogrified into "life-styles" sections. All over the country columns have sprouted up that reflect on and celebrate issues once thought to be of interest only to women—family, friendship, love, and loyalty. These ethical and personal outpourings, written and read without embarrassment by men and women alike, are teaching everyone that intimate connections must be brought back into business as well as personal life.

There are not too many women at the helm of huge newspapers that have the entire country as a constituency. One such newspaper, a relatively new phenomenon, is known behind the scenes as "McPaper." Sitting in its boardroom is a woman who seems to embody empathic business practices.

McPaper

They made fun of it at first and called *USA TODAY* "McPaper." It reminded many of McDonald's—instant, characterless—junk food journalism they called it. It wouldn't last a year, this new newspaper.

In September, 1987, McPaper celebrated its fifth year. Its father, the Gannett Company, expected to round out 1987 advertising revenues with more than $100 million, forty percent higher than the preceding year. Someone's obviously doing something right.

That someone is no one but Cathleen B. Black, forty-four years old, slim, blonde, blue-eyed, the adoptive mother of a new baby and publisher of an upbeat, upstart newspaper whose paid circulation of more than 1.5 million makes it the nation's second largest daily paper, after *The Wall Street Journal*.

Whomever I asked, wherever I poked, the term consistently applied to this powerhouse woman was "nice." She is described by one friend as "someone who always returns phone calls." George Lois, president of Lois Pitts Gershon Pon/GGK, the advertising agency that handles the *USA TODAY* account, says:

"People who work for her kill themselves for her, she's that nice. She's the most fun to work with of any person I've ever known, the most interesting, the most open, the most receptive. She doesn't hide her feelings. If she likes something, she goes nuts. If she doesn't, she drills you between the eyes. She's just a joy to work with."

"You never forget she's a woman," says one employee. "She's gorgeous for one thing, and she plays off that in subtle ways—she uses her sex, not sexually, but sensually. It's quite attractive."

"She's a doll," says *USA TODAY* editor Jeannie Williams. "There's only one word for her—nice."

When people speak of top-rung and powerful businesspeople, nice is not a word they often choose.

When Black became publisher of *USA TODAY*, she promised to overcome the hesitation of nervous and reluctant advertisers in the new newspaper with "enthusiasm, optimism, and water torture." She's a cheerleader, an optimistic, hardworking person.

Does Black think that women can lend special elements of feminine strength to the boardroom?

"It's clear that women can bring to the table a cooperative, participative kind of management style," Black says. "Women are more used to consensus building, for example—the establishing of support. And I'll never forget one woman who taught me about that."

Black tells the following story:

"Years ago, I sat on a board for the first time, a volunteer-type thing, and I went to a meeting and presented two or three new ideas, all brilliant, I thought, and one by one, they were shot down. The next day, a woman called me up—I don't know if a man would have done the same thing. It was such a *splendid*, cooperative gesture.

" 'Have you ever sat on a board before?' she asked. The answer, of course, was no.

" 'Well, we're going to have breakfast and I'm going to tell you how to do it.'

"So we had breakfast and she said to me, 'You know, what you've got to do is "seed" the board—plant an idea. Everyone likes to think he's the first to have heard something, so before you launch a new idea, make sure four or five people, who will be present, already know about it. Then they will support you.'

"She was a true friend, a cooperative agent. It was such a good lesson for me. None of us likes to be surprised at a meeting, if you think about it, good or bad. I don't like surprises and now I ask all my colleagues to tell me their ideas before the meeting."

When asked whether she allows herself to show vulnerability in her business dealings, Black's answer is swift.

"I think it's fine to show emotion, but I think you cannot be emotional; it's a subtle but important difference. Perhaps more than men, women tend to display pride, happiness, or sadness, but an emotional wreck in business is disaster.

"I'll tell you a little secret," she admits. "In situations where I feel most vulnerable, I'll turn to humor as a tool. I've observed many women do this in moments of stress, and they seem to do it somewhat better than men. Humor is a great gift because it is a great weapon. It deflects hostility, tension, or anger. Did you ever notice people who feel good about themselves generally have great wit?"

What makes for a powerful boss? I ask Black.

"It isn't necessarily a tough boss," she shoots back. "*Fortune Magazine* always lists the 'Ten Toughest Bosses in America . . .'; I'd rather be thought of as one of the Ten Best, not the Ten Toughest, and believe me—there is a difference."

What qualities do the "best" bosses possess, then? Black gives her personal list:

• Self-confidence

• Ability to share glory

• Caring personalities

• Decisive natures

• Commitment to colleagues and projects

• Enthusiastic skill

• Courage to surround one's self with people more skilled than one's self

Like Cathy Black, few of the top-rung corporate officers would openly claim the word tender, and yet none seemed to operate without the tender traits, claimed or not. Black's "quality" list is the quintessential power and tender list.

The Power of Pink

Consider the example of Mary Kay Ash who, in 1963, retired from twenty-five years in direct sales and founded Mary Kay Cosmetics. Her objective was to give women an open-ended opportunity, something she had never experienced in her career. In the early 1980s women were still walking "two paces behind the boss," who was invariably a man. She had met many women of tremendous capabilities whom she felt could have certainly gone to the top but who had been denied the chance simply because they were female bodies. She wanted to change all that. Interestingly enough, in 1963 the Civil Rights Law requiring equal pay for equal work regardless of sex was passed; it was also the time that the seed of the women's movement was beginning to take root.

During Mary Kay's brief retirement she decided to write a book about a "dream company" where there was room at the TOP for women. She felt that the needs of women in the workplace were not being met and was concerned about the social aspects as well as their financial aspirations. She thought back over her career and compiled a list of all of the good things about her work experiences, and another list of all those things that had frustrated her. Her goal was to share those experiences with women moving into the workforce and to help them solve problems unique to women in business. "I wanted to express a business philosophy based on the priorities that I had found so fundamental in keeping my own life and career in order: God first, family second, career third. Everything always seemed to work well in that order, and out of that order nothing seemed to work." To implement that philosophy, the "dream company" would follow the Golden Rule: Do unto others as you would have them do unto you. She wanted to create a business opportunity where women could have flexible hours to be with their families when they were needed and where they would be appreciated, recognized, and applauded for their efforts. While Mary Kay Ash's book was not written for twenty years, her thoughts became the foundation of her cosmetics firm, which celebrated its twenty-fifth anniversary in 1988.

Mary Kay's philosophy was not popular by early feminist standards when many feminists believed the only way women could succeed in business was to barge their way into a "man's world" and emulate them. By acting like men, women were forcing their way into a system men had dominated for centuries.

In contrast, Mary Kay Cosmetics was designed to emphasize the "go-give spirit," generously sharing knowledge and self with others. Although this spirit was never considered to be a "business secret," Ash was convinced that it was this special quality that would allow millions of women to find self-fulfillment.

In her former career Ash had always been disturbed when a male manager put down one of her ideas or suggestions with, "Mary Kay, you're thinking like a woman again." Certainly she was, because in those situations the companies were dealing with sales forces made up of women. "Thinking like a woman" was perhaps one of the keys to success that these male managers had not yet discovered. "Studies show that women do think differently from men, but such differences are in no way inferior or incompatible with 'the way a man thinks,'" says Ash.

Today Mary Kay Cosmetics flourishes more than ever as a people company built *with* and *for* women. The sales force includes many thousands of dynamic, independent businesswomen who run their own businesses, and the corporate staff includes many talented women in key positions, as well as men who seem to genuinely understand the tender side of power. Since the very first day, Mary Kay has used Tender Power to guide her sales force and also as a way to demonstrate to her customers that her company truly cares about their personal needs. "Thinking like a woman is always encouraged," says Ash.

"Being female is a tremendous advantage in a man's world. It is terribly important that we are careful not to form the habit of tuning out our sensitivities. Today, outstanding women perform in just about every area of business, government, and the arts and sciences. There is almost no kind of 'man's job,' from crane operator to politician, that some woman isn't doing somewhere and doing it well. The most successful of these women have found a way to balance their feminine qualities with their capabilities in the working world."

Many women are involved in organizations or relationships that have yet to recognize the value of the tender side of power. Perhaps this is why more women than ever before are starting their own businesses. Ash recognized this trend early on and has helped hundreds of thousands of women rediscover qualities that can help them succeed in all aspects of life. Mary Kay Beauty Consultants are independent businesswomen, building their own businesses, making their own decisions as to what level of success they want to achieve. While they are running their own businesses, they also have a tremendous support system from the corporation and from each other.

Ash believes most women first think of the tangible rewards they achieve in their businesses: the money they make, the cars they drive, the clothes they wear, the houses they live in; but many have learned that the intangible rewards are far more lasting and meaningful: the fulfillment, the peace of mind, and the joy of knowing that they are making a contribution, not only to their families and industry but to the nation and to the world! All of this has come about by embracing Tender Power as an operating philosophy, creating policies and practices that respect the needs of workers and employees and allow for compassionate family care. Ash, through her company, has created a world with real heroes and heroines, true models in every walk of life, a place where Tender Power is taught and encouraged so that everyone treats everyone else with mutual respect and consideration.

It should be acknowledged that it is easiest for women on the top rungs of corporate ladders to use reflective speech, to nurture down, to show caring. It is far more difficult from a lower-rung perspective to indulge in acts of disclosure and compassion. One fears giving away the competitive edge. Most women on the lower rungs are unable to pass through invisible barriers unless they act, in word and deed, like clones of successful men. They feel they must mirror the manners of the nonquestioning, invulnerable male executive or too often they hover just under the glass ceiling.

5

Under the Glass Ceiling: The View from Below

It's a tough place to be—just under that impenetrable barrier one can see through but cannot pass through to the scene above. Of all the positions in business, under the glass ceiling is where women find it most difficult to express their feminine voices; instead, they usually find themselves assuming a bland, androgynous personality. Those at the top may have the courage and the confidence that comes from having gotten there, but for those under the glass ceiling it's an act of bravery to act themselves. If one feels doubt, or is vulnerable, expressing it gets her into trouble. Women who have relied on intuition in the past find that this sense is devalued in favor of documented facts. That which is feminine and warm is considered silly and frivolous and not to be taken seriously. While women on the top rung can finally feel free to nurture down, if they only would, those in the middle are constantly trying to prove up. Sheila, a product manager for a dental equipment company in Denver, travels the country to meet customers (almost always men) to find out their needs and problems with her company's equipment. "I'm constantly trying to show how cool and clear-thinking I am. I think I'd do just about anything for a pat on the back from my superiors, and that won't come until the customers see me as 'one of the boys.' I've learned never to complain that I don't have enough time for family life or even enough time for me; somehow that's not what the male managers do. They grit their teeth and grin and bear it. I have to prove I can fit in."

It's interesting to note that many career specialists today also suggest that women stifle their pangs and shed anything that faintly whispers "female." Jinx Melia, for example, a career consultant and author of *Breaking into the Boardroom*, suggests that women emulate men and become "good bear fighters." She tells the story of the little boy playing soccer who was hit directly in the face with the ball. As he lay screaming in pain, his father yelled to the stricken boy, "Play with pain, Jay, play with pain." Women have never learned to play with pain, says Melia, and they need to.

Other career specialists give similar advice; for example, Betty Harragan, author of *Games Mother Never Taught You*, says: "When women had all the time in the world—in the fifties and sixties—to be sweet, nice, feminine—all the nurturing bull—it got them nowhere. Now, no one has time for that nonsense. You produce in the business world or you're out."

Unfortunately, without "that nonsense," as Harragan characterizes it, and with doing things the old way, women still are "out." According to a special U.S. Labor Department Report on the female work force, women are, without a doubt, still concentrated in the lower-paying industries and occupations—secretaries, cashiers, bookkeepers, registered nurses, and waitresses, to be specific. Nearly the same groups we saw ten years ago. On the management level, things aren't much better. If fifty percent of today's entry level managers are women, only about twenty-five percent of today's middle managers are women.

We finally have made inroads into the male marketplace; but, being in, we're just not advancing in the corporate hierarchy. Working just as hard as our male counterparts, trying to fit into the male mode, we're still stopping short where men advance. As the men push forward, unhindered by anything except their own talents, for women, there suddenly appears the oft-touted "glass ceiling." It's invisible, but inviolable.

Tara Roth Madden, author of *Women vs. Women: The Uncivil Business War*, thinks the reason might be that, as one program director in a New York women's research firm said, "Up to a certain point, brains and competence work. But then, fitting in becomes very important. It's at that point the barriers against women set in."

If she is correct, then trying to fit the male mold, "fitting in," is a barren prospect. We will never, never make it to the point where we look, feel, and sound like men, and thus will never blend in to the male society. Is it really hopeless? Is there a solution?

Madden has one. She suggests a "clarion call" for female role models. "Societies traditionally elevate strong and admirable individuals to role-model status," she says, "and all benefit by encouraging the young to follow in the inspirational footsteps of the more experienced."

Now, that makes sense.

No more fitting in. How about standing out?

Perhaps the best level, although admittedly the most difficult, for role models, to be conspicuously terrific, is a territory of women, not on the top, not on the bottom, but on this middle level of the work field. A concerted effort by strong, unsung heroines in middle management might finally crack that glass ceiling that hovers above. Role models must strive to stand out, say experts, not invisibly fit in.

It's true that many women who find themselves on the middle rung of the ladder to success are understandably doubtful about the good results to be derived from substituting cooperation for competition. They have seen the future, and it seems to be a picture of male-model success. Still, increasingly, there are others who insist upon doing it their way. They temper strength with caring acts, they refuse to feel embarrassed when they don't live up to the Corporate Amazon example, and they persist in their nurturing of those below. They try not to spend their time worrying that empowering others will detract from their own power.

Jenny Perez, an executive secretary for a paper merchant in Lombard, Illinois, says, "You're not successful till you've helped someone else. If you want to sit up there, aloof and isolated like the Wizard of Oz, scaring everyone with fake power, you'll never move on. Lending a hand makes you feel stronger in your soul and it makes you look stronger to others."

And Amy Gaskin, a bank manager in Dallas, says "I sure don't think power means coming off like a trucker. Women don't need sledge hammers and lassoes to make a point even if their men do."

These women in the middle who have learned to feel at home with their femininity smile when they read male-written management style books that praise the encouragement of creativity and the recognition of excellence and cooperation; they know these have been feminine tools forever. These women yearn for the day when these values are recognized as the distinctly feminine brand of leadership they really are.

Here are some voices of women who are often uncelebrated as role models or leadership material, unrecognized as legitimate style-setters and unrewarded by their industries. Still, they are genuine heroines, no matter how frazzled with discouragement they sometimes feel. They are women who know that the feminine traits are not to be dismissed, even though they're the first to admit that it's terribly difficult holding on to them in today's middle-level corporate climate.

If only we could multiply their potential power by the legions of other women in the middle, we could see that glass ceiling come tumbling down in shards.

Talk Reason to the Bread Man

Linda Hartmann is a middle manager at Hardees fast-food chain in Waverly, Tennessee, the "third largest fast-food chain in the United States," she proudly tells me. The people she manages and trains are the life's blood of any fast-food industry—the cashiers, cooks, assistant managers. Operations are her responsibility, and that means making sure the food is served properly and prepared hygienically. It is on middle managers like Hartmann that Hardees relies, and if Hardees is to get to be the *first* largest food chain in the United States, it is Hartmann and her colleagues who will get them there.

Linda is Tender Power. The soft southern accents of her voice belie the power part—but make no mistake, it's there.

"If my bread man delivers me bread that's not up to standard, or not properly coded or dated, and I throw a fit about it—he's going to say to himself, 'I can't stand that lady—I won't do nothin' good for her at all, if I can help it.' If he goes to a store managed by a man manager who says the same thing to him, he'll think to himself, 'Boy, that guy don't take nothing off nobody—he's a tough one.' It would defeat my purpose to act like a man. I don't think that either men or women deal well with women who react in a masculine way. My way is more diplomatic. I'd explain to the bread man that he's putting us both in a bad light if the bread is not up to standard. I'd point out the way in which the boss can come down on both of us. I'd operate with plausibility—make him see that he's doing us both a favor by doing right."

How does Linda deal, in her authentic voice, with employee relations. Her answer is—with reason.

"Men managers need instant gratification," she says. "Like—'I only want to tell you this one time—and that's it!' 'Get it to me in an hour—or else.'

"Well—that's just not a woman's style, as far as I can see. Even if it *is* a particular woman's style, it just doesn't cut ice with most people."

Hartmann mentions a cook with whom she's been having problems.

"I took her aside, very privately, very quietly. I asked whether there was a reason she wasn't following procedures; perhaps she was distracted because of some home problems? I listened to her gripes, her point of view. Together we talked about the best way to deal with it.

"The next day," says Hartmann, "I got a letter from her. 'Thanks for being so understanding,' she wrote. 'I'm sorry my work has not been up to standard—and I'll try to do better, I promise.'

"It's funny," says Hartmann. "Men can use women's style and it works great for them. Who can argue with being reasonable and compassionate? But women can *not* use the tough-guy stance and create loyal employees. It rings so harshly."

The Educator and the Nurse

Nursing and elementary education are two professions that traditionally have been almost exclusively peopled by women. Luckily, this is changing, but these fields still suffer from the economical deprivations and social devaluations seen in most woman-oriented enterprises. Much has been written about the female, and now male, teachers and nurses who daily are constricted by the airless weight of the same glass ceiling that hovers over their friends' mid-rung business careers. Much has been written, but little has been accomplished in the way of change.

Teachers are responsible for nothing less than the next generation's code of ethics—a heavy weight to bear. Yet they are often discouraged by low salaries, difficult working conditions, and something less than whole-hearted respect of a society that tends to give most of it to the more visible, more money-making, professionals. Yet it is educators and counselors on whom the burden rests to teach the values of Tender Power to the next generation. Without them we haven't a hope.

Ginny Ries is a guidance counselor in junior high school in Niles, Illinois. Niles may not be a playground for Café Society, but it is truly a learning ground for the really Beautiful People of the world. There, as in many small towns across America, and in a myriad different ways, the power of tenderness to make a difference is being taught.

"I don't think we're really different from anywhere else," says Ries. "We all tend to get caught up in our own concerns. I guess, in Niles, we really started to pay more attention to values when to our horror the town began to experience first-hand the rash of suicide attempts that seems to be plaguing young people nationwide. One night, I found myself sitting in the hospital emergency room with a little Oriental girl who was despondent and threatening to kill herself. Nothing we could do would get her to give us a commitment that she wouldn't try suicide. Her parents, new immigrants, wouldn't even come to the hospital because they felt they couldn't close their shop. To my own self-disgust, I caught myself thinking that if only I could get this whole thing resolved by five o'clock, I could still get home in plenty of time to put the chicken in the oven. No one was there for this child—not because we weren't caring, but because we didn't have the tools that told us how to connect with her and how to help her beyond lip service."

The Niles school system, to its credit, realizing that if adults were threatened by the growing despondency of some of its children, the peers of those children felt even more helpless. They were charged with keeping each other's terrible secrets and then living with guilt, knowing what might happen as a result of their silence.

The school acted. A team of professionals was called in, and an active suicide prevention program was started. Skilled experts lectured teachers and students, workshops called forth discussions, films were shown.

"One film in particular," remembers Ries, "taught the children that true empathy lies in taking active steps to help a friend when she confides she's suicidal—even if she asks you not to tell anyone. Both boys and girls were given permission to break the old, very male 'do-nothing/keep secrets' way of life and instead were encouraged to seek knowing help for their friends. Kids were taught to listen and feel responsibility. It was like shaking an emotional tree."

Networks of caring sprang up. The children of Niles, Illinois, began nurturing each other.

"The kids even began a dance clinic," says Ries. "Too many of them were feeling despondent and rejected because they couldn't dance—simple as that. It's something to see young people help each other into a social milieu!"

Guidance counselors, traditionally hired only to spur academic achievement, now have another function: They spend hours talking with teachers, finding ways to pass on values linked with empowering and sharing.

When the young people of Niles, Illinois, grow to adulthood, they will no doubt consider each other's humanity as well as the economic gains they can coax from one another. They will probably be as successful as anyone else on corporate ladders—maybe even more successful, because they will have learned the perils of being distant from their peers.

The practice of compassion can be learned. Nurturing and consideration grow to be a habit if started early enough. Instead of learning how to compete in a cutthroat world, people can learn how to excel in a connecting society. If new entrants from the new generation are to bring new values to the workplace, business must change its macho manners.

Another group of women who share the view from under the glass ceiling is nurses. On them falls the awesome burden of coaxing the sick to wellness. If there was ever a profession where connection, empathy, warmth, and empowering counted, it's nursing. If there was ever a person who was worth her weight in gold, it's a good nurse.

But nurses earn less than their weight in gold. Compassion, the very nature of their business, is sorely devalued.

Paula Starin has been a nurse in the critical care unit of a hospital in Nashville, Tennessee, for the last six years. She says that a nurse's care is often the difference between life and death, because "doctors don't have a whole lot of time to spend, and families' time with patients is very restricted in Critical Care. So it falls to the nurses," says Starin, "to draw up every bit of warmth they've got and send it on over to their patient."

The results are often dramatic. Studies have shown that just placing a hand on someone's wrist can lower a rapid pulse. Human contact acts as a potent stimulus for changes in cardiovascular functions, even when a patient is unconscious or comatose.

"I know of cases," says Starin, "where patients in coma, considered out of reach of all voice and other human contact, upon awakening, remember the caring voice of a nurse who never stopped talking to them, never stopped urging them back into life."

Tender Power was never so clearly illustrated.

Perhaps we really do take our caring professions for granted. Perhaps we relegate warmth and empowering to a few professionals and expect them to carry the burden for corporate America. This is unfortunate, because a world that devalues tenderness can't expect to continue reaping its advantages. Paula Starin says that the nursing profession is diminished by this devaluation. "There is a terrible shortage of nurses," she says, "and why not? The hours are long, the pay is terrible, the profession is underrated by the young. Sometimes nurses are even required to carry on with visible badges of what many see as signs of servility—the wearing of nurses' caps, for example. Nurses' caps are an old-fashioned and matronly affectation," Starin asserts. "Doctors are not required to wear caps."

Hospital administrations are often impersonal. Mary Lou Pepper from Elgin, Illinois, says, "I left hospital nursing because the administration acted as if I had no other life, even though I was a good employee. They didn't want to hear whenever I needed time off. I went to work as a private nurse for a woman doctor," says Pepper, "and things are real different. She stands up to give me her seat if she knows I'm tired. What a shocker that was. I was trained to stand up for the doctor. She even writes nice personal notes on my salary checks, like 'thanks for the extra time this week.'"

In a profession where the power of healing care is obvious, the rewards are few. As a result, many nurses have become overly competitive, angry, and backbiting of each other, asserts Starin. The old sisterly connections hardly exist at all in the field.

It has always been nurses trained to listen compassionately who have healed with a power not often displayed by doctors. Today, society hardly listens to the needs of nurses. The vocation, caught in the middle of an emphasis on personal advancement at the expense of giving, seems in mortal danger of professional thrombosis.

When the connecting values are put down, women begin to distrust their potency. They doubt themselves because others depreciate their worth. There's a sense among many women that when they do succeed, somehow it's an accident. If only the world knew how unsure of themselves they were, whisper their inner voices, they would be unmasked as imposters. The feeling is known, not surprisingly, as the Imposter Syndrome.

"I really question my abilities every day," says Marion Pritzker, a middle manager at a Des Moines, Iowa, pharmaceutical corporation. "I made better grades than most of my male peers in college; I used to think I was great but out here in the field, I feel like a fraud—like there's something the men instinctively know, that I'll never know. I spend a lot of time hoping my superiors won't find out that I'm not as good as they seem to think I am. My natural instinct, if there were women around, would be to ask questions when I don't know something—to open up and show my doubts—but I squelch that instinct. I think the men above and below me believe I *should already know* how to handle my work. Everyone else knows what they're doing, it seems, but me. Sure, I'd like to advance up the ranks, but right now I'm too busy just treading water. I trust few people. Women can't afford to trust in the business world."

The pressures women in the middle put on themselves to act in the male mode, to refrain from questioning and building affiliations, are massive, and in the end, self-defeating.

Managing with Intuition

One of the accusations most often leveled at women middle managers is that they can't make up their minds. In fact, say many critics, they have a distinct lack of decision-making skills.

Nonsense, says psychiatrist Theodore Rubin. "Women traditionally have made decisions in families or social relationships in one tenth of the time a male takes. Men ruminate and trust to a logical sequence of facts to lead them to a decision. Women bypass this type of thinking and trust their gut—the sum total of their experience," he tells Dr. Paula Bern in *How to Work for a Woman Boss*. She comments, "The trouble is now that women have moved into management levels in the workplace, they are fearful of using their so-called 'feminine intuition' or emotional reaction to a problem, and so they procrastinate in order to postpone decision making."

The lesson: Use what you've got; intuition is a powerful management tool. Women, under the glass ceiling, rarely pay enough attention today to the small, smart, interior voices. It is thought that these voices are not professional and only good for home.

In fact, it is this very intuition, women's super antennae, which men may possess but evidently ignore, that could save business failures time and time again. Bill Coors, chairman of the Coors Beer Company, tells the story of a psychology experiment. It is no longer used, he notes, because it isn't very nice. One needs, says Coors, a frog, a bucket of cold water, and a bucket of hot water. Put the frog in the cold water and it doesn't do a whole lot. Put the frog in the hot water and it jumps around making audible protests. Then, put the frog in the cold water and put the water over a low flame. The frog sits quietly. Before long, you have cooked frog. The temperature rises so slowly the frog doesn't sense the change. Coors says many managers are like that frog, not sensing change in the business environment until they're cooked.

Author Robert Waterman comments in his book *The Renewal Factor* that General Electric almost ended up as frog soup, because no one stopped to listen to the intuition that is often wiser than the most sophisticated merchandising studies. G.E. management determined from their studies that people were buying smaller cars and building smaller homes. So they hypothesized that people would also want smaller refrigerators and began to manufacture them. To the surprise of the folks at G.E., the company started losing money. Early customer response told them their reasoning was 180 degrees off target.

Any woman would have figured out, says a female G.E. employee, that since so many couples are both working, consumers want more, not less, storage space—to preclude frequent visits to the grocery. With all due respect to demographic studies and sophisticated merchandising, some simple feminine intuition could have saved General Electric a lot of time and money.

The tender trait of intuition is a business asset. If we don't use it, we'll lose it.

Let the Chips Fall

"You're in trouble if you do act tough—and in trouble if you don't," grins Lore Matthews, a computer programmer in a midwestern IBM office. "Relinquish your need for showing vulnerability, for building connections, for sharing—and you're a 'man-hater.' Display those needs and you fall into the trap of being labeled a 'sex goddess.' So, you might as well be yourself and let the chips fall as they may."

Indeed. This attitude seems to be most healthy, self-preserving, and encouraging to those who would like to see Tender Power prevail. Obsessive worrying that personal failures will be construed as gender failures will actually lead to failure, say experts. Claim your intuition as a tool. Give yourself credit for your warmth. True respect lies in self-respect.

Margaret Hennig and Anne Jardim, in their classic work *The Managerial Woman*, describe one middle manager who attempted to erase gender and make her woman characteristics as unnoticeable as she could. Her personal style, say the authors, was businesslike, resembling an "enlightened, genteel man." Her clothes were severe and she gave forth as "coldly rational and logical" a manner as she could muster, convinced that nothing more quickly turns others off than an emotional woman. And so, says the woman, "I often fought my own emotions, but never let that become visible to others."

As her career progressed, this middle manager says she started to notice she felt more secure in her job, didn't need to prove herself constantly, felt less like an imposter, and began to relax. She also wasn't quite as satisfied with her work, and she felt she was missing out on other aspects of life—marriage, motherhood, and the world outside, in general.

"For the first time," say the authors, statements by other women in the same position showed "a preoccupation with femininity. This was an issue which they had always been able to 'put away until later." Now, it became a dominant concern."

Many of these women, with a greater sense of self and a greater security at work, came to accept that "they no longer needed to avoid the symbols which they and others identified with 'traditional women.' As adolescents might do, they put on the uniforms of women—first to convince themselves, and second to test the legitimacy of assumptions and perceptions based on accepted definitions of femininity others held."

"They were women," say the authors, "they were managers, and they were capable of being both." Their relationships at work and at home became freer, more satisfying. And, for what it's worth—and it's worth plenty—most of the women in the Hennig-Jardim study broke through the glass ceiling, rising out of middle management to become presidents and vice presidents of their firms.

Evelyn Dunn is an insurance salesperson in Dallas, Texas. "The company I used to work for had an obnoxious dress code," she asserts. "They made a rule that only male management people could wear suits and ties to distinguish them from non-management males, she says. "Women, who were rarely management anyway, were encouraged (although not directly asked) to wear slacks: I think that management felt this sort of kept women in their place. No high falutin' pinstriped suits for us. Everyone hated that place, and no one worked harder than he or she had to work. The company I'm with today is so different. Now, I'm middle management, and this is the way we operate," says Dunn. "I've written it down . . ."

- Put yourself in the other person's moccasins.
- Treat others as though you work for them even though they work for you.
- Use incentives rather than quotas to get people to work their hardest.
- Stress cooperation. People don't have to love each other, but they do have to cooperate with each other.
- Teach, don't preach. Let other people, not just bosses, make decisions. When you give people power, you give them strength to make you strong.
- Don't spin people's wheels by challenging them; instead develop a win–win policy. When I win, you win. Do this by rewarding accomplishment and recognizing effort in tangible ways.

Some companies impose worse things on their employees than obnoxious dress codes. Many women working just under the glass ceiling often feel desperate about insidious time frames. If one drops out even temporarily to explore other choices or to nurture children, she loses her place on the corporate ladder. Many business experts reinforce this message. Even mothers advise daughters to concentrate on career "while you're young, because you'll lose too much ground to make back if you drop out."

You Can't Take the Escalator on the Way Up

Marilyn, who definitely doesn't want her last name used, is a senior buyer for a chain of fashion stores on the West Coast. She wants to grow up to be Liz Claiborne, she says, or maybe Donna Karan, and that has been the driving force of her life. Until recently.

"My husband Kurt and I didn't plan to have children. Who could take the time? We were devoted to our careers. We made ourselves as equal as possible in psyche and even in house responsibilities. I pushed him to be more sensitive and nurturing, while he gave me manly pep talks in the aggression department," she ruefully smiles. "We were truly a uni-sex couple."

Then, she became pregnant. The arrival of Jamie shattered all the "we're just the same" fantasies. Differences, deeply rooted in generations of Marilyns and Kurts, became acutely apparent.

"As soon as Jamie was home with us, I was *flattened* by the intensity of the emotion I felt," says Marilyn. "It's not that Kurt loved Jamie less, just that my feelings were so linked to some atavistic voice that suddenly was rumbling W–O–M–A–N. I still am madly ambitious, but it just doesn't feel right to go back to work yet. I can't tell you what a surprise that is! I'm conflicted by what my passion seems to be doing to my intellect. I feel like telling everyone in the park—'this is just temporary, I'm really going to be Donna Karan!'"

Kurt sheepishly says, "I know my wife is on her way up, and I liked having her salary. Still, I'd be lying if I didn't admit there's something in me that also likes the role of the breadwinner, these days. I feel manly. Still, when I'm juggling the bills, I also feel I'd like to see that salary again."

Marilyn and Kurt think they're having not postpartum depression, but postpartum identity crisis. Rigid, androgynous roles can't work anymore. Neither, it appears, do traditional roles of he goes to work, she stays home. A newer, broader, family identity seems to be required. They have a lot of figuring to do.

"On-the-way-up," says Marilyn, "doesn't seem like a smooth escalator ride to the top. It's more like an elevator journey, stopping and starting again. Eventually, I still hope to get to the top."

Women in the middle, just under the glass ceiling, not on the bottom and not on the top of the work hierarchy, do have their work cut out for them if they hope to incorporate tender values into their work lives. It will take the strongest of them to help each other and the men in their lives understand that dreaming big and working hard doesn't have to happen in a sterile, acquisitive, never-stop-driving-till-you-reach-the-top atmosphere. When women learn to attack issues, not each other, refuse to indulge in backbiting politics, feel free to be themselves without worrying about it, only then will Tender Power have a chance in big business.

Women in the middle have many problems, but one of the problems they can avoid is falling into the trap of inauthenticity. If men and women negate warmth and playfulness, and if they harden themselves to life outside of business, they fall back on instead of climb the ladder. At best, women who agree to live a life without connectedness usually manage only to march in place.

Sometimes it's just too hard. As one Nashville woman put it, "In a dog-eat-dog world, you gotta bite bones." Sometimes the glass ceiling seems to be made of steel.

So, tired of being on other people's payrolls, tired of fighting angry aggressive mentalities, many women have decided that they will not settle for a room of one's own; they want a business of their own.

When advertising agency D'Arcy Masius Benton & Bowles asked people to name their ideal jobs, what topped the list for women was "to be head of my own company."

6

The New Immigrants

Charlotte Taylor, a Washington, D.C., consultant, called female entrepreneurs "the new immigrants" in her book, *Women in the Business Game*. Her premise: Just as European immigrants started small family-owned businesses as the fastest route into the economic waters, women, "the new immigrants," are finding that starting and running their own businesses gives them opportunities to make money in environments that overlook the lack of Harvard MBAs.

Women, like all immigrants, face many problems in the existing work arena. There are quota restrictions, ancient prejudices, stereotypical judgments to face down. Many of us have tried the corporations and have mourned the loss of identity as we struggled, like all immigrants, to fit the prevailing mold. *Enough!* we cry in frustration. We can best be ourselves, on our own.

Entrepreneurial enterprises allow us to call our own shots, shape our own molds. Starting a business is not easy, but it can more easily allow for hours that include family, leisure, and self. As one middle manager said, "I know I will never make it to the top and keep my sanity. I feel like a closet female who has to use war words and sport terms and play-act the male game, all day long."

At forty-one, Marilyn Doates stood outside her Los Angeles office one day. At precisely the same moment, four doors down the hall opened, as if choreographed to do so. Four other women stepped out, each dressed like the other.

"And there we were. It was a riot—but not so funny. We looked like peas in a pod, except that our suits were gray, not green. We all had the same no-nonsense haircuts. We all looked at each other with some suspicion—'where is *she* going?' It was not supposed to be this way," said Marilyn. "The feminist movement had been about options and choices and individuality. It occurred to me that minute, that women had thrown away the very thing they fought so hard to get: a unique identity. That's it, I thought. And, I quit to open my own employment agency."

The old immigrants, those entrepreneurs of the past, were mostly men. If, in the old country, their fathers ran tailor shops, bakeries, and fruit businesses, they gravitated to the familiar and did similar things in the new country. Businesses grew. Italians, coming from the physical work ethic, plied the shovel, and in time became powerful businesspeople in sophisticated construction. Jews, stopped from entering corporate life by a plethora of prejudice, started their own tiny clothing operations and became leaders of the garment industry. Women, who had nothing to lose because they made nothing anyway, started beauty shops, dress shops, nursing services . . . businesses that plied the woman trade. Cosmetics tycoon Mary Kay Ash worked for a quarter of a century in a male corporate world that ignored her ideas, ignored promotions, ignored pay raises, and often handed her the information that she was "thinking just like a woman."

"I got into cosmetics," she remembers, "because I wanted to start a company where being a woman wasn't a liability."

Today, more and more women are finding the route to success lies in business where affiliation, cooperation, "thinking like a woman," is the most positive thing that can be said about a worker. It is women who own one in every four businesses, nearly a quarter of the thirteen million small businesses in the country, and they are starting these businesses at twice the rate of men, chalking up annual receipts of over 98 billion dollars. Women entrepreneurs are in it for the long run, and their successes range from being able to support a family to knocking the world on its head, like fashion designer Liz Claiborne. She built up her own company so well that in 1985 sales figures soared to more than 556 million dollars. Women are proving themselves on their own terms to be the kind of risk takers and innovators it was once thought only men could be.

For any one of a number of reasons, more and more women are beginning to initiate private enterprise. According to Dr. Frederick Hauser, clinical psychologist and chairman of the Department of Graduate Management at Pace University, "women tend to create an entrepreneurship as a means of recreating the family as they see it, after disappointment in the corporate family." Some women are merely looking for a way to work part-time or special hours. Others like the control, calling the shots.

Some women are ambitious on a personal level, some on a global level, some on an altruistic level.

Some are mothers proving that business life doesn't end with maternity. Mothers Work, for example, a 2.5 million dollar company, was founded by Rebecca Matthias, in Philadelphia, when she became pregnant and couldn't find maternity clothes suitable for her management job. Another mother, Lane Nemeth, founded Discovery Toys, a major manufacturer of educational toys, when she couldn't find high-quality playthings for her eleven-year-old daughter. Ann Piestrup, yet another mom, founded The Learning Company, one of the leading publishers of educational software for children. She concluded, as a teacher, that too many children were having difficulty learning from even the latest educational methods. Barbara Keck began a management consulting firm in New York so she could spend more time with her own kids. It grew to a twenty-person staff, half of whom are also MBA moms working part-time.

Some women, just plain disgusted with the androgynous uniform they were compelled to don in the traditional work field, were determined to try a better way. Some were scared stiff, but so eager to control their own destinies and the hours they could spend with their children, husbands, or aged parents, they decided to take a risk: They would go it without the protective umbrella of the male-dominated workplace. Some were thrilled with the idea of their own business, minus the glass ceiling. Some, successful in the corporation, were challenged by entrepreneurial horizons.

Women's energy and women's special skills, says *Working Woman Magazine*, are fueling an unprecedented boom in entrepreneurship.

Here are some profiles of different breeds of entrepreneurship, all marching to different drums, all celebrating both the idea and the use of Tender Power in their work.

Beyond Barbie

The first time Ruth Hendler became rich, and an entrepreneur, the issue was basically money, not empathy. She had observed her preteenage daughter play with grown-up paper dolls by the hour. The little girl had rejected the three-dimensional dolls because "they had the funny, little bodies of ten-year-olds—you know, the ones with fat bellies, no breasts, and dumb clothes. She yearned for grown-up dolls, the ones she could dream and role-play with; the ones which could represent her, all grown up—or the 'her' of her fantasies."

Already in the toy business, Ruth became especially interested in dolls. She and her husband Eliot visited Europe one year and serendipitously took their children Barbara and Kenneth with them. On a street in Lucerne, Switzerland, Barbara was fixated on the sight of a doll on a swing in the window of a toy shop, and the doll had *different outfits*. There were ski clothes, winter clothes, bathing suits—mother and daughter both couldn't resist.

"I bought one doll for her and one doll for me, and said to myself, 'What am I fooling around for? This is it.'

"I convinced Eliot to manufacture a fashion doll. At the time, little girls had few choices; they could either choose from the Tiny-Tears-Wets-Her-Diaper genre or the Madame Alexander collector items. You couldn't find a doll with breasts, with a waist, with *ankles* for God's sakes! You couldn't find a doll that would let a little girl interpret her dream of the future," remembers Handler.

So Barbie and Ken were born. Much beloved as well as much maligned, Barbie sells more than Cabbage Patch, Princess Di, and Betsy Wetsy combined. The doll confirmed Ruth's strong intuition. Little girls need to decipher the world around them through doll play.

Handler became part of the huge corporate world Barbie and Ken eventually created, and there she tried to retain her femininity.

"I worked hard at it. It isn't easy to be an executive in big business and still retain the womanly niceties. You find yourself getting impatient with people in the male mode. You tighten up on them. You may have to pound tables. I guess I was more sensitive to people than the men around me, but also tougher than I am now. That's because, I think, men who worked with me were themselves ill at ease. Treated me as some kind of a fluke. I had to earn the respect of every man in the business who had to test their macho to accept me."

The second time Ruth Handler became successful it was *truly* as an entrepreneur. When she had given birth to the plastic Ken and Barbie, she was young, strong, and thought all things were possible. Barbie and Ken represented a perfect world. In the real world, though, perfect Barbies and Kens don't exist; indeed, in the real world, people are sometimes short, fat, imperfect, and ill. Barbie never had a sniffle.

Several years ago Ruth discovered she had cancer and, like thousands of other women, endured a mastectomy. Sometime after her surgery she decided to buy a prosthetic device, a false breast—not quite as perky as Barbie's but one, nevertheless, that would make her feel better.

"I didn't want to look like a freak. Look, you can be a very good person and have no breasts at all, but if you have one breast and you walk around unbalanced, you're going to look funny. Women must have two matching sides."

At least, that's what Ruth thinks. So she checked out what was available and was, she remembers, "humiliated" by the sales clerks in the stores.

"Remember, I had been in a position of great power. I was at the top of my world, could do no wrong, was providing little girls with an expression of their dreams, of their potential, and *Whammo!*—this kind of thing happens to me. I knew no one at the time who had lost a breast and it was just an awful experience.

"There were two major problems. One was that the sales clerks in large department stores didn't want to wait on me. They were repelled by what they saw and by their own fears, so compassion and professionalism gave way to brusqueness. The other problem was that they didn't really have a product to put on me, one that was worthy of all our efforts. At that time, what was available to women who'd undergone mastectomies were globs. Just globs. There is no other name for it. You put this glob into what was called a surgical brassiere. The brassiere managed to make even your surviving breast look ugly because it pressed it down and distorted its natural shape—supposedly so you'd at least be evenly misshaped. What logic. The fools who designed those surgical bras had to be men or women who didn't understand other women. They were too conscious of the economies of production and they weren't worried about consumers' feelings or sensitivities. Having empathy for what they perceived as a 'deformed' person didn't make good business sense."

Ruth's surgery was on a June 16th. In August, she went back to work wearing the glob, or, as they called it then, "the form." She was so self-conscious at the obvious mismatch that she began to wear sweaters and vests under suits to obscure her chest. *That* lasted for about five minutes. She was determined to make things better for women like herself—and while she was at it, she was determined to turn a tidy profit, tender and business power going hand in hand, as far as she was concerned. Knowing what she knew about plastics and, for that matter, nicely balanced breasts, through Barbie, Ruth understood what needed to be done. Wearing a brand new entrepreneur hat, she began again.

Today, she is the owner and chief executive officer of a business called *Nearly Me*. Women throughout the world have new access to prosthetic devices that feel and look comfortable and natural. Ruth, when she can, personally supervises many fittings. Her connection with women, her empathy and understanding, have combined to create yet another blockbuster entrepreneurial success. In an interesting transition from a Barbie breast to a postcancer breast, Ruth's authentic, caring voice was heard.

A Helping Hand

Carol O'Connell took the chores that had long imprisoned women and made them into a route to self-worth. She never trained to be an entrepreneur, never even thought about it—but, that job at the deli was getting her down.

"I wasn't even making much money. All my life, I'd felt I wanted to help other women—and there I was, selling them meat, somehow, a less than satisfying enterprise."

Carol had started as an elementary school teacher in Michigan, but after seven years of that, with a new baby, she felt torn between her students, her husband, and her child. She and her husband moved back home to Matamoros, Pennsylvania, where Carol spent the first two years nurturing her child.

"Then, I felt antsy, and took the first job I could find—at the meat counter of our local delicatessen. When I was pregnant with my second child, the bottom fell out of my life: My husband decided he didn't like being married. There I was—two kids, a job at a deli, and a whole lot of anxiety."

How to gain control of her life? She began to look around.

"In so many ways, women were asked to do it all and get less. Little things like mail, for instance: When I was divorced, somehow I stopped receiving my Christmas cards, tax checks—*all* my mail. I went down to inquire at the post office and discovered that my ex-husband was receiving it all. 'Whichever name appears first on any given envelope, that person gets the envelope,' said the mail clerk. What incredible blindness toward women! What mail is ever addressed *Mrs.* and Mr., or even *Ms.* and Mr.?"

Such general inequities of life got Carol thinking. Working women were expected to do it all—the house and the job. How could she help women, and profit in her own business? She had a vision of a career woman longing to play with her baby and instead, being faced with mounds of housework.

"Many working women tell their child's caretakers to concentrate on the kid and forget about the toilets—and that's wonderful. Still, when the woman comes home there are all those dirty toilets staring at her."

The answer was a maid service. There was nothing low-class about cleaning homes. Women had been doing it for centuries. She would begin a business to be run by a woman (herself) who would work, dust rag in hand, along with other women, to service the needs of still other women. The difference between now and past centuries is that this time, the women would receive fair pay.

Carol contacted other female entrepreneurs in the business. Networking "you'd be proud of" went on. She couldn't believe the generosity of other women who were willing to empower her, willing to share their business prowess. "Instead of competition, I experienced caring."

Daisymaids was born. (Those houses would be fresh as a daisy!) Carol hired eight women and began to look for clients. They were easy to find. She had hit on a service whose time was right. The relationship between boss and workers was superb.

"We share a camaraderie. There's nothing of the distance and impersonal flavor of big business, in our organization," says O'Connell. "A mutually concerned group that instills a sense of self-worth in each other isn't a bad group to work with, I think." If you're a male, don't both applying for work at Daisymaids. Why not?

"Men don't understand about the details. They don't take much pride in clean homes. They don't come up with tips like peanut butter takes off certain rug stains. Women draw from their own experience, and in this particular business, that counts. Also, women don't tend to jockey for position so much—there's little backbiting. They consider it a business—something house cleaning should always have been, anyway. A service business—like any other."

Carol, like many other women, seems to have found a balance. She fulfills her work needs without sloughing off on her emotional life. Her own business allows part-time hours—something she and her workers value at this time in their lives. She has no desire to march to someone else's beat—and indeed, she marches away from the traditional workplace, convinced that her steps, at her own speed, are toward greater personal progress.

"I'm not interested in making a fortune," she says, "only in calling my own shots and feeling good about myself and what I can offer to others."

Service businesses differ from product businesses: one sells labor, the other sells things. Although it's a long way from selling the labor to clean toilets to, say, selling cosmetics, the roads each entrepreneur might travel can be remarkably similar if the approach to selling is consistent with their personal convictions. Because Carol O'Connell had the courage of her convictions, she was sure-footed about her approach. She was going to use empathy, cooperation, and other tender traits to get ahead, and she did.

Ironically, she was more successful at the start than another entrepreneur, far more famous and powerful than she. The more famous entrepreneur had to learn from experience, she says, to trust her intuition and her instinctive sense of how to do business, before her business had a shot at success.

A Velvet Glove

Polly Bergen is very show business. Many people remember her in her own Polly Bergen television show, as well as the many films in which she appeared.

In 1965, Polly, who believes in leading more than one life, felt impelled to indulge her penchant for business. Having always controlled her glitzy, star image, she decided to become an entrepreneur, and to control—in deed but not in name—her own cosmetics company. The company was called Oil of The Turtle, not *Polly Bergen's* Oil of The Turtle because, Bergen felt, "using my own name would be a handicap. By and large women with highly visible, show business personalities were considered bubbleheads, called upon for image, but not management. I wanted to be both, so I served as spokeswoman and kept the fact of my ownership rather secret for a while. It worked. I used my own, natural, velvet glove type of management instead of the sledge-hammer variety, and the company grew by leaps and bounds. I loved it—and found that I managed the business part wonderfully—and very much on my own."

Women, says Bergen, are not the most accomplished team players. They're not often brought up to concentrate on team sports, the military or huge corporations. Historically, says the star, they've run it all on their own—the house, the kids, the structure of family life. They're *primed* to run *small* organizations!

"I was a terrific entrepreneur," says Bergen, "when I followed my gut. At one time, four hundred women across the country were selling my line.

I remembered each of their birthdays, each of their children's birthdays; I took them out for lunch. I used every bit of nurturing there was in me and when, for a short time, the company hit some trouble and was very short of cash flow, most of these women stayed on at greatly reduced salaries—because we cared about each other. So, never tell me that women can't use their instinctive caring, nurturing traits to make good money."

The trouble came when Bergen began to distrust her instincts, began to think she would grow even more quickly by operating in a male mode.

"It was real proof that we women often 'do it to ourselves,'" she remembers. "When the company began to get really big and earn serious money, I became fearful. 'Perhaps I'm not smart enough to run such a huge enterprise' thought I, falling into the bubblehead trap that some men have been laying on us for years. Would you believe I hired a man to come in and run it—absolutely a man's man? I moved into the advertising/marketing/creative end of the business.

"That man walked in and almost destroyed my company."

She learned a lesson, but she didn't learn it well enough. Bergen sold Oil of The Turtle in 1975, but stayed on as CEO for three years.

"I was absolutely worthless. The only woman, surrounded by men, I could get nothing done. They gave me credit for being creative, for being able to sell, but credibility to run the company? None. I simply couldn't stand up to them, using their crummy techniques."

Polly Bergen is giving herself another chance. At the moment, she has started a shoe company and a jewelry company that will also feature handbags and belts. As owner and chairwoman of the board, she will retain control for the business as well as the creative end of these two entrepreneurial efforts. It's not easy, but she's hopeful.

"I think that entrepreneurship is the wave of the future for women," says Bergen. "I may be wrong, but when we feel we have to play hardball by men's rules in giant corporations, very few of us will succeed; and, to be realistic, hardball is what's required in the big business world. It'll change—little by little, as the small business grows up to be the large corporation."

One small business that has high hopes of growing up to be such an enterprise was begun by an entrepreneur whose only experience had been behind the lines in support rather than in leadership positions.

A Case for Support

"If the women's movement failed anyone, along with the marvelous strides it made for many, it's failed us—the support network," says Melba Duncan, president of The Duncan Group, Inc., which specializes in the recruitment and placement of executive secretaries, office administrators, and administrative assistants.

Everyone can't be CEOs, or senior management, and there is a huge need for a support system that can efficiently and professionally buoy up the top echelon so it can get on with its work, she maintains. It seems to Duncan that despite lip service, militant feminists don't truly address themselves to the real needs of the middle and lower echelons. A support layer works with pride and earns respect from professionalism, not grandstand stances, she says.

Duncan, who started as a "file girl—they didn't even call us women, then," gives quick credit to the women's movement for calling attention to the indignities, but she worries about overreactions to "imagined indignities." She herself moved up quickly through the ranks from secretary to executive assistant for Pete Peterson, then Lehman's chairman of the board.

"I did not consider it beneath my dignity to bring Pete a cup of coffee," she smiles.

Finally, after many years as support for top executives, Duncan left to become her own boss. She still feels passionately about the meaning of support and about what she believes has been an unintentional disservice by well-meaning feminists.

"Take the coffee issue—just because it's always brought up," she says. "I'm a woman and I'm black—a minority on two counts right there—and if anything, particularly sensitive to the issue of servility. I have to tell you, there's a difference between courtesy and servility. I am convinced that women who feel nurturing and gracious ought to be able to express these personality assets through small acts of courtesy without feeling 'used.' One must use judgment. I draw the line at peeling and serving papaya, as one client suggested. But, I personally feel it's an outrage to make an issue of the serving of coffee as being menial and not a professional act. Power comes from being well suited to one's position, from having a strong presence—and that doesn't mean shrieking and that doesn't mean fearing graciousness. For a woman to parrot new rules that would have her refuse serving coffee as part of a prestigious position in a dignified atmosphere may well exclude her from the most marvelous opportunities. Perhaps it's a small point," notes Duncan, "but I resent a mentality that dictates 'if you serve, you are demeaned.'"

Duncan revels in the role of entrepreneur. "Owning one's own business allows me to be soft and feminine, as well as competent. It works for me, here; if I were striving to compete on a middle management level, I'm convinced I'd have trouble being heard."

In the end, she feels that a great asset to the female entrepreneur is the trait her mother had been pushing, sometimes unasked, for as long as Duncan can remember. "It's dignity," says the gray-suited, lace-handkerchiefed boss. "Dignity breeds the kind of success I'm after. Calling the shots in my own business is the way I go for dignity. Bringing a cup of coffee to my own employee gains me even more dignity."

Duncan is grace personified, and her strength inspires her working crew who seem to genuinely like and feel comfortable with her. Will that personalized touch last as the business grows? One waits to see.

It might be noted that many entrepreneurs mention a common pitfall that seems to entrap quite a few. Sensations of power can be heady. It is easy to understand why some men became more tyrannical than they suspected they could as they rose to become bosses. Women fall into the same snare, and it often affects their personal as well as their professional behavior.

"I almost lost a marriage when I stopped being the woman he married to become the successful entrepreneur," says Lee LeGrand of Huntsville, Alabama. "My office was in my home and downstairs was where I, as director of a corporation, ruled the roost. Upstairs, I continued, out of habit, being director.

"Directing, however, didn't work upstairs. My husband didn't have a whole lot of ego to begin with, and I was killing what was left.

"'Well, that's your husband's problem,' said my business partner. But of course, it became mine as well," sighed Lee.

Many women, intoxicated by new power, forget tender. Impatience reigns in personal confrontations where patience once lived. Yesterday, they were resigned to "making do" on their husband's modest salaries; now bringing in twice those salaries they become insensitive to male feelings. Instead of equally sharing the head-of-the-family position, they begin to usurp the title for themselves. This is not what feminism or Tender Power is about, at all.

Patience is surely one of the most tender traits. Some of us have more patience than others. Some of us, like Rachel Ericson.

Untapped Power

They were childhood sweethearts. She, soft, shoulder-length blonde hair—a spunky person. He, abrasive, diamond-in-the-rough brilliant, tough, given to four-letter words in every sentence. You either liked him or you couldn't stand him, this Ronnie.

They married when she was seventeen, and he went into his dad's construction business. He made it thrive.

She stayed at home with the kids, always patient.

On his fiftieth birthday, without warning, Ronnie began a true mid-life crisis. He worried obsessively about death, dyed his hair, and entered a state of massive depression. There was, to Rachel's horror, even another woman.

"I had such mixed emotions," she remembers, "but most of all, I knew he was in trouble. At night, the bed vibrated with his sobs. He didn't know why he was crying, but he couldn't stop."

Rachel hung on. She pushed the other woman to the back of her mind as only a symptom of something worse. She loved Ronnie. She would wait out the tough times. Patience.

Puttering around, alone in his basement, Ronnie, a passionate fisherman, came upon a novel way to create aquariums that would operate on a stunningly original waste-cleaning system. You wouldn't ever have to change their water. The puttering became an obsession. He'd build tank after tank—some for food fish, some for lobsters, some for tropical fish; all the fish thrived amazingly.

His tanks were his salvation. They were the only things that interested Ronnie. Little by little, the blackest part of the depression seemed to lift. A three-pack-a-day smoker, Ronnie would lie on his back, deep into the night, dragging on his cigarettes and talking about tanks to Rachel. She listened, exhausted, but willing to grab at any straw that would tug him back to life.

Ronnie left the construction business and began to spend full time on his obsession. "He worked day and much of the night, on the filtration system," says Rachel. "At six in the morning he'd be in our factory; alone in a 15,000-square-foot building, with a kerosene heater, he built tank after tank with only his own two hands."

"I was going bananas, but I knew that he had to make a success on his own, not his dad's business. It was his idea of manliness—not mine. But, the depression was loosening. No matter what it cost, I had to help him hold on."

Often, in the hours before dawn, Ronnie, wide awake, would go down to the kitchen, Rachel sleepily tagging behind. Both would work with her Mixmaster trying to develop foam that could be used to simulate the protein waste that had to be filtered out of the aquariums.

Rachel learned, much against her inclination, how to build aquariums. "I didn't have an engineering background," she remembers, "but, I was living with this thing. It was my most powerless period, although, truthfully, I never remember feeling I had any power of any sort.

"Worst of all, it soon became apparent that I was going to have to be the one to sell these tanks. Who else cared? Who else believed in him? I'd never sold one single solitary thing in my life."

Ronnie's idea was to get the tanks into supermarkets, diners and fish stores, where wholesalers and retailers would be able to promise absolutely fresh fish to their customers. The tanks that had been available up to now were always scummy, thick with density, and the fish tasted the same.

Rachel learned the mechanics of the product. She developed a spiel; she flirted a little with the buyers. Dressing her prettiest, she began making the rounds, using every tool of persuasion she had ever used on her kids. Miraculously enough, she began to sell. One diner owner, then another, bought a tank. Ronnie was turning them out single-handed. Then, another order and another. Food Emporium, a supermarket chain, ordered many. Customers could now choose a fresh brook trout, swimming on 68th Street in Manhattan, for dinner.

Ronnie slowly was getting better. He stopped seeing the other woman. He and Rachel went on a trip and she "played at being his girlfriend, not his wife of thirty-two years. It was beautiful," she says.

Incredibly, the business prospered. Rachel was the sole salesperson. She began to enjoy the sense of power. In a year, Ronnie hired twenty people to work for him and help build the tanks, by the secret method only he and she knew.

Four nights after Ronnie's fifty-eighth birthday, he clutched at his chest. In three minutes, in Rachel's arms, he died.

At his funeral, she told my husband, an old fishing buddy of Ronnie's, that it took her about sixty seconds to decide to keep on with the business. She would take Ronnie's place somehow. She hadn't his engineering knowledge, but "to carry on his dream would be to carry on the man. I felt panic and fear at the monumental task ahead. I had to run this enormous company. Would I lose it? I would not lose it, I told myself."

She hasn't. She found new sources of untapped power in herself. The devotion, admiration, and patience she had for her husband—the same qualities that stopped her from walking out when she knew there was another woman and much trouble, is now a force of profound strength in a business that grows mightily, each day.

The route Rachel Ericson chose would not be the route a "new" woman would probably choose. In a generation that's grown up not accepting anything that smacks of second-class citizenship, Rachel's choice would be intolerable to me, or to many others who are, at least, half responsible for the soaring divorce rate in this country.

But, Rachel had her own "intolerable." A mate's inner torture was the intolerable for this woman. Who's to say that a little more of this brand of tenderness from males and females wouldn't bring a new kind of power to modern-day relationships?

It was the power choice for Rachel, as it turned out. She's an entrepreneur on her way up; in her fifties, she might have been a woman lost and frightened. Her future is bright with possibility. This is a woman-run family business. Rachel's taken her daughters into the business. Ronnie probably would have been too macho to allow that kind of thing to go on.

Not-for-Profit Entrepreneurs

There's a shining new breed of entrepreneurs out there. Legions of women are starting and succeeding at their own not-for-profit businesses. These entrepreneurs are women who give more than lip service to their nurturing instincts. They are women who affirm their own lives by enriching the lives of others. They are the modern-day equivalent of the likes of Margaret Sanger, Sojourner Truth, and Susan B. Anthony.

These women, no one who knows them doubts, could make tons of dollars from their enterprises. They almost always have the generally astute business "smarts" of the most powerful chief executive officers in any Fortune 500 company.

They choose a different way.

Their way is to focus on a specific lack they feel in their worlds. They want to change the world, make it better. What do they get out of it? Usually a sense of accomplishment, the gratitude of others, and, at least, a fair living from their enterprise, if they are successful. No one ever said not-for-profit entrepreneurs have to be impoverished.

This commitment to others' needs makes the world livable. Women who have the tenderness and the power necessary to work primarily for others' benefit are everywhere, sometimes quite unsung except by those to whom they give the power to sing.

Here are three such women, very different, very powerful, very tender.

The Nurturing Network

Mary Cunningham, as noted earlier, has had more than her share of dazzling success along with a good portion of melodramatic headlines. As corporate vice president of strategic planning for the Bendix Corporation, she enjoyed a meteoric rise and, from many, admiration for her clear-eyed business approaches. What's more, she has the Harvard MBA and substantial personal income to finance any profit-making enterprise that might catch her interest. Smart money would bet on that enterprise, given Cunningham's proven business acumen.

But that's not what she chooses to do these days.

Whatever did happen to Mary Cunningham, you may well ask, after that whole brouhaha when she and her boss William Agee, chairman of the board at Bendix, resigned in the aftermath of what now seems a rather silly love scandal? The consensus of opinion has it that Cunningham was a scapegoat of the system, a woman who had committed the grave sin (in that very straightjacketed male corporate world of the early eighties) of falling in love with the boss (and he with her). Despite her business accomplishments, public opinion refused to see anything but scandal, and both were punished by being forced out of the corporation. As she says, "the rumor, gossip, and innuendo was a tool, a mechanism of an organization that wanted to rid itself of a woman who had made it too far."

So, what happened to Mary Cunningham? For one thing, she married Agee. For another, she went to work for Seagram, with exactly the same title, reporting to CEO Edgar Bronfman, to prove that she could land on her feet and succeed with self-vindicating glory in an equally demanding executive role.

All this she did before she left Seagram to have two babies, Mary Alana and William, Jr.

And today? Is Mary hard at work at yet another corporate success story? Hard at work, yes. Corporations, no. She, as a matter of fact, is using every bit of her skill, connections, and energy as a not-for-profit entrepreneur. She has created a business out of nurturing.

The business Cunningham founded is called The Nurturing Network. Located in Osterville, Massachusetts, it is a not-for-profit organization that bypasses religious, political, or moral views. It casts no judgments and makes no accusations. What it does do is provide arrangements for a birth alternative, because, Mary says, "there is no greater tragedy than that of a woman who feels forced to have an abortion."

No matter whether one is pro choice or pro life, distinctions that often become confused in the claiming, few can argue the value of an organization that truly offers alternatives to pregnant women who desire them. The polarization of the abortion debate appalled Cunningham, and so, without taking sides, Cunningham, following her business instincts, found a businesslike way to help those who are not happy about their pregnancies but are uncomfortable with the idea of abortion. It was a way that would not disparage any woman's right to her own body, but would provide every woman with the practical ways and means to go another route, if she wished.

Cunningham has a tender touch, but a powerful business manner, and she's gone about empowering her new project as she would any fledgling business. First of all, she's drawn in some heavyweight firms, some among the Fortune 500. The firms have agreed to temporarily employ her clients and provide mentors as well as senior executives who will shepherd their progress. There are almost a thousand members of The Nurturing Network in addition to businesses; one hundred universities, for example, have been recruited to help women who, perhaps embarrassed by the situation in which they find themselves, wish to temporarily transfer their study sites so that they can continue their education through to the end of their pregnancies. The Network also includes homes in which pregnant women may live and families to nurture them. The Nurturing Network is currently applying to become an adoption agency as well, to serve those clients who wish to put their babies up for adoption. If mothers choose to keep their babies, the Network will help them obtain child care so they can return to school or career. Confidentiality and privacy are guaranteed.

"If, eight years ago, Corporate America showed me a rough, tough side," says Cunningham, "setting up this network has shown me its warm, human, caring side. It's inspiring to see the number of people who are seeking an outlet to do something good. And this is a way to directly affect a woman's life," she says.

A good way to think of nurturing, says Mary Cunningham, is to consider it "life gardening." She defines it as the ability to "protect, to shelter, to encourage to grow and develop."

Here is a woman whose problems at Bendix came, in part, because she couldn't choose work over love, or love over work; she refused to throw tenderness out of the marketplace.

Perhaps, in her new entrepreneurial venture, she can finally succeed in combining the fruits of work and love. Perhaps, as she offers choice to other women in tough situations, she will find her own proper niche. Cunningham was motivated by altruistic considerations as well as by an idea that appealed to her strong business instinct. There are other women whose motivation is far more intensely personal.

I Will Find a Cure

You'd never know it to look at her. Lee Ducat, small, blonde, elegantly dressed, perfectly coiffed and made up, resembles a beautiful society woman. Nothing could be further from the truth; she is a working lioness, albeit with a low and sexy roar.

When her little boy was nine and diagnosed with juvenile diabetes, the doctor told her it was an "okay" disease and easily controllable. But what Lee found out was that it wasn't okay; the disease was almost impossible to control, even if her little boy did all the right things, took his insulin shots, and ate no sugar. She gave up her job as a programmer at a local television station and decided to fight the disease that threatened to make her child's life sadder and shorter. Lee began laying the foundation for a grass roots organization that would soon be officially chartered as The Juvenile Diabetes Foundation. The organization is now international, with over one hundred and seventy chapters.

Today, Lee wheels, deals, cajoles, and pleads with government and big-business groups in an ongoing effort to find that cure for her son and millions of other sufferers. Every day she finds herself at yet another business meeting, trying to raise funds for research.

"I used to go into these meetings toe-to-toe with possible adversaries who I sensed were more interested in funding weapons research than in finding a cure for diabetes. These are harsh aggressive people I'm talking about—people who control the purse strings of major corporations and of the government economy itself. I went in expecting and prepared for combat—not prepared for calm discourse or reasoning. I'm a mother whose kid's life hangs in the balance and my anger and hard-as-nails approach worked, up to a point. But it didn't work fast enough or go far enough. I sensed I was losing some possible allies because it wasn't all that natural to me to come on macho. I was willing to fight with teeth and claws and whatever else it took for this cause, but willingness wasn't the issue. Effectiveness was."

The years progressed, and as Lee was drawn deeper into heavy duty negotiations, her style became more light than heavy. She began to trust her natural inclination toward softer dealmaking. She began to explore her unique female psyche to find the tools that had always worked in her personal life.

"I can only liken it to that new Japanese bullet train," she says today. "Instead of plowing through the landscape, faster than the speed of light, deafening reverberations, ignoring everything in its way, not seeing the landscape as a whole—as the bullet train is designed to do—I tend to move more like a cat these days, like a wise, old feline.

"You know how a cat comes into a room, kind of rubs against your legs to sense the territory, kind of checks out the atmosphere before she moves? Never, ever does she make it a question of sound and fury. That cat gets whatever she wants, gets to be fed, stroked, paid attention to—gets what she came for!" says Lee Ducat.

When Ducat is about to meet with the international president of Procter & Gamble to see him on sponsoring a telethon, something he's never done before, she does her homework before the meeting. She researches everything she can find out about the president of Procter & Gamble so she's prepared to deal with him on a human level. She finds out about his family, his pet charities, his hobbies, the books he likes to read. She also researches the background of other people at the meeting, particularly those who might likely be in opposition—and she plans responses to those objections before they're even made. She often makes personal contact with people before she is to meet them officially. She uses the age-old woman trait of connection and bonding to win points before the game is even technically begun.

Most of all, she relies on intuition.

"I trust my instincts," she says, "more than I ever used to. I think about someone's probable reaction, visualize myself responding with smiles and strong, quiet argument—and, it's amazing! Much more often than not, just what I've visualized happens. Go figure that out—I really can't!

"We're talking negotiation," says Lee. "Empathy is the biggest negotiation tool. I must try to understand where the other person's coming from to make points for my side."

She's a classic. She's also not above claiming those elusive "feminine wiles" as part of her strength.

"Whatever works, I use. I'm going to find a cure for my son. I can't tell you how many meetings I've attended where some powerful man just happened to sweet-talk me into giving up more than maybe I was prepared to give up. Men use this all the time—why should women throw away a perfectly good tool?"

Some day soon you'll read about a scientific breakthrough. Some scientist will find a way to transplant the beta cells of the pancreas gland that manufacture insulin—which diabetics need to live. Whether or not Ducat's name will be mentioned, you can be assured that it wouldn't have happened without Tender Power—Lee Ducat's brand, in particular.

Some women's motivation to succeed is both personal and altruistic. They begin first by helping themselves, and then they are ignited by the sparks of larger possibilities. Something in their feminine psyches teaches them that the combination of tenderness and power can result in a change as big as reconstituting the way an education should progress.

Empowerer of the Young

Madaha (in African, "rolling hills and sand") Kinsey married too young, she says; and in her early twenties she found herself a divorce statistic and the main support of a baby daughter. She was soon to dig down very deep into a well of resources she didn't yet know she possessed—she would become an entrepreneur for her community. Her inborn strength and her tender, loving spirit were to combine into awesome power.

At first Madaha Kinsey felt very much alone in New York. A teacher in a ghetto elementary school, she decided, with the help of her family, "to take off a year or so to nurture my daughter, Saran. After nine months, I was climbing the walls. Also, the money problem loomed large; if we planned to eat, I had to work—but I couldn't bear to leave my baby."

Part-time work was the solution, she thought, and she applied to work for a tutoring service that, through contracts with government agencies, serviced hundreds of foster care children throughout the city.

"I was appalled when I was hired. No one asked me about my teaching techniques, no one asked me what materials I'd use—all I needed was a license to be hired. I could have been an ax murderer."

She thought she could do better.

Five hundred dollars borrowed from her mother bought her business cards, advertisements for teachers, and a screen to separate Saran from the children who came to be tutored. Her apartment number was 6B. Madaha soon changed that to a more professional *Suite* 6B. The tutoring service grew, and when Saran was three and a half, Madaha placed her in a day care facility.

"I checked it out thoroughly—one must, you know—and continue to do so. I had a strong family support system, but if I didn't I would have created a friend support system. Businesswomen with kids must link with each other."

Links for Madaha had, since her earliest days, meant family. Her Uncle Vic was a hero to her, because he taught her to be independent, her own boss. It was he, the family liberal, who supported her new "natural" hairdo and her reading of authors like Erica Jong, "who taught me to celebrate womanness." Madaha's mother, from the old school, was appalled by her young daughter's growing rebellion, and "there was adolescent fury at play in my home, for many years." It was years later—when Madaha, Saran, and Saran's old-world grandmother took a trip to Africa together, the three women, the three generations—"when I fell in love with my mother. My mom saw the old African women cooking on coal pots and immediately remembered her own mom doing the same in America. The strength of that shared connection and heritage made such a new and powerful bond between me, my daughter, and my mother. My mother had been a nag—and all of a sudden, Saran and I both saw the nag as a New Woman, an African, a Sister. One way of coping, I've since learned, is to try to look at familiar people in a new way."

The tutoring service grew. Kinsey made time to travel the Manhattan subways weekly with her small daughter, who took music and dance lessons unavailable locally.

What happened next, says Madaha, was that both she and Saran grew weary of that subway. There was nothing else to do but expand the tutoring service into a school where children might nourish their souls as well as their brains.

"I saw in my own community children who were taught to read and write but who were not given the tools of the special graces of life—art, music, poetry, dance. I thought I could make a school where I might bestow a different kind of power into an intellectually impoverished community."

Mindbuilders was born. Small black and Hispanic children would attend this nonprofit, creative arts center, where her goal was to instill "in each student, through a demanding curriculum and focused, caring instruction, a positive self-concept, self-discipline, and a sensitivity to others.

"It would give our children the tools to enter a competitive world as well as tools to enrich their souls."

The program began in the basement of the Crawford Memorial Methodist Church in the Bronx, New York, with a handful of students. Since then, Kinsey has shepherded the program to service more than a thousand students (with a waiting list almost as long). Its more permanent headquarters, these days, is a former school that has become, almost overnight, "a neighborhood institution," says Kinsey. Classes range from Suzuki-method violin classes to dance, from remedial reading to a professionally run drama group for teens. Several full-time employees and about fifty part-time instructors compose the staff. Alone, Kinsey has knocked on government and private sector doors, getting funding from the State Council of the Arts, the National Endowment for the Humanities, New York City, and private individuals.

She has coped in business, head on, meeting prejudice against her as a woman, as a black, and as an inexperienced businessperson. And she has tapped the heart of the community.

In order to buy the building to house the school, she asked middle-class and poor families to pledge their bankbooks, their homes, possibly their futures, to stand behind a loan from Chemical Bank that Kinsey had managed to secure; a loan that would bring power to the children. True to Madaha's word, the loan was repaid as promised, and the bankbooks—the collateral—were returned to the people.

On the day of the dedication ceremonies hundreds of people came to honor the woman who brought them a promise come true. Politicians, press, family, and friends cheered a lady who someone dubbed "a great soul." Two small boys played a violin concerto. The new school was viable. There wasn't a dry eye in the place.

Soft-spoken, with a dancer's body and a radiant smile, Madaha Kinsey has the look of a woman who is delighted with new-found power within herself. Kinsey says, "My daughter has a role model who has succeeded and who loves success. More important, I think I've showed her that she can retain her tenderness and her vulnerability, and still gain power. And, if you ask me what that means, it means a true sense of self-worth. It came to me, this knowledge I finally had self-worth, one day when I looked around my apartment. On the wall was my art work, a poem of Saran's, and the hamster and various buttons that belong to my permanent 'adopted daughter'—a young woman named Diane who's had a rough life and who has added to our family nourishment by living with us for the last few years. On the wall, also, hangs a silhouette of an African mother and daughter engaged in pounding grain: They are the connective link with our heritage.

"But what was missing from my home was a bed. I'd slept on a futon for years, never finding time to go out and buy a more traditional sleeping arrangement."

"'Hey—wait a minute. I deserve a real bed.' I remember saying. 'Look what I've built, look what I've accomplished.'"

The futon went. Kinsey, an entrepreneur of astounding power and tenderness, will never again sleep on the floor.

Madaha has overcome. Given her powerful ambition and organizational talents, she might well have knocked them dead in the corporate world. Instead, she uses her gentle power to service her community, and in doing so, has satisfied her own dream, earns a good personal living, and has an enormously satisfying life-style. She does it her way.

And so, many entrepreneurs, the new brand of immigrants, are putting the tender back into power plays. Whether they run profit-making or not-for-profit businesses, they play a crucial role in the humanizing of business practices.

There is another societal step on which powerful women have earned firm footholds; and that step is in the sphere of the professional. The professional woman owns great prestige and usually economic clout.

There are certainly humanistic professions in our country like teaching and nursing. Here and elsewhere personal influence is enormous, but, if truth be known, public power and respect is minimal, one more sign of the depreciation in America of caring values.

The fact remains that, when it comes to public respect and commensurate earnings, other professionals like doctors, lawyers, architects, and journalists have always had more personal appeal and stature. When judges enter courtrooms, people stand. Most politicians are treated with awe by an admiring public and sometimes even by an unadmiring public.

If tenderness is to be employed in these power professions, to which large groups of women have lately come, it is women who must introduce and practice it primarily from atavistic memory. Tenderness is rarely found in graduate school course catalogues and certainly not in the job description of an attending physician or newspaper journalist.

7

Professional Tender Power

Many women today choose to travel certain professional routes that in the past were closed to them. Women today are architects, lawyers, doctors, politicians, social welfare planners, and journalists, and they move through many levels of learning and experience to attain their professional goals. Granted, along with a diploma, is power, not tender.

The question is: Can practitioners of Tender Power change the landscape of the professions? Is the practice of medicine or the rendering of justice improved with more compassionate, connecting traits? Many think not: All that's required of good doctoring or good lawyering is a knowledge of the medicine or of the law. The other stuff muddies the field.

I believe that the opposite is true.

Certainly, in medicine, we're hearing new information about the mind/body effect. Many practitioners agree with Dr. Herbert Benson, associate professor of medicine at Harvard Medical School, who says, "perhaps the most important quality you should sense in a physician is that the physician cares for you." His words echo prescient earlier specialists like Dr. Francis Weld Peabody, the first director of the Thorndike Memorial Laboratory of Harvard Medical School. In his 1927 classic, *The Care of the Patient*, Dr. Peabody wrote, "One of the essential qualities of the clinician is interest in humanity, for the secret of the care of the patient is in caring for the patient."

If feminine traits of caring and kindness are effective in medicine, cannot these traits affect as well the arguments of a lawyer, the architectural designs of a draftsperson, or the votes of politicians who directly influence the development of various humanistic public interests?

What follows are some profiles of professionals who think about Tender Power, whether they call it that or not.

Justice is a Beauty

I check out the front of a Blumberg form, the ubiquitous legal document found on every lawyer's desk. There on the cover she is, the woman who is Justice. Straight as an arrow she stands, long hair streaming, eyes blindfolded, sword handle in her left hand, scale in her right. If ever there was an embodiment of Tender Power, it is Justice, who is quite a beauty, I might add. Waiting in the outer office to Judge Marie Lambert's chambers, I witness the following dispensation of justice (or nonjustice, depending on who's telling the story) with some alarm.

The judge's secretary, who doubles as an officer of the court (a police-woman, in plain terms), sits at her desk. I wait for my appointment along with two middle-aged Chinese men who are also waiting for something. The young woman approaches the two men and tells them gently that they must have an appointment, that whatever injustice they have come to see the judge about will have to go through proper channels. The men become furious, disruptive. They begin to yell loudly in Chinese. I change my seat. She asks them to leave, but they refuse and begin to gesticulate. The secretary rushes to her purse and seizes her policewoman's badge, which she firmly displays to the angry men. This makes them angrier. I stand now as far away from them as I can get. The secretary seizes each man by the arm and hustles the two of them out of the office. I'm amazed they go, because she's one quarter their collective size.

When she comes back, she is abashed, and says to me, "I guess there was nothing tender about that, but at least I didn't go for the gun."

She was right. Tender Power has its limitations, sometimes in situations not nearly as dramatic as the above.

It's my turn, and I'm ushered in to Judge Lambert's chambers. Seated, she nevertheless seems larger than life. A deep, deep look at me—then, a broad, warm smile. She asks me to wait a moment while she finishes giving some instructions to her law clerk. Law clerk is a prestigious position—usually the plum handed to the top student in the graduating class. In this case, the clerk is Linda Sosnowitz, and it is she with whom I have been corresponding, asking for this interview with Judge Lambert. I am glad to wait, because it gives me a chance to look around at my surroundings, which remind me of a Daumier print. The room is large, and darkly paneled. We sit at a massive wooden conference table, heavy with patina. This is the Surrogate's Court, a court of great importance. Every front page story seems to land in Judge Lambert's jurisdiction; recently, for example, she handled the tragic case of Travis Christian, a/k/a Mitchell Steinberg, whose caretakers are accused of murdering his adoptive sister, Lisa Steinberg. The room reeks Justice, from the heavy red floral drapes on the wall to the dozens of fat legal tomes in the bookcases. But then, the eye falls to a tiny, hand-painted sign on the judge's desk that reads, "Whatever women do, they must do twice as well as men, to be thought half as good. Luckily, this is not difficult."

Judge Lambert, it appears, is my kind of judge.

"When I began to practice law," says Judge Lambert, "there were few women trying cases. I had to make a decision whether as a trial lawyer before a jury, I'd do better for my client looking and acting like a man or looking and acting like me. I wanted to have the jury understand I was a caring person who cared about my clients—but I wanted them also to trust my strength and intelligence. I chose me.

"When the jury saw me, I looked like their wives and daughters, a woman to whom they could relate. That gave me points. Then, my work preparation did the rest. Even in the beginning, I didn't lose status acting warm and womanly and, my verdicts were larger than most of the men lawyers. So, I knew I was on the right track—acting myself."

I listen to the judge and I think that it is remarkable that I have heard this almost bromide response—be yourself—from every successful woman. It is about as useful, in a way, as saying, "a stitch in time saves nine." We all started out as ourselves, but all the influences, pressures, accommodations we made along the way took us miles from ourselves. Still, the women I speak with, including Judge Lambert, are no dummies, bound by cliché. They have something very definite in mind, I think. They speak of the essential nature of women when they speak of "be yourself."

"Women have the greatest ability to listen," she tells me. "I find that when I sit there, as a judge, I listen, I hear what's said to me, and sometimes they don't think I hear, but I hear. What's more, I have great empathy for those who come before me, and if you don't think empathy strengthens our system, you're wrong. At the moment, I'm getting many AIDS cases— who owns the property when one partner dies?—and I feel such compassion, not only for the families who have lost a child to this disease but also for the lovers, for the other victims. . . ."

I ask the judge if the Surrogate's Court, which traditionally hears cases dealing with estates, is best served by having a judge, male or female, who considers connections and feelings as well as law.

"I don't think this court is only about law, at all. It's a court not for the dead, but for the living. It's the living that have to leave my courtroom feeling that they've received justice, and the only way you do this is to temper the law with compassion," she says.

What about women's intuition? Does something as devalued as that have a place in a court of law?

"I *always* feel I have an intuitive feeling about the law. They kid me in the office about it. I may not know the facts when a case first comes in but when I say I *know* there's a case here, I *feel* that I'm right, everyone perks up and takes notice because over the years I've been proven right. Maybe it's knowing that the law is based on common law and common law is based on common sense. . . . but whatever, when I get a strong feeling, an intuition, I'm usually right. Let me give you an example."

And she does. I promised not to use the names of the people involved in this headline-grabbing case. Judge Lambert tells me of a situation that looked "very black and white" on the surface. A homosexual man marries a much older woman, and within two years she dies and he has all her money.

"Sounds pretty clear-cut, right? He's a bounder, right?" asks the judge. "Naturally, because a huge sum of money is involved, the woman's children are enraged, and they sue.

"So you listen with your head, but also with your woman's intuition," says the judge. "You hear how the man never left the woman, how he had doctors around the clock for her, how she was happy when he was there, how she glowed when she heard he was coming."

And you hear, continues the judge, about how awful the children thought he was and how awful he thought the children were, and it turns out that there is more to this case than what you actually hear, because you have to intuit further. What slowly comes out, to a person who uses empathy and sensitivity, apart from cold legal facts, the judge implies, is that there is another thing going on here: Maybe it's not the husband who was manipulative, nor the children—maybe the woman herself was manipulative and scheming . . . maybe there's a third story, the *real* story.

I am awed by the power of this judge, and by the tender, humane way she thinks. Others in the system are awed as well. One male attorney says, "I have never, ever heard one negative comment about this judge; she is totally respected and admired."

The judge excuses herself for a minute to conduct a short conference outside of her chambers, and I am shocked to note that she *wheels* herself out of the office. All this time she has been sitting in a wheelchair and I didn't even notice! Her injury is temporary, law clerk Sosnowitz assures me, but I have seen so many strong people who somehow lose the *sense* of power when they are placed, even temporarily, in a vulnerable physical position. Not this woman.

Linda Sosnowitz is an attorney who is just beginning to juggle home and career, tender and power, hoping to find her own balance in it all. Sosnowitz is married to a man who does try to help, to share the problems of the dual career couple but it's never, ever an equal sharing, says the attorney. For instance,

"They think that the toilet paper just materializes, just gets there," she says. "I'm not talking about helping with child care—these are all smart men, they know about nurturing, and all that; I'm not even talking about house cleaning—it's easy to hire someone to come in and help occasionally. It's this: Young men, like my husband, are highly successful and organized in their careers. Most of their mothers were home organizing for their fathers, so they're used to an organized home. The young women, like me, who grew up expecting to have careers, sort of internalized, as well, these organizational skills from our mothers, so we automatically assume those roles, even though we have additional career roles. It's sort of a joint expectation, a very subtle thing; today, with both husband and wife on equal career tracks, the woman is *still* the one who makes sure the toilet paper gets to the bathroom, and the man is *still* the one who never gives it a moment's thought. There are times," confides Sosnowitz, "when your circuits overload, when there's just one too many things you should have done that you didn't. If the workplace you go to is not humanized, as this court is, you could just explode, I guess. Judge Lambert is a very serious person, but she is also a very informal and natural woman, so I am lucky to be here."

The judge returns. I ask her, finally, if centuries of women's mediation, eons of making peace with children and husbands, soothing ruffled feathers, compromising, conciliating, is something women should value, or should we learn tougher, firmer stances?

Judge Lambert believes in the former, as well as the latter. "You don't get legislation passed unless you allow for shifting and fixing, changing, and compromise. You don't do well *anywhere* unless you can accommodate. This doesn't make your voice inaudible."

Power, she tells me then, can be tender and gentle, but never inaudible—even literally.

"I had this young lawyer appear before me, and she spoke so softly you couldn't hear her, and her witness followed her lead and spoke even more softly, and I guess I was a little sharp with her," says the judge. "The next thing you know, the attorney's eyes filled with tears and I cleared the courtroom.

"Well, it turned out this trial was her first. If I had known that, I would have been not quite so sharp. Imagine how scary it must be to walk into that imposing, awesome place, and have to convince a judge and jury, who seem miles away, way up there. . . . But, I explained to the young lawyer that being a woman didn't mean that she had to speak softly, because I could never rule in her favor if I couldn't hear her! Tender doesn't mean Caspar Milquetoast!"

The judge has a parting bit of advice. If you want to retain the best parts of womanness and still be powerful, find a mentor. Search for someone, literally, who seems to do it all brilliantly. Then, don't exactly imitate her, but *use* her techniques, follow her lead. It sounds simplistic, but it works. Soon you'll end up with a blend of you and what was so great about her.

The law, it is interesting to note, seems to be trying to change the status quo so that its original representation of Justice as a woman will ring true. Derek Bok, president of Harvard University, says, "Over the next generation, I predict society's greatest opportunities will lie in tapping the human inclinations toward collaboration and compromise rather than stirring our proclivities for competition and rivalry."

If the administrators of justice can strengthen their art and craft by melding their caring with power, can the administrators of mercy—the medical profession—do the same?

The Doctor Is in—And She's Caring

Dr. Ann Halsell Applebaum, an associate clinical professor of psychiatry at Cornell Medical Center and unit chief at New York Hospital's Westchester Division, says she sees many young professional women who seem to be "aping the behavior of young men," fitting husbands and children into their lives in a quite mechanical fashion.

"They say things like, 'I'll have one now,' and if they happen to be young doctors in training and they turn that child over to a housekeeper in order to finish their residency training, that's really okay, they think, because they'll have another one in a few years and have more time for that one. It's pretty bloodcurdling, when you think of it."

On the bright side, says Dr. Applebaum, even young, extremely aggressive-in-the-masculine-mode women, "tend to fall in love with their babies; even though they were planning this robotlike New American Family, they get hooked on their children and everything turns out pretty well."

Many female doctors and female hospital administrators in powerful positions have softened up their edges, notes Dr. Applebaum. Arriving at the top gives license to speak in more authentic voices. It's some of the younger women who are "leaner and meaner in a striving kind of way that's sort of cold and worrisome to me," she says.

What will happen to the children of these women, I ask Dr. Applebaum. What is the psychiatric forecast?

"I'm dying to know," she answers. "The results aren't in—it's too early. But, I predict they'll be filled with longings, if they've only had role models in the achievement-is-all mode. They won't be too different from the very wealthy children we've seen for years, who have been so neglected they either have no attachments or connections only to nannies. A pattern of maternal neglect in the presence of plenty has been around for centuries, really. Today, that is replicated in the striving, upper-middle-class families where the child is once again relegated to the role of an adornment or possession."

Dr. Applebaum points out that the lean, mean, professional machine kind of mother is not the rule in medicine; in fact, the opposite is often true.

"It's interesting to note," she comments, "that the medical schools are filling up with women who constitute between twenty and forty percent of the classes, right now. These women, in my observation, are harassed unmercifully, not by their professor, but by their male colleagues whose envy is sometimes palpable. One of these young female medical students, bewildered by the antipathy of male colleagues, went to the gynecology clinic with a personal disorder of her own, and there she discovered a reason for male jealousy. The nurse asked if her problem was an emergency. 'If it is,' said the nurse, 'you can see the male gynecologist immediately. If it can wait two or three months, I'll be able to give you an appointment with the woman gynecologist.' That kind of competition terrifies the male doctors!"

Why is the female doctor more popular? Because, it would seem, she doesn't hurt, for one reason. Knowing what an intrusive examination feels like, she's more likely to be kindlier and more gentle, report many women. And, although not all female doctors are supportive and empathic, more appear to ask the right questions, and listen, really listen, to the answers, than their male counterparts.

Women are flooding the psychiatric ranks, too, says Dr. Applebaum, and they are very good for the most part.

"There *are* gender differences," says the doctor. "Ten thousand years of being chattel has certainly programmed women in the arts of seduction, and one of the best arts of seduction that there is, is listening. What finer occupational trait could a psychiatrist have?"

I tell Dr. Applebaum about a young doctor, a gynecologist fresh out of medical school, who recently opened an office and took, as a professional partner, a young male colleague from her graduating class at school. It took her no time at all to fit the stirrups on their examining table with warm, cozy, knitted booties. She knew, from experience, how irritating it was to be made to wait in doctors' examining rooms. Since keeping a patient waiting was, sometimes, unavoidable, she directed the receptionist to keep a pot of brewing tea on the ready. Her patients were warmed and delighted. By such caring acts, she humanized the office.

Her partner didn't quite see it that way.

"We're serving up medicine here, not playing house," he announced. "The booties and tea have to go."

Who went, not long afterward, was the female doctor, to open a practice of her own where she might continue to dispense empathy along with medicine.

Dr. Applebaum nods with understanding.

Dr. Beth Cohen, twenty-eight years old and no relation to the author, was in her last year as a resident at a major hospital when I interviewed her.

She makes some interesting points. In medical school, says Dr. Cohen, the women students were even more aggressive, even tougher, than their male counterparts. "They had to be that way to survive," she says. Once out, once practicing, she finds that women practice far more "humane medicine—at least they do when they allow their womanly instincts and their empathy to interact with patients."

She, for instance, is far less liable to get irritated when women call in the middle of the night (and it is always the women, she says, never the men, who call the doctors for their sick babies) to ask a not-so-brilliant question.

"I think about how I'm sure I will be when I have a baby," she says, "and I can totally understand the middle-of-the-night fear and worry a parent can feel. What kind of doctor would feel angry at having sleep interrupted? If I did feel irritation, I'd know I was in the wrong business. A friend of mine told me she did just that—called the pediatrician at three in the morning because her child's temperature was uncomfortably high, and she's a doctor herself!"

What made Dr. Cohen choose medicine? "I love kids—it's as simple as that. And my brand of medicine was never going to be anything but pediatrics where I get to be a kid again, play with the babies, horse around with the older ones . . .

"I guess," muses Beth, "there's something motherly in me already, even before I'm a mother. I pull this quality out, and it's more important than being correct in every single diagnosis. It's no accident that today half of the pediatricians are women. They sensitize the practice.

"Any doctor can give out antibiotics for every virus, that's not good medicine. Good medicine is touching, listening to, caring for, patients. They used to say that doctors should keep their emotional distance from those they treat. That, in my opinion, is awful medicine."

Asked about the mind/body connection, Dr. Cohen says she's certain that positive feelings increase healing. "A doctor who makes a nurturing connection with a patient is more likely to effect a cure," she says. "And women in family medicine have it over men physicians, because they are definitely more nurturing. Women are more likely to touch the kids, ruffle hair, hug, hold out their hands and say 'give me five!' In my experience, the male doctors seem to make more verbal than physical contact when they're not actually examining."

What about Dr. Cohen's own personal plans—does she want it all?

"Sure," she says. "But I know I'm not going to have it all at this speed. Just having myself to worry about, I have not a moment to breathe. When I have a family, I will have to make compromises. Part-time is a strong option. I won't want to work full-time when I have a family. I'm a doctor, around kids all the time, and I think, in those first couple of years, it's essential to bond. Look—I went into medicine because I loved other people's kids—I suspect, I'll love my own, as well, and want to spend a lot of time with them. . . . although, never twenty-four hours a day. Part-time work, three days a week, say, is the optimum."

Shortly after I spoke with Dr. Cohen, I visited a friend in the cardiac care unit. Attending to her needs, after bypass surgery, was Dr. Jill Kalman, an intern in internal medicine. I was struck by the fact that Dr. Kalman had brought a book to my friend, a book that would answer the questions that come in the still, dark hours of the night. Dr. Kalman didn't just recommend a book; she had, of her own volition, gone out and bought it for her patient. It was lovely to see this energetic, young woman physician kneeling on the floor to get closer to my friend's face, holding the sick person's hand, wiping her brow. I'd never seen such tactile involvement by a doctor before.

"When I was in medical school," Dr. Kalman told me, "I remember hearing a lecture from an eminent male physician. 'Get very physical,' he told us. 'Nothing makes for worse medicine than putting a wall between the doctor and the patient.' I never forgot it. Now," she smiles as she tells me, "I always sit on my patient's bed to make eye contact, or I kneel to bring our eyes on an even level. It's important to be a person and not merely an authority on a pedestal."

Yes, it is the women doctors in internal medicine, just like in pediatrics, who make nurturing contact, more than the males, she says. I am not shocked by the information. Yes, she takes home her worries about her patients, "which isn't terrific, but it's worse when I don't care about a patient and take home nothing," she says.

And yes, Dr. Kalman, who is married, is worried about what she'll do when she has children.

"There will definitely have to be compromises made, and the compromises will be on the side of the time spent practicing medicine, not on the side of the family," she says. "I'm never going to be the star cardiologist, because I won't put in the hours I'd have to take away from my children. I know that now, even before I have them. Sure, deciding to be a doctor, a caring and good doctor, is a great commitment; still, my life will have balance, that I tell you now."

I can't tell if it's a professional trend or if it's the fact of their femaleness, but many young women doctors to whom I spoke all intended to practice fewer hours of medicine in order to spend more time with their families. These physicians loved their profession, but they were not willing to practice it in the male mode—long, long, endless days of doctoring. Fewer hours—deeper connections with patients is their mode.

Many of us are convinced it is these young women who will bring the tenderness, so long gone from the scene, back to medicine. It is these women who will make medicine more powerful in the human sense, and therefore, more healing. The old family doctor who made house calls may never return, but his compassionate quality may yet be back as more and more women opt for the new, connective kind of medical practice.

Dr. Sheila Jackman is director of the Division of Human Sexuality of the Albert Einstein School of Medicine. Part of her job is to lecture the young, third-year medical students.

"What do I tell them?" she asks me. "Well, for one thing, I tell them that here, in their third year of learning to be doctors, they know less about people than they did three years ago. They've learned that all the answers are in the books. They forget how to intuit messages by really *listening* to patients."

For instance, she says, "We often role-play situations. I tell my students that I am a forty-four-year-old woman who needs a hysterectomy. I ask the doctors-to-be if my sex life will be changed. Almost every one of those students immediately start talking about replacement estrogen therapy, uteruses, and dryness.

"Almost never do the students think to ask, 'Well, what's your sex life like now?' It's only treatment and medicine they're concerned with—not a woman's expectations, fears, humanity, and life-style.

"Book statistics tend to take the person out of the physician."

Humanist Architecture

Bricks and glass and steel and rulers can take the person out of the architect as well. But if medicine and law can be influenced by humanist traits long associated with women, can a high-rise building be as well? Susan Gross, a recent graduate of the Columbia University Graduate School of Architecture, Preservation and Planning, thinks it can.

The assignment was to design a movie theater and a place that would act as a museum to honor film and film makers. A prestigious prize hung in the balance. The second-year students had their work cut out for them, remembers Gross.

"I thought deeply about what a film was and decided that it had a lot to do with entering a dream state. One's first dream, it followed, would be one's experience in the womb. Therefore, the enjoyment of film would be enhanced in a dark, womblike place," says Gross.

Her project became a "spirally motion" to end underground in a dark, nurturant, womblike place. She wanted, she says, to transform a tactile sensuality—warmth itself—into an architectural form. She thought about planning space that would become more restrictive, protective, and enveloping. She lowered ceiling heights, closed window apertures, and darkened the interior to create an environment that would feel safe and personal. Did her movie theater work? Well, it was different from her classmate's. And he won the prize.

His project consisted of a magnificently cold, austere, box-design, elevated on a huge tripod about one hundred and fifty feet into the air. It seemed to be on stilts, suspended mid-sky. "I admired the verve," says Gross, "but, I don't think it's sour grapes to say that I believe that people would feel isolated and uncomfortable watching a film in that cold, beautiful box. It seemed antithetical to humans.

"No question—in our first year in the school of architecture, there were obvious differences in male and female projects. Not that men's designs are always more stark or bold—surely women design this way, as well, but—I hate to be trite—it comes down to towers. Men seem to build these phallic monuments to themselves."

Toward the end of the graduate school program, notes Susan, most of the women seemed to have gravitated toward the male ethos. One of the class's early projects, she recalls, consisted of building models of housing developments. "One female classmate spoke of her row of attached homes as a 'string of pearls,' " says Gross. By the end of the year, she was referring to it in purely technical, but far less colorful terminology. Gross is not sure that was a sign of progress.

During the school year, remembers Susan, it was often a struggle to retain a feminine ethos. This was partially so because many male students tended to claim the profession as masculine in spirit and nature—even language. This became graphically apparent during a dinner shared by male and female architecture students. As the women spoke in terms of bricks, steel, and concrete, one young man thought it sounded "funny" to hear such "masculine" materials bandied about in the conversation of the female architects—a chauvinistic attitude that naturally enraged the young women.

Gross's goal? "To translate powerful ideas into powerful, but human, architecture," she says.

There is clearly no such thing as purely male or purely female structures, but gender can influence, and Susan hopes to build structures that encompass both male and female gentleness as well as purist design techniques. Her final project comes close, she says.

"It's a structure to honor the spirit of Amelia Earhart—an institute where people and the media can come to research space and the qualities of heroism," she says.

Gross's structure, as she envisions it, would be built on a pier located on New York's Hudson River. The pier would not be horizontal as most are, but would instead swell up gradually from the water's ever-changing surface. Shadows of Earhart's planes would be engraved onto the pier and as the tide rose and fell, the airplane images would appear and disappear—a mystery, as Earhart herself will always be. Soaring from the pier and seemingly rising from the water would be a splendid, rounded structure comprised of airy grids and struts. It would house the air and space museum and in a dramatic paean to Earhart's spirit, her three airplanes would also be exhibited on three "floating" levels.

To Susan Gross, this building would be a balance of spirit and pure design, a triumph of humanistic architecture. The essence of poetry, science, and symbolism would meld with pristine power.

Sounds like Tender Power, to me.

If law, medicine, and architecture can be made stronger disciplines with a bias toward humanism, is there any place at all for tender in politics?

Apart from in-the-clouds idealism, can the rough-and-tumble game that politicians play derive more influence when it is tempered with sympathetic and feeling ideals?

"Politics Make Strange Bedfellows." (Charles Dudley Warner)

But if you ask Martin Oppenheimer, *politicians*, he'll say, make perfectly fine bedfellows. His wife, New York state senator Suzi Oppenheimer, an admitted workaholic, is a woman who has enough warmth and nurturing to take care of him, their four children, and thousands of loyal constituents, as well.

"It's critical to nurture in government as well as the home," she says to me. "The information we're gathering in government studies points shockingly to the almost inescapable cycle: If you're raised with abuse, you abuse. If you're raised with nurturing, you nurture. I can't imagine why such clear-cut statistics don't compel legislators to sponsor serious education in the art of nurture."

Oppenheimer is a woman who has done it all, but in sequences, a life plan that is drawing the interest of more and more assertive women.

"My background is business, my Master's comes from Columbia Business School, and when I was pushing thirty and very aware of the biological clock, I knew I had to get down to business, particularly because we wanted a large family. I had four kids in a little less than seven years, and when we were pregnant with the fourth (it has always been a joint effort, this parenting), we moved to the suburbs because I'd always wanted to be involved in community life."

In short order, Suzi took on the traditional women's roles, and it was clear that she was a born leader. She joined the PTA and soon became president. She joined the League of Women Voters and soon became president. When her youngest was just entering elementary school, she decided to run for mayor of her small town, Mamaroneck, New York—and she soon became Mayor Suzi, a position she held for eight years.

Now in her second term as state senator, Suzi explores political options on the issues she's chosen to be hers.

"I feel that it's up to women to humanize the political arena, since it doesn't seem to be a top priority of men. I'm the officer of the Legislative Women's Caucus, which is comprised of eighteen women from the assembly and five from the senate and together we have carved out for ourselves all issues pertaining to women and children. We champion, among other things, the search to find human ways of caring for the elderly, the young, ourselves. Women must have support and respite, or else the wonderful gains we've made will break us."

We hear, states Suzi, that men are risk takers and that's why they succeed.

It's the women who are risking everything, really. "It is the core of women, its essence being humor, nurturing, and the networking that we do so well, that will give substance and a safety net to the risks we take." It is, moreover, caring that makes the difference between a person and a plastic candidate. Caring will bring young people into the political arena—an arena currently turning them off, says Suzi. We've been barring emotion from politics, lately.

"Once," says Senator Oppenheimer, "when I was mayor, I was attending a board hearing that met to discuss the issue of community group homes for the retarded. The community consensus was to keep the retarded away from our pretty place.

"I remember becoming quite emotional—I even cried—something I'm not crazy about seeing politicians do—as I made an impassioned appeal to allow these homes into our neighborhood."

The community, she remembers, was not happy with the stance she took.

"I received so much angry mail, the pundits thought I was finished. Who wanted stumbling, bumbling people living next door? But, you know what? The same community returned me to office with even a greater margin of victory than the year before. The public will forgive you not doing what they want if your principle is humane. I believe that. I believe America is yearning for niceness. Is that womanly? Or masculine? I don't know. It surely is human. I'm not such a paragon of virtue, but I want my four kids to live in a human environment."

Is it an accident that when women are in politics, the tender, human level of politics tends to rise? The question is—how to get women like Suzi in the drivers' seats? A National Women's Political Caucus Poll in 1987 found that Americans are quite easy with the idea of having women on school boards and in lower-level governmental positions. When we see Tender Power in charge, we get used to it, and we're accustomed to seeing women on these levels. As women rise in the hierarchy, the comfort level with their presence at the top will also rise. The trick is to push for the rise.

Listen to Patricia Schroeder, congresswoman from Denver, Colorado, who ran for the presidency and then changed her mind. She is a direct, exciting presence, and should not be counted out as far as the future is concerned. She is particularly well known for a lack of pedantry in her speeches. She gets right to the heart of human power.

Says Schroeder:

We need to protect the family against economic hardship. It takes two incomes to achieve the family income of one person working just three years ago. We don't have child care. We don't have equal pay for comparable work, we don't have employment practices that allow part-time work with benefits, and we don't have parental leave. You can be fired for having a baby in this country. Our tax code encourages people to raise thoroughbred horses, not children.

There is no question that our economics, politics, and business practices today seem dreadfully out of sync with the long-held concept of the great, big-hearted America. Labor-saving technologies seem to be giving us more, not less, work. Instead of returning to the pride of creativity and individuality, the enjoyment of family and friends, time to grow vegetables as well as relationships, we Americans have been burying ourselves in slavish drudgery and treadmill climbs to the top. Perhaps, by putting sensitive women in the nation's drivers' seats, we will finally return to a balance of life, love, recreation, and hard work. Perhaps men and women alike can celebrate human connection again, along with human achievement.

Liz

Connection is irrevocably meshed with achievement when it comes to the power that Liz Smith holds. What power does a gossip columnist have?

If you are a writer, and you want your book to sell, get Liz Smith to mention it in her column or on her television program. If you are a director, and you want people to come to see your film, you better hope Liz likes it. If you are a moviegoer, whether you know it or not, the films you see and the stars that appear in them are in subtle ways prescribed by Liz Smith's messages to the public. And, if you are a star, you very much want to be on Liz's "good person" list, because she can make or break you by what she reports. The public believes her. Whether you have thought about it or not, someone like Liz Smith, by her reportage, dictates standards of entertainment, glamour, and often morality in America. It wasn't always so.

Liz's predecessors—Hedda Hopper, Dorothy Kilgallen, Louella Parsons—were always treated as comic characters. Although journalists by profession, gossip columnists were never *really* considered journalists. They all seemed so sneaky, petty, untrustworthy; even when we were fascinated by their stories, we wouldn't want to bear the brunt of their terrible, probing power. Gossip columnists fed us the foibles of Hollywood, but they did nothing to enhance the status of their profession—not until the humanizing force of Liz Smith gave "gossip" a new name. It is Liz's tenderness that brings the gods and goddesses down to our level, making them seem like real people we might actually know, maybe even be friends with. It is Liz's tenderness that makes her (unheard of in gossip-column history) such a friend and favorite of the glitzy, glamorous movie-star community. And make no mistake; Liz's great power is derived from her capacity to connect with others, from her empathy with those in trouble, from her humanity.

I met Liz at Pearl's, New York's famous Chinese restaurant where people go to eat lemon chicken and be seen by Liz. Her table (the best) was visible from the door, and as we spoke many stared at her famous face, stopped by to say hello, and to be seen.

"How can you be in this business and be a nice human being, a warm woman? Your business is to dish out dirt," I asked Liz.

"My business is to tell the truth," she answered. "I get the truth because I convince the film community that its best interest lies in letting my column break the news. I think if you just give people a chance, let them tell their side and have their day to answer back . . . they're grateful. And it gives you points. To tell you the truth, the press has such a terrible reputation now, that if you just treat people fairly, they think they're being treated extra well."

Fairness usually has less to do with equity than it has to do with avoiding those super-sensitive, killingly vulnerable spots everyone protects in himself. To go for the jugular is inhumane, and Liz rarely aims for the kill. She respects the fragile layers with which others shield their most secret secrets. One would think that a gossip columnist's job is to rip away the layers in every instance. The gossip columnist who conducts her inquiries according to that precept would have a difficult time inspiring trust within those on whom she must depend for stories. Liz's predecessors were neither trusting nor trustworthy: Their stories for the most part were catty rather than revelatory.

Liz operates on a different level. She uses her intuition to tell her what's news and what is nobody's business.

Is women's intuition a myth? Is being sensitive to others a weakness?

"Women are definitely more intuitive than men," says Liz. "Also, it appears they've been socialized to be more sensitive. That's good. Wouldn't you hate to be a man? They have to seem so brave, so stiff-upper-lip, and they have to go to war and they end up so—constipated in expression! Women should like to be perceived as vulnerable; it's a tremendous asset to be thought of as sensitive. Still, don't make the mistake of thinking all women are sweet and kind. The Apaches always turned their victims over to their women who thought up the most delicious tortures." Contrary to Liz, there are many who feel that caring too much about others' feelings is a detriment in any business. One would think it certainly would be a detriment in a profession where the point is to "get the dirt" no matter how it damages the object of the story. Liz says this might be so and confesses that she actually thinks she's a terrible reporter because, "If I were more aggressive, I could get more news, but I'm always folding up and whispering, 'Oh, you don't want to say that . . .'"

Liz is not a terrible reporter. She's the first one to get the story. She's the best. Part of it has to do with her ability to inspire trust, but part is also due to her ability to defuse a situation when a furious movie star feels that even Liz, despite her sensitivity, has told one too many secrets. Then Liz calls on yet another ancient female trait. She smooths over, she conciliates, she listens.

"There are a lot of unpleasant aspects of my job," she says slowly. "When people call up screaming, I kind of deflect their anger—my mother taught me to do that—'Well, what *is* it you'd like to say?'—or, 'What have I got wrong?' I guess that I'm good at mollifying them to some extent, good at making people see that what's been said isn't so damaging after all. I know many of my friends in the movement like you to say women are not manipulative, but manipulating, modifying, conciliating—those are human traits. I'll tell you something: I meet male stars who are so used to having women fall down dead over them, they start manipulating *you* before you open your mouth."

Another thing Liz does, is flirt. She does not feel it is demeaning to women to use sex appeal.

"I couldn't live if I couldn't flirt," she asserts. "When I want to accomplish something, if I go directly over a guy, push him around, use tough clout, scare him—I get nowhere. If I kid around, tell jokes, act womanly—well, who are we kidding? It works. Men do the same thing—they better not try to take away that tool from us. I grew up flirting, and even now, at my great age . . . well, I mean a man always likes when you flirt with him, no matter how old you are!"

Many women entering journalism tend to take on the protective coloring of androgyny. They are fearful that looking different and acting different from their male counterparts will mark them as somehow less forceful and less efficient.

"I think it's important to look good and that means looking different from men, no matter what artifice we employ," says Liz. "I wouldn't want to be in one of those businesses where women take on protective clothing to avoid being noticed, to avoid calling attention to themselves. . . . all those miserable little gray suits.

"Powerful women also means acting different from men," says Liz. "Although I know some wonderfully gentle men, most don't show it. Gentle manners distinguishes powerful women. True power says please and thank you. There is nothing that more obviously separates the powerful from the powerless than graciousness.

"If there's any one good thing that comes along with power, it's this," she answers. "If you're a nice person, a caring person, you can use power to make yourself and other people more comfortable. If you abuse power, you tend to lose it. You know, I think it's hard for women in particular to misuse power: They always get trapped."

"You're not tough on your staff?" I asked Liz.

"Oh, I yell and carry on," she says grimly, "but no one ever pays attention to me. Call that power?"

I do. That's exactly what I call it. It is professional, not amateur, power. It is very human.

Professional power is on the rise in the female population. The proportion of women to men who receive higher academic degrees is slowly increasing.

Male-to-female ratios in engineering, medicine, and law schools particularly are getting smaller. Clearly, women who have fought for the opportunity to join the elite professional world have no trouble meeting its requirements.

Still, underneath the aggressive, competitive personality of the new professional woman lies an older feminine identity. Sometimes the two do battle. It's encouraging to know that for all those women who struggle daily with the idea that they have to choose between being caring and being professionally dynamic, there are other women who insist on being both.

"I once saw an advertisement for tank tee shirts and women's boxer shorts underwear," says Marlene McNeil, an engineer for Chrysler Corporation in Detroit. "I cut it out and saved it because it got me ticked off. 'Did you ever think you'd be so at ease in a man's world?' it read. 'Because suddenly what was once purely male territory is now where you're looking your best.'

"People who write those ads are living in the dark ages," says Marlene. "They still think that women who attain male power should want to look and act like men. Most women are about as comfortable wearing those stupid jockey shorts as they are about imitating men's behavior at work. That's why jockey shorts for women died a very quick death."

Perhaps professional women can be the new role models for younger women on the way up. Academic success has allowed them to develop strong egos, and career success has given them the courage of their convictions. If anyone can bring a humanistic ethos onto the job, they can. If anyone can tenderize the workplace, they can.

8

Tenderizing the Workplace

There are tender solutions to the tough problems of the marketplace. If tenderness in the largest sense of the word were really employed in the marketplace, the benefits to the bottom line would be enormous. Humor, empathic listening, and a feeling of family as corporate policy are management devices of compelling power, as the Japanese model of success has proven. Order-giving is far less potent than effective participation and communication among the staff. CEOs and managers with strong people skills and sensitive to the importance of feedback and the existence of life after work will be the ones who attract the best worker power. A growing discontent with the ethics of the eighties has been spreading from the top down.

"We're seeing the politics of greed and self-aggrandizement coming to an end," says Jeremy Karpatkin, a political party organizer. The politics of greed—careerism, adulation of wealth, a cult of restrictiveness, a disregard for the needy and the dominance of the male businessperson—are becoming yesterday's politics. The country's mood and the direction of the marketplace is awakening to the human needs of its workers. Self-centered behavior somehow seems less attractive than community spirit. New interest in moral, spiritual, and family growth appears to be taking center stage.

From a global perspective, some countries, as we shall see, are doing a better job than we are at tenderizing the marketplace. The good news is that it is never too late to start.

Instilling nurturing methods to increase worker participation is one way to humanize the workplace. Changing the physical plant of offices is another way: Softening hard-edge ambiance by greenery and artwork has been found to put workers in corporations in much better moods.

Probably at the very heart of tenderizing the workplace is the recognition that love, family, and labor can be integrated. Some companies pay no credence to the need for social innovation. By failing to provide child care and leisure time they lose employee loyalty and productivity. Controlling, combative competition, the economics of the warrior mentality, are no longer viable. Too many people hate the warrior mentality. Too many people yearn for a more caring, livable work environment.

Ultimately, in redefining success for both men and women, firms will have to give both men and women quantity as well as quality time to spend with families and even by themselves. Dr. Willard Gaylin, president of the Institute of Society, Ethics, and the Life Sciences, in Hastings-on-Hudson, New York, says we have to reeducate people to what's really important, to reevaluate the meaning of status. Imagine if people really believed, he says, that being a family was at least as valuable as accumulating "those little pieces of green paper!"

Family, Dr. Gaylin and other experts point out, doesn't have to be mom, dad, and the kids, but family in the largest sense of the word—connecting colleagues, attaching friends, as well as blood relatives. Not everyone wants spouses and children, but almost every human does need to connect with the larger human family—and the time to do so.

"Work until you drop" appears to be a modus operandi that is as dissatisfying to men as it is to women. Over half of all employed men, fifty-three percent, in a D'Arcy Masius Benton & Bowles study, chose *having to go to work* as the one activity they would like someone else to do. Perhaps it's not work per se they dislike, but unrelenting, uncaring work.

The warrior mentality in the marketplace has got to go. It's leaving only a few of us very rich and too many of us unfulfilled. Blunting the warrior mentality is not simply a woman's challenge. But it is women who must push men to speak out for humanizing changes. Let's not kid ourselves; of course men are capable of tenderness, but it wasn't until women entered the workplace that family issues, for example, were given a hearing and a legitimate place. Men will not do it by themselves. They have been taught for eons that you shouldn't bring your personal life to the office—and quite understandably so. If your son had a toothache, there was always a wife or a mother-in-law at home to take him to the dentist. Now the wives and the mothers-in-law are in the next office down, and personal life must come to work.

More than a decade ago Hennig and Jardim wrote of women in their classic *The Managerial Woman* that, "their personal lives were being mortgaged to pay for their careers." Things haven't changed much to this very date. In a 1986 report on corporate women for *The Wall Street Journal*, Amanda Bennett wrote that "agonizing conflicts between family and career haven't eased much, and may, in fact, be intensified for newcomers. . . . young women are much more conflicted about how they're going to balance career and kids. It's tormenting them."

It's time.

Tenderizing the marketplace must have first priority. Here are some ways it can be done.

Lighten Up

It seems appropriate to begin with humor as a way to tenderize the workplace. There are many who have accused women of not having a sense of humor because women don't laugh at jokes that make fun of their desire to succeed in the workplace. Women don't laugh because it isn't funny.

Anyone who cares to investigate will note that it is women who have traditionally used humor to get along in the world, whether a light touch to diffuse tension at the dinner table or black humor, softening the frustration that women have shared over countless cups of coffee. It has always been women who understood about the power of humor.

Now, appropriately, it is a woman who, among others, is at the forefront of a brilliant and very modern use of humor. Dr. Barbara Mackoff, a Seattle-based, Harvard-trained psychologist, provides clinically tested techniques of corporate humor on the job.

"Humor is the ultimate power tool," says Dr. Mackoff, "and punchlines bolster the bottom line."

Dr. Mackoff has conducted workshops at IBM, Hewlett-Packard, the American Institute of Banking, and the United States Forest Service, among other corporations. The workshops are geared to help managers and staff see challenging or threatening situations in terms of their comic potential. It is a way to loosen up potentially volatile situations.

Dr. Mackoff creates an agenda of corporate slang, in-jokes, and visualization techniques. She encouraged one person, for example, to think of the theme from *Jaws* whenever a certain supervisor approached, and another to picture himself as Tarzan because his office was "such a zoo."

"It's silent comedy, and you can do it in your own head," says the psychologist, "all it takes is practice."

The interest in the psychological and gentling effects of humor is a sign of the times. With restructurings, takeovers, and layoffs sweeping the corporate world, employee insecurity, and hostility at super-high levels, employees come to see, says Dr. Mackoff, "that most of the foul-ups, snafus, and face-to-face encounters that rob us of the energy we need to cope can be diffused with interior humor. I see power as the ability to get things done," says Dr. Mackoff. "Tell me what the people in your organization are laughing at and I'll tell you what kind of organizational power exists."

Corporate Kidcare

Tenderizing the workplace means doing something about kids, and there's nothing funny about that concept.

If corporations don't love being in the business of kidcare, too bad. It's either that or "lose highly trained employees to diaper duty and tricycles for ten years," says *Working Woman Magazine*. According to surveys, 2500 companies (up from 600 in 1982, but still not nearly enough) offer some kind of child care assistance. It may be reference and referral services, subsidies or vouchers that parents can redeem, discounts at specified centers, reimbursement accounts in which pretax dollars are held back from salaries to pay for child care, funding of child care centers, or, in the most tender of companies, on-site child care centers. Providing kidcare is not altruism; it is to the corporation's benefit that women feel free in conscience and spirit; how can they give their most powerful talents if they're worried about their children?

Although experts differ as to whether or not very tiny children should be left in child care, present reality dictates that, since more than half of all new mothers remain in the job market, substitute child care, as the 1987 Census Bureau report indicated, is here to stay. In 1987 two thirds of all school-age children had working mothers, and for the first time even most mothers of babies under a year old were employed. Thirty-seven percent of the children in need of substitute mothering end up in informal care situations with a friend across town, or with a lady down the street who watches several children besides her own. Twenty-three percent of children who need substitute mothers are in formal day care centers. As more women go to work, fewer are available for overseeing others' children.

Dr. Michael Rothenberg, co-author of the latest edition of *Dr. Spock's Baby and Child Care*, says that by 1990 eighty percent of mothers with children under one will be working and looking for child care. "And where are they going to find it? It's a nightmare."

It's a nightmare because salary and job benefits of caretakers are not improving fast enough to attract people to the field. Most full-time child care workers earn less than $10,000 per year, which is less than we pay animal caretakers or parking lot attendants.

No one can fairly say that the person who devotes her days to guarding your child ought to do it for peanuts. Corporation contributions, government subsidies, private industry taxation—all must combine to offer more tender, more powerful, and more fair child care arrangements.

Parental Leave

What if you want to take care of your own children?

Betty Friedan says that it's not enough to grant maternity and paternity leaves after the birth of a child. The leave must be granted, says Friedan, in some combination of paid and unpaid time—and this is the important part—while people retain whatever seniority they've earned. Too many men and women, in the first flush of gratitude to the corporation's largess in granting leaves, found themselves back at square one when they returned to work. They were not given the same or an equivalent job, and they lost their pension entitlements. Where, asks Friedan, "is the social debate, the social demand, the movement pressure that will put this issue on the national-policy level, where it belongs?"

This nation, says Friedan, is "the only industrial country, besides South Africa, without a national policy of parental leave! The difficulties women are having with putting it all together are treated as each woman's own individual problem. So it's back to either kids or career—and that's where I came in! Either-or is a no-win."

Other governments have put such policies on a national level, in the gentlest but most imperative of manners—and they have succeeded. Case in point: Sweden. Letty Cottin Pogrebin discusses the Swedish male sex role and how the concept of "nurturing men" came to be a true government priority.

"How did they do it?" asks Letty. "They did it by running print and television campaigns showing men, hairy-chested, bearded, *enormous* men, with little teensy, weensy babies, the men giving bottles and changing diapers with this accompanying message: 'He's all man so he can easily take care of a child without imperiling his masculinity . . .'"

Then, the Postmaster-General of Sweden took paternity leave, but he didn't do it quietly. The government chose to show his picture in every newspaper, saying, "I have grown children, my children came and went, they were strangers, I never knew them. With my second family, I'm not going to make that mistake. Take time off to bond with your children."

Result? Eighteen percent of Swedish men take time off when a child is born, to bond with that child. Eighteen percent is surely a tiny figure when compared to all men in Sweden, but, notes Letty, "it's light years away from the time when eighteen percent of American men take time off to do the same."

Betty Friedan suggests that in the second stage of the women's movement, "Where women seem to be moving out of the home to fulfill themselves in a man's world of work, men seem to be disentangling themselves from definition by success in the work world and shifting towards a new definition of themselves in the family and other new dimensions of self-fulfillment."

It may take real courage to encourage this kind of tenderness because, as psychiatrist Willard Gaylin observes, "We're prepared to let a woman enter the corporate world, but we're not prepared to let a man leave." Anthropologist Patricia A. McBroom says that "The experience of men and women in other cultures holds out the hope that if men are brought close to their children as nurturant parents, the entire system will reflect a change in the masculine ethos with far-reaching effects on the social order, including our patterns of work."

The macho warrior ethos, says McBroom, does not survive very well when men have the same responsibilities and rights as women within the family structure.

The power of masculine tenderness is enormous, and corporations and governments can foster it if women push companies and governments for humanizing parental leave.

Flex-Time

A tender solution to the human need for self-time, invented by a German woman chemist and imported to the American corporation in the seventies, is Flex-Time—the system of choosing one's own starting and quitting times, within certain limits set by management. Now, it is used by some twelve million employees (not including many freelance, managerial, and sales employees who have always worked on more flexible schedules). It has been estimated, says *Working Woman Magazine*, that another twenty million professionals work part-time permanently. All this has given way to yet another form of Flex-Time known as job-sharing; two women share one job and each puts in the hours and responsibilities she feels her family life can sustain without damage. Many bosses feel that job-sharing gives them twice the labor for one salary. Flexible alternatives give women and men a chance to have careers, private lives, and a home life without sacrificing anything.

Eldercare

Within the next ten years the new hot issue is going to be eldercare, say many experts. In late 1985, a *Wall Street Journal* study noted that aging parents, traditionally the woman's responsibility, will become a top priority for which the corporation will have to find tender solutions—or risk losing newfound woman power.

"Often caring for a parent results in cutting down hours at work, or even quitting jobs," says the *Journal*, as twenty-eight percent of those surveyed by the newspaper had already done. The conflict between career and caretaking is likely to get worse; as the population of elderly people inexorably grows, their situation in life grows inexorably sadder.

We live in a time when the issues of concern, compassion, and caring hardly have a place at all in governmental policy. With all the rhetoric heard around election time, tenderness in the practice of government power is a word with little meaning. On January 1, 1988, an explosive surge in health insurance premiums stunned thousands of employers and millions of workers nationwide. Rate increases of up to seventy percent gave the lie to the administration's vow that medical costs were being brought under control. Almost worst of all in this front-page *New York Times* release was the report that thirty-one million elderly and disabled Americans covered by Medicare were going to have their premiums raised by 38.5 percent! People with no way to make more money, nowhere to turn, are in despair. Some of them can turn to their children, but whom can their children turn to? In another time it was hard enough to care for elderly parents, but usually there was at least a woman home tending the stove, the children, and those parents. Today, with almost everyone at the office, care for the elderly, many of whom will not even be able to afford Medicare any longer, becomes a crisis situation. Clearly, something is terribly wrong with the value systems of those who make the big decisions.

Elaine Wilk Cohen, spokeswoman for Pathfinders/Eldercare, a private counseling group in Scarsdale, New York, says that by 1999, when about five million Americans will be over eighty-five, caring for the aged will become one of the most urgent concerns of business. Employees caring for older relatives, she says, are late more often and are less productive than other workers; according to a University of Michigan study, such workers are even more likely to be depressed than their elderly charges!

"There's no question that the emotional and financial strains of caring for an elderly parent, despite the best-intentioned son, usually falls on a daughter or daughter-in-law," notes Cohen. "Because Americans are living longer, a typical life span often hits the eighties, even the nineties. These daughters are besieged by sadness, feelings of entrapment, and depression that's caused by knowing that things are not going to get better."

Giving an example of what she calls a typical "division of labor" in parental caretaking, Cohen tells of the aged father who suffered a stroke.

"The man's son paid his bills. All his finances were neatly in order. But," says Cohen, "it was the woman who took time off from work to go with her father-in-law to the hospital in the ambulance. It was the woman who visited most often and on whose shoulders fell the primary care of her aged mother-in-law.

"It was the woman who schlepped, made soup, and nurtured," says Cohen. "The son mostly looked sad."

Some grown children can divorce themselves from the care of elderly parents. Others can't face themselves if they don't act responsibly. For these people, there are corporate good guys suddenly appearing on the scene. Some private counseling groups like Pathfinders/Eldercare offer seminars to corporations intended to open up "eldercare" communications between workers and management. A few of these corporations are showing increased sensitivity to the new problems. Pepsico, for example, issues a sourcebook featuring sections on psychological and physical changes in older people and sources of state agencies where one can find information about finances, housing, transportation, and other services. Other large companies showing heart are American Express, Mobil Oil, Ciba-Geigy, and Johnson & Johnson.

Many corporations set up corporate accounts for employees that are not subject to income or Social Security taxes, and employees can draw from these funds when they need them for eldercare. Stride Rite, a children's shoe manufacturing corporation, is considering building a day care center near corporate headquarters in Cambridge, Massachusetts, where employees can bring their elderly parents as well as their children. This center, the quintessential expression of corporate empathy, will sponsor programs of physical therapy, field trips, social activities, and even some intergenerational programs like cooking classes.

When Work and Home Collide: Getting the Government Interested

A funny thing happened to me on the way to Congressman Bill Green's office—and it wasn't funny at all. I was literally on my way out the door to interview this member of the United States House of Representatives on the subject of caring for the aged; I wanted to see what the government had in mind in the way of providing some help to women who are the caretakers of their elderly parents, when the call came in.

It was my father. My mother, whose eighty-fifth birthday we had just celebrated, had fallen. She was in agony.

I called to cancel. I was sure the congressman would understand.

Two weeks later, having cancelled six other interviews, I managed to meet with Congressman Green. I was fresh from hospitals, doctors, frantic with worry about the hiatus in my work schedule, pressured now with a myriad of extra burdens. Who would cook and shop for my parents, who would make sure my mother's medication was properly administered, who would tend to my dad's needs until my mother was well? Me, that's who. Somehow.

"When work and home collide," says the congressman, after asking about my mother, "it usually is women who are caught in the impact. Normally, I would not tend to support the government's mandating of benefits that have not been bargained for by the trade unions, but in this case, it is pretty clear that the union movement in the United States is not particularly feminist oriented. In fact, if you look at the history of the ERA, you'll note that initially trade unions vigorously opposed it on the grounds it would cost men jobs," he says.

Green thinks the U.S. government ought to tell employers that yes, they must provide at least some unpaid leave for eldercare or other family needs. Yes, the government ought to operate with compassion. And yes, parental leave is also a big issue.

"But, there are problems," he assures me. Although the parental leave he has in mind would assure fringe benefits like health insurance and a guarantee that employees could return to their earned status, the leave would cover, at most, only a matter of weeks or months.

"Also, we've got to yet determine the size of the business enterprise that would be required to promise time off; as it stands now," says the congressman, "we figure we could start with a business with more than fifty employees, as a compromise—and then, work downward from there. It's obvious that a person who employs only one might find it difficult to absorb the losses involved in this project."

The congressman makes it very clear that we're not even discussing government subsidies here—as many other technologically advanced societies provide for child care and eldercare. The issue is employer contributions.

I ask if there are any other bills on the congressional agenda designed to provide more than empathy to older people.

The congressman digs deep and finally mentions a pending bill that would improve Medicare benefits. I must be patient, says Congressman Green. Bills and proposals must wend their way through the legislative process, says Congressman Green, whose heart may be in the right place, but whose information is not particularly current: One week after my interview with the congressman, news that Medicare premiums for the elderly would *rise* 38.5 percent was on the front page! So much for governmental Tender Power.

If there ever was a time for a government to adopt the traditional womanly traits of caring, cooperation, and empathy, it's now, just a few years from the turn of a new century. Power without tenderness is wreaking havoc.

I came away from Congressman Green, pleased to see that the issues of child care and eldercare are on the minds of our legislators. But the stronger feeling I had was that women had a mighty struggle ahead, mightier than they might anticipate, to *keep* the issues from being mere token appeasement policy. When work and home collide, two weeks of unpaid leave is not going to mean a whole lot.

Big Business—Listen!

Men and women individually can promote the concept of Tender Power, but Big Business will do its share, too, if Big Business is watching market research studies. A major study called "Fears and Fantasies of the American Consumer" recently addressed itself to finding out how advertisers could best reach the modern consumer. D'Arcy Masius Benton & Bowles sent mailings to four thousand households. They concluded their study with advice to advertisers based on the current American state of mind, as they found it.

First, advertisers could best sell products, they suggest, by *Making Emotion Relevant*.

"Our study reveals," says the advertising company, "that Americans, above all, prize the emotional connections they share with other people."

If advertisers show a product "helping to bring people closer together or helping to make moments together special," they would sell tons of the product, advises DMB&B.

It's clear that American Telephone and Telegraph came to the same conclusion as DMB&B. The advertising campaign that suggests "Reach Out and Touch Someone" is increasing telephone revenues masterfully.

Second, advertisers need to *Make Empowering Others Relevant*. "Show characters in ads helping each other or getting through problems together," suggest DMB&B. Celebrity spokespeople who are widely perceived as caring about people also sell products. Corporate rewards for noteworthy acts of altruism spur employees to greater heights. Visible corporate support for projects that give others strength and address human needs, like the Ronald McDonald Houses, sell the product as well.

Apart from advertising studies, other experts on the American business scene have novel ideas on how management can increase productivity by the use of tender traits. Tom Peters, co-author of *In Search of Excellence* and *A Passion for Excellence*, is convinced that one of the oldest feminine traits, the ability to connect through listening, has always distinguished superior leaders. Now, says Peters, with global competition from the Japanese at its zenith, it's even more important to train business managers to connect with their clients with improved listening practices. Really hearing what others say not only humanizes the marketplace, it raises the profit margin. The following is what good listeners do, says Tom Peters. They

1. *Listen with intensity.* That often means face-to-face human contact, not just "getting out from behind the desk, but getting rid of the desk." Peters suggests that managers give their customers home telephone numbers as well as toll-free numbers to get uninhibited and personalized feedback.

2. *Listen naively.* This means listening without preformed judgments. Hang out in the marketplace, be on the road, closely observe customers, dealers, and salespeople to get a whiff of trends, says the expert. "By observing California's youngsters on roller skates, a Sony engineer came up with the concept of the Walkman, a portable cassette player," says Peters.

3. *Act fast.* Good listeners act fast to change the status quo on the basis of what they hear.

4. *Ask dumb questions.* Listen to the answers. It's the dumb, elementary questions that hit pay dirt.

5. *Break down barriers.* Patient listening is powerful listening. Resistance to change is often overcome in chatty sit-downs with managers and underlings. Peters mentions the hospital administrator and her strategy, "Eat Your Way Through the Medical Staff": During about seventy-five easy-going lunches that included both doctors and other staff, the hospital administrator engineered over the course of a year a revolutionary upgrade in relations between the medical staff and the rest of the hospital.

6. *Take notes. Promise feedback. Deliver.* Send thank-you notes to individuals and groups, perhaps summarizing what you thought you heard within twenty-four hours of a meeting. Taking notes lets the other person know you're serious and you're engaged in listening. The male administrative model of the last fifty years consisted of giving and taking orders. Diligent listening is the feminine model of operation, the one that can transform and tenderize the marketplace.

All this is not so amazing. There is profit in humanizing the workplace. If it is true that women are disclaiming the tender traits of compassion, cooperation, and nurture, they're running against the tides of change. Tender is power—and profit.

Retrenchment from the Way It Is: A Temporary Solution

A new book burst upon the scene in 1985, and it was the subject of much talk in locker rooms, boardrooms, and over coffee—wherever women met. It is called *Women Like Us,* and in her subtitle, author Liz Gallese tells precisely *which* women like us she's thinking about: *What Is Happening to the Women of the Harvard Business School, Class of '75—The Women Who Had the First Chance to Make It to the Top?*

Gallese interviewed eighty-two women in this Harvard class and found out some fascinating things. Among them is the fact that "women who succeed are most often those who choose to live their lives in a man's world. Small wonder why these women are such a select few," says the author. The group, she notes, paid a substantial price for whatever success they achieved: "Well into the fourth decade of their lives, fewer than three fifths were married and one third were still single; only twenty-four had children; thirty-five had been in therapy."

Is this a denouncement of women at work or, heaven forbid, Harvard Business School? Absolutely not. Women, however, says the author, seem lately to be retrenching from *big* business (studies show that women expect lower salaries and often choose jobs that are less powerful than those men choose) because they have a "reluctance to forfeit what is uniquely theirs, their femininity. . . . The women's reluctance to forfeit their entire selves for the sake of their careers, moreover, strikes me," says the author, "as a particularly thoughtful and intelligent attitude. For no matter how often a particular woman may choose to deny the feminine side of herself, the fact remains that women, as a group, are society's childbearers and that is something else that will not change. While the choice to have a child is an individual one for each woman, there is no choice for the female sex as a whole, and to deny that is shortsighted at best, sheer stupidity at worst."

What this means, in short, is that all women truly are responsible to each other in the search for realistic solutions. If some women refuse to do it the male way, if they find they must retrench from the male-designed workplaces to find their way in entrepreneurial enterprise, the women who remain should not stay silent and acquiescent. The battle to secure child and elder care, work flexibility, and other reformations must be continued until women can find equal business footings under their own feminine colors, on their own terms.

It can't be said enough: We haven't succeeded so well acting as male clones. Perhaps, in the wake of some women's retrenchment, a pulling back from flopping around in male shoes, the Harvard Class of 1990, insisting on traditional women's values, will really make it to the top, and what's more, will graduate to caring and warmed lives as well as big business, with the highest honors.

A Breeding Ground for the Feminine Ethos

A tenderized marketplace can be a new breeding ground for men and women with awakened sensitivity to the feminine ethos. A tenderized marketplace can herald a brave new direction as we move toward the twenty-first century.

The nineteenth and twentieth centuries have seen a time when achievement and performance at work became the most important thing in the lives of men. The male of the species, so busy at his job, has had little time or energy left for play, for maintaining relationships, for caring for the young, old, or sickly. It was only reasonable to expect that young women, watching their fathers and husbands put career ahead of all else, did the same when they entered the marketplace. How much we've all lost.

But, people are talking. For the first time in generations, people are talking of discontent. Men, as well as women, are hoping for change.

This is a phenomenal hope to cherish. Tenderizing the marketplace must give power to the economy, because when people work in a caring and attending environment, when people are afforded time to nurture their young and bond with each other, when people are encouraged to breathe deep of quality leisure time, production must soar.

Tenderizing the marketplace could change the way the world plies its trade.

Then, and only then, can the real work begin. When we feel challenged but not threatened by work, we will have more strength to teach our children the feminine ethos. At their earliest stages, we could blot out the "compete-until-you-drop" ethos and substitute more humanizing lessons.

How soon can we begin to redesign the value systems of the littlest people? As soon as they look us in the eye. Before they start asking the hard questions.

9

Tender Wings of Power

How does a woman learn about tender *and* about power? How does a man learn that the combination is not only possible but potent; not only potent but a very natural feeling? At what stages in their lives can young people come face-to-face with functioning cooperation, empathy, and connection?

At the tenderest ages, it is possible to transmit the awesome strength of feminine power to both little boys *and* little girls. Power is given wings by the teaching of humanistic values.

Developmental stages in a young woman's life put her in positions where tender and power can either do battle or work together splendidly—depending on who the young woman, her parents, and her teachers are, and depending also on her own experiences and observations.

I don't pretend to know why my son opted to play with guns (which stopped, incidentally, as soon as the military became a real option) and my daughter opted for dolls and nurturing. I don't pretend to know why most of the children in the various kindergartens in which I substitute-taught did the same thing, despite their different parental backgrounds. As a feminist, I know in my heart of hearts that aggressiveness or connectedness as gender traits are not written in stone, and yet—*there were those kids* (and there still are according to today's kindergarten teachers)—boys shooting and building with blocks, girls cuddling those dolls. Put a little girl in the blocks corner and she builds as well as, and often better than, the little guys. Put a little guy in the doll corner and he sets up house. But, put no one anywhere and you'll see more girls than boys, on their own, drift over to the doll corner—the nurturing department.

So even if gender traits are not inscribed in stone, few can deny that tendencies toward aggressiveness and team play seem to be more dominant in boys, and tendencies toward empathy and nurturing consistently seem to be more dominant in girls. Whether these tendencies are a matter of social teaching or genes is academic: What's practical is that power and tenderness can be taught. What's monumental is the absolute truth that if both power and tenderness are taught to both sexes, the resulting energy is awesome.

It's not happening. We're not passing down the tender messages—only the messages of power. Listen to what Mary Anne Dolan, a syndicated columnist and Los Angeles television commentator, says in the *New York Times* as she discusses the hopes she had when she rose to the editorship of a major metropolitan newspaper, excited about pulling other women up the ranks in her wake.

"This was a moment when the promise of the women's movement could be fulfilled," writes Dolan. "We had permission at last. The joint belonged to us! We would bring all those 'female' qualities we had been boasting about on placards for years in through the front door, into the open of the newsroom. We would be a family. Between male and female would be respect and generosity and adaptability and warmth and comity and nurturing. Such an environment would make the most of our talents and, centrally, of our work. We would have honest conflict and competition, but also compromise and consensus and, therefore, success. We would make mincemeat of the male business model. . . ."

Then, writes Dolan, wistfully, "Looking back I can say that of the women I appointed to top-level positions, only one truly resisted the clichéd power traps and rose to the kind of heights Betty Friedan predicted when she wrote *The Feminine Mystique* twenty-five years ago. Only one learned to 'compete not as a woman or a man but as a human being . . .' Nor did all the women in positions of responsibility abuse their power," says Dolan. "What happened was that, by and large, they took on the worst—sometimes hilarious—aspects of the stereotypical corporate ladder-climbing male. As soon as masthead status was achieved, the power grab began.

"The number of formal meetings with 'boss' at the head of the table quadrupled; there were pre-meetings and post-meetings. Words like 'facilitate' and 'strategize' came into vogue. Everyone was suddenly afraid that somebody else knew something she didn't. Or had a more impressive title.

"Office geography became as important in what had once been our cranky 'Citizen Kane' newsroom as it is in the West Wing of the White House. Secretaries began acting like palace guards.

"There were memos everywhere, multi-copies and held with brightly colored plastic paper clips representing various fiefdoms. If you didn't have a 'record' of a conversation, the conversation hadn't taken place.

"Where there was opportunity to deal with people openly and with ease, many female managers were wary. They acted out a script that was part Osgood Conklin, part J.R. Ewing, part M.B.A./One-Minute-Manager and a tiny bit Mom. Many spent a good deal of time seeking out the nearest male authority figures."

Discouraged by seeing women downplay their instinctive skills at interacting and delegating, saddened by seeing women "completely rejecting their own femininity and becoming sexist counterparts," Dolan asks if we can avoid imitating the worst rather than the best of the male model. She argues for passing on a different set of standards, humanizing standards, to our children.

As Dolan watched the women in her organization go along with an ancient creed—"power first" (for lack of female models, she says)—she saw them passing down to future generations only a fearful "I want" without a joyful "I am."

Have status and money without the philosophical underpinnings of humanity become the only rewards of the feminist movement? The women's movement was about much more than status and money, insists Dolan. It was about choice and cooperation with men, not about imitation of men. There are, says the journalist, historical and worthy differences in the experiences and values of women that are vitally important to pass down to our children.

The Female Legacy

Dr. Karen Hopenwasser is clinical professor of psychiatry at the New York Hospital-Cornell Medical Center. She specializes in matters of gender.

"Indeed, there *are* differences in boys and girls, men and women, that we ought to understand without being bound to stereotypes," she says.

There are, first of all, biological differences, says the doctor, and they differ from person to person. There are also differences in social forces, which are internalized early in the life of women and men. And, says the doctor, there are differences that are both biological and a social construction as well, like mothering or fathering and expectations of what it is to be a good parent.

Social forces, purposeful communication, and the feminine lessons of connectedness, caring, and nurturing are early felt and eminently teachable to boys and girls. When can we start?

Dr. Eleanor Galenson, clinical professor of psychiatry at the Mount Sinai Hospital in New York and co-director of the hospital's Infant Psychiatry Unit, says, "somewhere around twelve months, babies begin to explore their mothers' faces (and certainly, their fathers' as well, if they are around). They put their fingers in their parents' mouths, they touch their parents' hair, and this kind of thing tells us the baby is aware that there's someone out there, separate from her. The baby begins to know she can move on her own steam. It is a monumental period in life.

"Between fourteen and sixteen months, many little girls already display the beginnings of semi-symbolic, tender doll play. They take dolls, which always stand for themselves, as well as others, rock them, put bottles in their mouths, cover them with blankets. This tells us that the child has already absorbed some of the nurturing and connection lessons; it is the beginning of the realization that she can do to another person what is being done to her."

It is interesting to note, says Dr. Galenson, that gender differences show up very early. It's "highly unusual" for boys to take dolls and nurture them in the same way. What's more, says Dr. Galenson, "It's almost universal that girls alone do this."

When a child begins school, she or he reaches another monumental peak of life. This stage is of utmost importance in the development of the tender traits that will balance and humanize the adult power to come. Social differences begin to come to the fore. Little boys and little girls learn what will be possible for them. It is the time when children gather information from the world, enough information to question, enough information from which to draw subtle inferences.

Dr. Karen Hopenwasser gives a real-life example of such observation and questioning from the experience of her own four-year-old daughter.

"My child attends a wonderful school, a premiere place where the teacher is truly interested in gender issues and equal rights for girls," says the doctor. "One of the first things she chose as the basis of her curriculum was 'trucks.' Four-year-olds, she thinks, are already struggling with issues of power and strength, and although normally it's the boys who are interested in playing with trucks and the girls play in the doll corner, this was a curriculum that was going to be about power for both boys and girls. So trucks it was and of course, the little girls showed as much interest as the little boys."

But then, says the doctor, the little girls began noting the construction areas where trucks were primarily found, and who were they seeing at these truck sites? Male construction workers. Although the teacher wished to convey to the girls that trucks were a domain to which the girls had access, the reality is that most girls will still learn to identify trucks and construction with men.

But, the doctor continues, all was far from lost. The important part of the lesson began when the children began questioning. What came out of the nursery school truck curriculum was not so much "do women drive trucks, are women construction workers?" but "what *can* girls do?"

The answer, of course, is everything. It is at this early stage that astute parents and teachers can instill the idea of *possibility*. So many things are possible. One can play in the doll corner. One can even drive the trucks into the doll corner and feel the power of wheels without sacrificing the joy of nurture. It doesn't have to be one or the other—it can be both at once.

Tender traits, like gender equality, are skills that can be taught like mathematics, swimming, or any other skill. The possibility of being a compassionate person who is able to make powerful affiliations is there for every child. Astute parents and teachers can begin the training for tenderness in the same methodical way they start their children off in the pursuit of reading skills.

Empathy, for example, is a skill that can be taught and learned as soundly as one learns to play the piano or ride a horse. Once learned, empathy is a subtle route to gaining influence and power. A four-year-old who points to a woman in a supermarket and cries out to her mother, "Look at that fat lady!" will probably be hushed by her mother and ignored, at least outwardly, by the woman who is singled out. An adult who loudly whispers almost the same thing to a friend is judged much more harshly, however. The difference is not just a matter of politeness: We don't expect a four-year-old to be empathic in the same way an adult should be.

Empathy is the human ability to creep into another's shoes and understand her feelings. How would the four-year-old feel, her mother asks her, if she were very heavy and bursting out of her clothes and someone else jeered? Unlike a propensity toward intelligence or blondeness (a matter of genes) a propensity toward empathy is a skill even young children can learn.

What's in it for empathic children? Studies have shown that they tend to do better in school, in social situations, and in their careers when they are grown. They also tend, not surprisingly, to make the best marriages.

The earliest signs of empathy are not empathy at all.

Crying newborns in a nursery trigger the crying of other newborns, not because one group feels sorry for the other but because the sound of crying, like any loud noise, creates discomfort at this age. At two, a child can respond to her mother's tears and offer a hug or even a favorite toy in sympathy. Psychologists disagree, however, as to whether or not this is true empathy. It may simply be a reaction to the unhappiness a child feels when seeing a parent in distress, a subtle threat to his or her sense of well-being. A child really begins to understand what another child is feeling when, at age four or five, he comforts a friend who's been bruised from a fall. This empathic child has been taught by example to comfort another by offering a loving touch or a happy distraction. His parents have shown him what to do, because they offered loving touches and distractions when he bruised himself. Another child, one who has not been taught how to deal with her feelings of empathy, may push or hit a hurting friend; the other child's crying has made her uncomfortable. She can put herself in the place of the hurt child, but she does not know what to do with her empathy, how to express it. So she pushes, simply to relieve herself of her own frustration. She reacts with aggression because she has not been taught to act with compassion and with comforting gestures.

Studies show that girls develop more empathy, and at an earlier age, than boys. "There is a very high correlation between a mother's empathy and a daughter's empathy," says Norma D. Feshback, chairwoman of the Department of Education at the University of California at Los Angeles, "but that's not true with boys."

Tender traits not only temper power, they deliver it. Dr. Feshback's research, along with that of other experts, indicates that one can predict how well children will do academically and socially in the fourth or fifth grade by looking at how empathic they were some years ago.

Children who are more empathic also tend to be better at resolving conflicts, says child expert Lawrence Kutner. They are therefore more readily perceived as leaders by others. More empathic boys turn out to be less aggressive boys and more generous boys.

How do you encourage empathy?

1. Infants and toddlers mirror the way their parents treat them when they are frightened, cranky, and irritable. A baby who is left to cry for hours or a toddler who is readily spanked is not apt to learn much empathy from her caretakers.

2. In preschool astute teachers and parents can begin talking about how other people *feel*, and about how children should *act* when they observe pain or sadness.

3. As children grow, values should be discussed and decision making on hypothetical problems should be encouraged both at school and at home. How can unexpressed feelings be discerned? How can people encourage others to share their hurts and disclose their secrets? How can comfort best be offered? All these are apt ways to teach the skill of empathy.

Unhappily, though, at crucial life stages, many children are not lucky enough to run into astute teachers and parents. Instead, boys are often trained to pursue thoughtless power, and too many girls are encouraged in the act of self-sacrifice—the relinquishing of feminine strengths. In fact, both boys and girls are often taught in subtle ways that displaying respectful traits like cooperation and comity will hold them back from business advancement.

In certain situations, unfortunately, that message may be accurate. Surrounded in the most competitive marketplaces by men and women who won't give an inch, a nurturing, caring person can easily be vanquished. Instincts to cooperate and share in such a marketplace are irrelevant at best and self-defeating at worst.

So what happens to children who, taught to treasure the tender traits, later when they grow up find themselves in such ruthlessly competitive environments? Realism predicts they simply won't be satisfied. However, realism also suggests that many of these children, steeped in compassion and intuition, will also have the judgment to quickly recognize situations in which warmth won't work. They may choose to tough it out, or change jobs, but they won't feel vanquished when their basic values are not acknowledged by those who are threatened or bored with cooperation and caring.

A fascinating theory comes from authors Sarah Hardesty and Nehama Jacobs who studied women in Corporate America. They conclude that change will not occur until the *men* in charge of corporations are convinced that change will help them. It's men who must be taught to understand how good compassion and empowering feel. Luckily, a growing number of corporations seem to be in the mood for attitudinal revampment, judging from the many new books on the subject of management. Indeed, many men would be greatly relieved if it were considered acceptable to trade a single-minded treadmill to the top for more time out for family and personal pleasure.

But, to shape a company that sees beyond mindless job achievement, one must really start with the children. Young people, trained from the earliest years to cooperate rather than separate, negotiate rather than dictate, and care rather than conquer, can act as agents of change in the history of American business.

Teen Power

The teenage years are rife with double messages. Young men and women are bombarded by conflicting sights and sounds in a potpourri of media. The one unmistakable message they do receive is that tender is an anachronism, superfluous. Despite some perfunctory homage by parents to the values of cooperation, kindness, and sharing, the lie comes barging through: Tenderness and power cannot coexist. That is what most young people really hear.

On the one hand, teens are treated to the obligatory lessons of sharing from parents and teachers; on the other hand, they have Madonna-like images egging them on to self-centeredness.

Parents may preach that it's what you are, not what you look like that counts, but idols like Michael Jackson bid emulation of multiple face-lifts.

Empower others is the unwritten legacy of generations of women. Seize control is what too many kids learn at school. In order to become president of the class, of the corporation, of the world, insular self-promotion is the way to go. Group actions count for little. Whoever has the most followers wins.

Nancy is a fourteen-year-old student in a midwestern city high school.

"They give you lots of lectures about team play," she says, "but it's a load of bull. The person who really gets the awards is the captain of the volleyball team, not the players."

What about morality? Nancy says:

"Kids cheat quite openly. It's cool. The teacher leaves the room because, like, she *pretends* we're bound by an honor system, but anyone with smarts knows the highest scorer, not the most honest person, gets into the best colleges. Even if I felt like tutoring my friend in math, which I sometimes feel bad about, I won't. I need to keep my edge."

Keeping the edge, for many teens, especially those who live in large cities, is often about physical self-protection. Kids learn to put up emotional and also physical barriers to their persons. How do you teach a young woman about connections and trust when in an age of drugs and mugs she may well need to learn to fight back?

Karate schools and courses in self-defense dot the landscape; their purpose is to teach young people how to respond to violence in the traditionally male mode—by counterattack. Very often, responding in kind to violence works. Some teenagers take beautifully to guerilla tactics, karate clips, knee-to-the-groin kind of defense against the not-so-rare crazies that abound. Surely, it can't hurt to learn the art of physical self-defense.

Still, there are some teens, both male and female, who would not, who *could not*, defend themselves in such a way. It's just not part of their authentic selves to respond to violence with more of the same. There must be another way.

There is—a tender way, that, believe it or not, is often more powerful than the most abusive violence.

Dr. Deborah Prothrow-Stith, an assistant professor of medicine at Boston University School of Medicine and chair of the Boston Task Force on Adolescent Issues, is an activist who says she is going "to leave the world in better shape than I found it."

When people talk about Dr. Prothrow-Stith, they are apt to repeat the story that circulates in the Boston schools about a student, a Quaker, who was regularly picked on by a bully. One day, the bully actually punched the student, but the student didn't hit back. Instead, he quietly asked, "Why did you hit me?" The bully began to cry and ran away.

It's a true story, says the doctor, but she doesn't use it in class, "because no one believes it."

Instead, she gives a course that is entirely believable to students.

"I think that public health models like those applied to smoking and fitness can be applied to other programs, such as violence," she notes. Using law enforcement statistics, and energetic audience participation, her ten-week course in the prevention of violence by body language, words, and thoughts seems to have dramatically decreased the number of fights and other kinds of violence in the Boston schools where it is offered. Clergy, social workers, and neighborhood community workers are showing interest in strength that is spurred by gentleness instead of violence. It is another example of a different kind of power that can be taught to children in all stages of development—particularly the teen years.

During these teen years the issue of sex, as one father grimly puts it, "rears its ugly head." "Men," he told his daughter, "are animals." What can this young woman think of the subtle messages she's getting— messages that warn her against sharing of intimacy. The instincts bred in her for generations, the instinct to allow vulnerability and to encourage caring, are given short shrift in a society that takes its lead from men's tendency to insist on distance. What's more, her dad's message is reinforced daily by the consumer advertisements that bombard her with messages of impersonal gratification.

"I see this big ad for Obsession perfume in the department store," says the daughter. "This lady is standing there naked, and the guy is kissing her breasts. They're not even looking at each other. And the Guess? jeans ads. I love Guess? jeans, but the people in the ads are always in some kind of trouble, some confrontation. I always think the woman looks like she's scared of the man, who looks like he's going to hurt her. They're enticing in a way, but they just bother me."

Small wonder. The message of loving and powerful sensuality is destroyed by an insinuation that reads "sex equals violence."

There are other mixed messages that young women hear as they grow. Another, in particular, is confusing.

There Are No Limits

We tell our teenage daughters they can do it all—and then we tell them not to sacrifice family. We tell our daughters we want them to succeed in the male mode—be a doctor, a lawyer, a stockbroker—and then we tell them to stay as sweet as they are.

The No Limits message freed us for a while, but, because of its innuendos, today we know it's imprisoning. Rightly so. No Limits is a lie. There are always limits. Unfortunately, the limits are rarely honored or even acknowledged. Witness an advertisement that appeared in the *New York Times* on September 8, 1988. It featured a sketch of a chic, slick, unharried woman in her "devastating little, black dress." The designer of the fashion, announced the advertisement, "creates for the woman who often works twelve hour days but never fails to put family and friends first."

Never fails to put family and friends first? It is insulting to the world of women who work from nine to nine, arriving home at perhaps ten P.M., to suggest that they can do it all, be Superwomen, even if they do wear devastating little, black dresses. Doing it all is a burden that no one ever even suggested men carry on their shoulders.

Women were denied options for so long we paid no attention when *Future Shock* author Alvin Toffler warned that "choice may become over-choice, and freedom, unfreedom." When we teach young women that if only they work as hard as they can, and if only they're brave and good, they can have it all, without compromise, we're perpetuating a myth and aggravating an insult. Certainly women, like men, can lead full and balanced lives with career and family success, but no one can do it all at once, relinquishing nothing—not men, not women. Certainly, when we teach our daughters that they can easily succeed at climbing to the top of their corporations while they raise their children, work at their marriages, take care of their aged parents, nurture their friends, and dust their chandeliers, we're not telling the whole story. We're not telling about the limits to energy, patience, caring, and time.

The one constant, in all my years of teaching and mothering, was the adolescent outrage at *having to decide*. Before they even graduate from high school, young men and women are asked to choose probable career paths. Young women, in particular, are encouraged by their achieving mothers not to waste time mooning around thinking of husbands and children. Make up your minds—you're at that stage of life where it's important to be decisive, say counselors and parents.

As young women progress through their adolescence, they do continually seem to be asked to sacrifice what psychiatrist Jean Baker Miller calls affiliation; what sociologist Jess Bernard calls "the female ethos of love/duty"; and what many spiritual leaders call simply "love of others." Young women report feeling cheated by the choices of their parents and ambivalent about the choices that a feminism, not of their making, seems to expect. They honor the women's movement but hate feeling they have to sacrifice the "old stuff that was pretty good stuff."

The myth of No Limits feeds into the myth of Immediate Perfection. If our daughters shouldn't compromise the dream of equality, they must still modify the methods of getting it all. The trick is to refrain from imparting the message to our young heirs that, if they lag, or even fail, at one or more stages of their lives, they're inadequate; it must have been something they did wrong. That's the male modus operandi. If a woman doesn't start her career right out of college, if instead, she marries in "the old way," does some nurturing, and *then* proceeds to the top, it may just work as well. If a man decides to try on a few career hats before committing to a life plan (as now, many young people are indeed expected to do), is he to be castigated for not being "serious"?

Is it not possible to treasure the old familiar female bromide that encourages adjusting, fixing, shifting priorities, conciliating, changing minds? What would be so terrible if men and women were taught to handle their careers in open-end stages, as they handle their growth patterns? Parents should not demand instant "right decisions" and instant perfection from what *seems* the appropriate stage for those perfect decisions. Young people must trust in timing, luck, and politics as much as in making conscious, irrevocable choices.

Higher Education

Although the tenets of Tender Power can and should be taught to boys and girls throughout the early and middle years, one of the most powerful impacts can be made at the university level, those years just before the real world is tackled. Higher education is a perfect time to prepare young men and women for business and personal lives that encompass humanistic values.

On the rolling green plains of North Texas, such a model of education exists. It happens to be, not surprisingly, a university run with women at its helm.

The great majority of university administrations are male dominated. Ninety percent of American college and university presidents are men, as are nine out of ten full professors. No wonder that most college administrations are designed to conduct the male hierarchical model, which can be described as probably "rigid, dictatorial, usually aggressive, sometimes militaristic, occasionally confrontational," says the *New York Times* in an article on Texas Woman's University. The president of Texas Woman's University in Denton is Shirley Chater. The top four administrators of the university are also women. They practice, among them, a form of university management that is highly moral and therefore, think many, highly educational. It is based on the "female model," what Carol Pearson, the author of a monograph on women for the American Counsel on Education, describes as "standing up for one's principles and being assertive without looking for enemies, being gentle and respectful even of the people who are your detractors." This model does not preclude rigor and toughness, says Patricia Sullivan, a school administrator. "If we have to play hardball with somebody out there, we will."

President Chater, before she came to T.W.U., held high posts in organizations run by men. She remembers constant jockeying for power. These are some of the principles, in contrast to those of the male-run organizations, that she has instituted at T.W.U. management levels:

1. She advises her staff to be candid, open, and vulnerable. "You can take risks, you can make a mistake, and it won't be held against you for the rest of the year." This style of management inspires creative thinking, she says, because those who don't fear taking risks usually extend themselves further.

2. Chater advocates empowering. Power, she holds, is both fluid and regenerative. "The more power you give, the more you generate."

3. She advocates the sharing of ideas on management and course content by the student body. Students are encouraged to take part in their own education: The matching corporate theory, say T.W.U. adminis-

trators, is that managers who are allowed to take part in the decision-making process learn better and thus are better managers.

4. The management model of the university tends to encourage a high administrative turnover, says Chater—a practice almost unheard of in typical male management styles. Thus, the president allows for and even encourages self-replacement. "Each of my vice presidents could easily be a college president," says Chater with both delight and feigned dismay. In the best corporate management, administrators teach those on the rungs below how to take over top administration jobs. The theory is that there is always a higher rung to which one can aspire.

5. University management encourages women to deal in "studied collaboration and habitual consensus." Cooperation is a trait most warmly admired and revered.

By structuring the academic curriculum to follow the form in which the university is actually managed, lessons in humanism are graphically offered. Higher education, nationwide, would do well to study the model of Tender Power presented at Texas Woman's University.

Tender Wings of Power

So, if we are to give our children wings, if we are to teach them that influence and power are strengthened with caring values, we must consciously go about teaching them to build humanistic value systems. How do we do it?

It can't be accomplished by moralizing: Often behavior of moralists contradicts their actions. Some religious people love their neighbors on the Sabbath and spend the rest of the week in fearsome competition with them. A laissez-faire attitude is also ineffective, because young people experience confusion and conflict when left totally to their own devices. Role modeling, although effective, also has its problems, because young people today have so many disparate role models, including parents, teachers, friends, rock stars, and politicians. Who is the best to emulate? Sometimes it's impossible to decide.

What's left? In his youth Floyd Patterson, once heavyweight champion of the world, attended the Wiltwyck School for Boys, a correction institute for young men who had gone wrong. At Wiltwyck he first heard about the Golden Rule. Doing unto others as you would have them do unto you, an old-fashioned but still extraordinarily contemporary idea.

Punishment, said Patterson, taught kids only how to punish, and scolding taught them how to scold. Showing them understanding taught them to understand. They learned cooperation by cooperating.

One young Nashville mother carries the Golden Rule one step further. "In every situation with my children," she says, "I have two choices. I can either react or respond. When they act selfishly or rashly, my instinctive choice would be reaction—NO YOU CAN'T! Instead, I try to take ten seconds to regroup so I can respond, 'Why do *you* think it would be a poor idea?' "

It's an interesting approach, "do unto others." Respond, rather than react. Responding accelerates children's ability to choose caring values for themselves.

Finally, choosing caring values and learning to cherish them is only preliminary to publicly affirming them. If young people are to bring humanism into their lives, they have to have the courage of their convictions. They have to learn to act on principle. Acting on principle bestows not only a sense of power, but true power. People who put into practice that which they instinctively feel is life affirming, connecting, and *right*, are the best teachers for the next generation. People like the following three:

I work in a very competitive atmosphere where the goal is to succeed at any cost. When a woman has a baby, the deal is to have it quickly and get right back to work; you can show its picture every now and then, but don't let it occupy your mind too much. Well, I couldn't do it. I was terrified, but I marched into my boss's office a week before I gave birth and told her I'd need six months. What's more, I expected to come back at exactly the level I'd left. And, I'd work at home, keep in touch, and not disappoint anyone. To my absolute amazement—she looked at me hard and said—okay. Just like that. Okay. It started a trend in the office.

Joyce, a twenty-nine-year-old product manager

There was this guy at work, this clumsy fool. He wasn't really a fool, just one of those guys who puts his foot into trouble every time he takes a step. I kind of liked him, and to tell you the truth, I felt sorry for him. You learn to stay detached in this business, to stay uninvolved with other people's problems. Trouble rubs off. A misfit makes friends with other misfits, right? Well, maybe I would have stayed clear in college, but I felt like such a rat turning my back on this kid. So, I made friends with him. I invited him to my home. We talked. I told him about the pitfalls. I liked the guy. My wife did, too. Well, I just felt better about myself and it wasn't self-destruct for me either. It happens that the president of this agency took me aside and thanked me for setting the poor guy straight. He said he thought I ought to set up a support group system in the office—it would be good for business. The clumsy fool? He's only the most creative guy in the world. Probably my best friend now.

Alan, a thirty-one-year-old advertising executive

My friend's dog died. He cried and he didn't want to show me he cried, so he hid. So I cried, too, and hid with him. So we both cried. Then the bunk felt like crying. Then we all played volley ball.

Kevin, a seven-year-old sleep-away camper

Change is in the wind.

10

Opting Out

Infancy's the tender fountain,
Power may with beauty flow,
Mother's first to guide the streamlets,
From them souls unresting grow—
Grown on for the good or evil,
Sunshine streamed or evil hurled;
For the hand that rocks the cradle
Is the hand that rules the world.

William Ross Wallace,
"The Hand That Rocks the Cradle
Is the Hand That Rules the World"

Can You Go Home Again?

Donna is a full-time university professor in Fort Wayne, Indiana. She's worked many years for this prestigious position. When she became pregnant with her second child, she called to tell me that she was taking three months' leave after the baby's birth.

The week before Donna was to return to her job, she called again.

"I can't—I just can't," she said. "Sherry, I'm nursing this infant. I am so nervous to go back. I'm torn to shreds."

"Don't be silly," I reassured her. "You'll get back to the work atmosphere with all the fascinating people in your classes and with the knowledge that you have a good nanny taking care of the baby. You'll be just fine."

She wasn't so sure.

Ten days later, she called again. "It's all over," she said. "I quit."

My advice had been facile and unthinking. I have been a strong advocate of the "you-can-do-it-all" philosophy. The only thing is, it hasn't been me trying to do it all.

Last week I met with Donna to hear what had happened.

"First of all," she said, "I love my job—it's the best one I ever had. I was almost up for tenure. I longed to return. Second of all, it was important to me that I go back after I gave birth to prove that I was truly professional. That's what professional people do, isn't it?"

Donna had worked right on through her due date. She delivered about five days after she left her desk. For a while she felt that "it's okay, I can really do this. I kept in touch with school, every day, and I planned for my return . . ."

Her salary was no small consideration.

"It would have taken us out of the red," she says. "My husband, Mal, just out of medical school, had taken his first job, and we were so looking forward to two salaries—a real livable income, for once."

Toward the end of her three-months' leave, Donna began to feel tortured. It seemed unnatural to leave a nursing baby. But she squelched the feeling that was tugging at her and, on the day she was to return,

"I put my breast pump into my pocketbook so I could express the milk, if I felt uncomfortable. I got all dressed up—I'd planned what I'd wear my first day back for weeks—and on the way I felt great. 'I'm lucky to be away from the diapers and the vomit; I'm going to be able to do this!' I kept whispering to myself.

"When I got to my classroom everyone was lovely. All these welcome back memos were on my desk. 'What a terrific place, I'm so lucky I can adjust,' I thought.

"Then, my milk let down—you know that sensation of milk flowing toward the nipple that occurs in nursing mothers whenever they even hear a strange baby cry, or see a milk carton? I wasn't surprised, but then I got emotional and started to cry. Even then, I was okay.

"'This is normal,' I told myself. 'It's your first day. You'll adjust. It's okay to cry.'"

But it wasn't okay for Donna. She cried for three hours. Then she said, "I understood that I didn't *want* to adjust."

That was that. She didn't even finish the day. She went into her department chairman's office and said, "I can't do it." Immediately she experienced an enormous tide of relief.

"I flew home," she remembers, "and it was crazy! I felt like Rocky—like there should be swelling music accompanying me. . . . 'Mama's coming home!' I sang to my son in my head. . . . 'I'm coming!'"

The last decade has seen thousands and thousands of women returning to work immediately after childbirth. For many, an early return to career is fine and right, no question of that. For many others, though, embarrassed to go against the tide, embarrassed by their urgent need to nurture, embarrassed at finding themselves so in love with their babies that separation is literally painful, a speedy return to work takes a great emotional toll. But for Donna, the decision was made. She would buck the tide.

"This is the introduction to LIFE," says Donna. "*Year One*. Acquiring language. Developing emotional stability. Learning to love. Do you *know* what happens in that first year? It's massive!"

For some aggressive, career-oriented young women, the shock of realizing that they must choose between the power of that unexpected bond and their dreams and aspirations is awesome. For one thing, support is slim.

"I knew I was going to let certain people down who had no doubt I could do the whole thing," Donna says. "My mother, for example, was disappointed. It wasn't going to be 'my daughter, the professor' anymore. And, certain friends. 'How *could* you?' I know they think that. It's as if, single-handed, I was bringing the women's movement to a screaming halt. And," Donna sighs, "even myself. I've lost my identity, in many ways. I am truly mourning the loss of my job. How will I know what's passé in the field, what's happening, what ideas are new? I feel as if I had this 'in' and I blew it away. I feel like a wimp in many ways. I let the school and my students down."

For another thing, and even worse, muses Donna, "you kind of feel, 'oh boy, now I'm going to *raise* a wimp—a mommy's boy who will be too dependent on me.'"

There are clearly, in this day, in this age, negatives for those who feel they must try to find some power at home when answering the pull of tender.

On the other hand, there are some positives—arguments to be made for heeding the call. Not every new mother feels it, but certainly many do. Power is not a sorority for working women alone. A certain inner confidence is to be gained when, knowing one is following one's strongest instincts, one chooses, in defiance of current dogma, to stay home. For some, heeding that call is power. Moreover, those who decide they can afford to stay home, at least for a few years, are not alone in the wisdom of their decision. There is increasing support for it from both peers and child care experts.

"Many of my most intellectual friends," says Donna, "my most sophisticated, successful career friends have done this. Wendy, an MBA who started her own business, chucked it all, for a while, to be home with her babies. My friend Viva, my friend Kim, a successful editor and the smartest friend I have—good-bye work, for now, they say. Not everyone, of course. My sister-in-law, who just had a baby, has gone back to work easily—and, if you can, that's fine. Of course, it's true that so many young women can no longer afford to choose; the family's survival depends on their income. But there are some of us who can take some time off if we tighten our belts or make other arrangements to work part-time—and we should not be made to feel unworthy of a career if we opt out to nurse our families for a while."

Sometimes, muses Donna, when she feels she's lost all cachet in the world, when she has to write "same" on forms that ask for home and work numbers, when she is bored and aggravated with the cooing and the cooking and the diapers—it's particularly difficult.

"I think of what I gave up. When I worked, and had someplace to go, I really pasted myself together. I functioned, I was bright and clever, no matter how I felt that day. But now?—I'm in my smelly nightgown, all morning some mornings. The house is a mess; I have no structure. It's a struggle not having lesson plans to write. Still, no matter how bad the feelings about myself get, I know I have to follow my instincts. I think it's right to be home with my baby."

In the last generation, it took nerve to go out and work. Today, it takes the same courage to choose family, even temporarily. It takes power to be selfless—to give up one's work identity. Selflessness is out of fashion today. Women are considered archaic if they concentrate on home and family, if they choose the disempowerment that comes from opting out of a career.

When one woman can choose power at home, and another can choose power at work, and both can feel unembarrassed and correct in their choices, women's rights will have come full circle. The circle will be complete only when industry makes allowances and provisions for both choices for all women.

"Do you know what?" says Donna. "Everyone can find rationalizations for saying what she's doing is right. If you go to work, there are a million rationalizations for the correctness of that action—the kids grow up more independent, resilient, blah, blah, blah. If you stay home, there are a million rationalizations for doing that—you are making connections with your flesh and blood, you're doing the most important work there is, blah, blah, blah. For me, the latter obviously has stronger rationalizations. I can't help but think that here we are in the Brave New World and it's really the Dark Ages when so many women, who wish not to, have to miss out on all this mothering."

Power is to be found in the workplace, surely; but another kind of strength is found in being able to reject the seduction of work and the sometimes disdain of respected peers, and in the economic sacrifices implicit in choosing home. The women's movement never intended to cast shame on those who chose home and family; but we feminists who are honest must surely admit that shame in staying home is, for many, a by-product of feminism.

It is not difficult to find child care experts who enthusiastically support the choices of some working mothers to return home for at least the early months of their children's lives.

Dr. Eleanor Galenson, clinical professor of psychiatry at the Mt. Sinai Hospital in New York and co-director of the hospital's Infant Psychiatry Clinic, says the pressures and policies of the times are creating alarming character and identity problems in some children. She and other experts trace the problems back to those early, formative years.

These days, says Dr. Galenson, something rather dismaying is taking place. "We see less and less pretend play, fewer and fewer children, in general, expressing sympathy and caring for one another."

In nursery schools, she explains, it was quite common in the past to see one small child cry in sympathy for another's tears. An empathic three-year-old would give a toy to a sobbing peer to comfort him. But certainly in boys, and even in girls, this kind of empathy is showing up less frequently. Dr. Galenson is convinced it is because of "split-mothering"—or the "nanny effect"—prevalent in the current culture.

"Today I saw a little girl of two and a half who never played with dolls at all," says the doctor. "She has been taken care of by a twenty-seven-year-old nanny who is the least motherly person in the world, a child herself. The two babies are taking care of each other and the smallest baby, the two-year-old, is a very angry child with little sense of doing to others what should be done for her."

Women on the fast track today who leave their babies full-time with caretakers may have problems in the future, concludes Dr. Galenson, who is convinced that we are deluding ourselves with talk of quality versus quantity time.

"I hate those terms," she says. "The so-called quality time usually occurs at the end of a working day where both mother and baby are exhausted and it is wreaking havoc. New figures show us that children placed in day care from the age of three months, compared to a similar group raised at home, look dandy when studied for the first two or three years, but then at ages four or five, across the board, they show clear tendencies toward more anger, irritability, and hostile aggression."

Another point: Many experts, including Dr. Galenson, maintain that the ability to connect—traditionally a strong "woman" skill—is healthy and good. The healthiest young people, all of them agree, are those who eventually become self-reliant, not iron-curtain separate from their parents. But, say many experts, healthy separation is not likely without strong mother connections in the first place.

"The increased number of separation anxiety cases we've been seeing in the last few years," says Dr. Galenson, "seems to involve those children who have never really felt connected to their mothers in the earliest stages of life."

One study that backs up Dr. Galenson's theories was quietly advanced by the academic community and even more quietly published in the *New York Times* in late November of 1987. Although it created controversy in the day care/child development expert circles, it was hardly noticed at all by the public.

Dr. Jay Belsky, professor of human development at Pennsylvania State University, analyzed five studies involving 491 young children placed in unfamiliar circumstances—that is, day care centers. The experiment was designed to measure the quality of the emotional tie an infant has for the person who usually cares for her. Implications of these arrangements are vital to understand because they affect not only the child's sense of trust and security but also future relationships with others. Dr. Belsky found evidence of less secure attachments when extensive nonmaternal day care was initiated in the first year of life. Further, the *Times* reports that Belsky cites a "disquieting trend in the evidence on older children." Dr. Belsky notes that he finds "more aggressive and noncompliant behavior among five-year-olds who, as infants, had extensive center-based care." Older preschoolers, it was found, were described as more anxious and hyperactive than infants who had experienced maternal care rather than "split-mothering."

The implications of the new studies are staggering, and they are creating the predicted waves of anxiety among the experts. After all, the reality is that almost two million women cannot or will not chuck their jobs to mother their infants. The majority of mothers of children one year old or younger are in the labor force—51.9 percent of them, according to the most recent data from the Bureau of Labor statistics. If the implication is that more than half of the 3.7 million children under a year old are going to have problems from the current common practice of total day care in the first year of life, where does that leave us?

Is this a call to arms, a prod to hysteria for those working mothers who opt to use, who *must* use, the current day care system? Of course not. For each study that points in one direction, a good researcher can find another that points to an opposite conclusion. For instance, there was an earlier study done by a Harvard team that involved sixty Boston infants. The study was conducted by Dr. Jerome Kagan of Harvard; its conclusion was, "A day care center staffed by conscientious and nurturant adults during the first two and a half years of life does not seem to produce a psychological profile very much different from the one created by rearing totally in the home." The family is such a potent emotional force, concludes Kagan, that it overrides some of the negative effects. Results like this surely give great support to mothers who cannot, or don't wish to, remain at home with their infants.

Nevertheless, it *is* a controversial issue, one that in many cases has been swept under the table. All is not black and white. Even if it serves women's psyches well to say that babies do beautifully with other-than-mother nurturant care, the opposite may be the truth. It's important to understand that we just don't know what the truth is; the problem is so new it precludes extensive study. So doesn't it make sense to say that, despite its popularity with the thousands of working mothers who need or want to "do it all, all at once," the notion of substitute mothering in the earliest, most vulnerable years needs a closer look? New research compels us to take that closer look.

Doesn't it make sense also to acknowledge that the home life of Clair and Cliff Huxtable (Phylicia Rashad and Bill Cosby) is an impossible-to-emulate fantasy? Clair, a law firm partner, impeccably dressed for success in a stunning pastel outfit, comes home daily to a home not graced with household help, opens an immaculate oven in that pastel suit, and bastes a perfect roast that miraculously appears in her kitchen. Invariably, Clair has plenty of quality and quantity time and energy to spend helping with homework and dispensing parental advice. Admittedly, she has a lot of help from Dr. Cliff, who rarely seems to be at his office. Perhaps if he had to work full-time, she might have chosen to stay home for a while. In the American sit-com family, choices are always possible.

For most who might like to consider spending the early months at home with their babies, choices simply don't exist. In 1987 seven million Americans were raising children alone. And nine times out of ten these solitary parents were women. Unmarried mothers, widows, separated or divorced women, all were struggling to make ends meet. Their median income was just one third of the median incomes of couples with children. (Upon divorce, the average woman's income drops to 70 percent of its predivorce level, according to University of Michigan researchers Greg J. Duncan and Saul D. Hoffman.) These women cannot even consider the luxury of spending time with their babies during the formative months. Nor can most married women consider dropping out of the workplace, even for a day. In 1985 the median income of all baby-boom households (consisting of those born between 1946 and 1964) was between $25,000 and $34,000, every penny of which seemed desperately needed when one considered the fact that the average baby cost between $3000 and $5000 before the first year, not including the average cost of $3200 for hospital delivery. A year's worth of disposable diapers cost over $500!

Although one should be aware of the faction of child experts that advises close maternal supervision in the first years, and one should never disparage women who choose and are able to stay home for a while, common sense tells us that most women can't go home again. What's the answer?

Tenderized Child Care Is the Answer

None of us knows all the answers, but all of us should know that America must at least make a start toward providing options for those parents who wish to spend more time with their babies and still stay on course to success in business.

The power of vote and protest has brought about reform in other countries. Why not this one? Government, labor, and private management can be made to listen to concerned parents who insist upon parental leave for those who wish it. In addition, money will have to be earmarked for better salaries, working conditions, and training for caretakers. If women can't or won't take parental leave, they must be assured of stellar substitute caretakers. The well-being of the nation, not just parents' peace of mind, depends on reform in this area. For starters, enforceable minimum federal standards on day care issues of staff/child ratio, qualifications of caregivers, group size, parent involvement, and health and safety measures must be provided by this government. "Federal standards are essential to any bill," says Michigan Representative Dale Kildee. "Besides the horror stories we hear of children being hurt while unattended, we also have kids sitting around vegetating in front of the television all day."

Those in the business of advice-giving don't have much to say to women who opt out of the workplace to claim a kinship with the legions of mothers before them. If advice on how to manage is offered, the words are usually as empty and as facile as those I offered to Donna when she first expressed her own angst to me.

"Keep your perspective," is one prescriptive. "You aren't quitting *the* job—it's only *a* job. With your education and experience, you can find a new job when you're ready."

For some women a change of perspective will prove useful. But what if your job isn't *just* a job? What if it's one that you have carefully nurtured for years, one that carries a position, rank, and salary that would almost certainly be lost if you chose to leave it for a year or so, or even more?

"Learn to play the piano; set goals for yourself," is another point of view. "Go out to lunch; read a book; get part-time help; enroll the children in a day care program one or two mornings a week." Maybe yes and maybe no. That advice seems pure mush: reading a book, playing the piano, going out to lunch. Not the answer for a woman who has chosen to stay home to raise her children, for a while, but who eventually wants to reclaim a grown-up business life.

"Maintain your professional ties." This is better advice. Free-lance work, when possible, keeps a finger in the pot. Subscribing to trade publications and attending meetings of professional groups will help you to feel ready for business life when you do return—even at a loss of rank and salary.

Other countries have better answers, it seems. Other places, at this writing, encourage the emerging new feelings of so many women.

In a *Wall Street Journal* article, bylined from London, journalist Joann Lublin speaks about "hope for the curse of the working mummy." British working women, she says, tend to leave work and stay home for an average of three and a half years after they have their babies. This represents a period three times as long, on average, as the time American women stay home for maternity leave. The loss of trained women in their working prime, the frustration of their upward occupational mobility, says Lublin, aggravates a shrinking labor pool of young workers (there are increasingly fewer eighteen-year-olds in the U.K.) and creates enormous new training costs for companies.

In 1981 the National Westminster Bank thought of an answer. Their solution has attracted about two dozen U.K. private and public companies, including other banks, retailers, engineering companies, and several government agencies and unions.

The bank's answer is: career-break plans. By using different strategies, according to the career field, arrangements are made to allow promising professionals and managers to resume their careers without loss of seniority, pay, or status after child-rearing leaves of up to five years. The women, says Lublin, "stay in touch during their prolonged absences by working a few weeks a year, receiving monthly information packs, and attending employer-subsidized refresher training."

From the vantage point of some employers like John Shrigley, a personnel director of GEC Marconi Ltd, a big U.K. electronics firm, the career-break notion "isn't philanthropy, but the best use of an investment."

What happened to the concerted voices of the American women vocal and powerful enough to negotiate marketplace entry changes in the male-dominated work world? Where are the same voices, demanding some kind of graduated reentry plan for the growing number of women who opt for staying home for a while? The voices, sadly enough, are inaudible, if there at all.

In fact, says Lublin, one American research associate expressed amazement at the fact that some U.K. employers *voluntarily* attempt to accommodate working mothers, while in the United States business groups are presently fighting a federal bill that would require employers to offer a mere four and a half months of unpaid leave for parents of newborns. The Brits have gone "light years beyond" what the proposed Family and Parental Leave Act would accomplish, says the associate.

Opting Out and Feeling Good

First of all, if you do decide to take time off from the workplace, don't feel guilty if two weeks at home make you feel ready for the loony bin. It does not benefit mother or baby to tether an unwilling woman to the house. If you are aching with eagerness to get back on the job—get the best care you can for your child, then fly!

But what if the idea is appealing and practical? The best approach, says Dr. Galenson, is for mothers to arrange to get off a full-time work track and onto at least a part-time track for the first two years of their infants' lives. "Even if this means loss of money or advancement, whatever part-time arrangement that can be made for only two years is, in my judgment, absolutely essential to a child's development. That first year is crucial—the second year, almost as important. At the end of that time, the little one has a base of connectedness. You can *never* get back what you don't put in." concludes the doctor.

Again, this is startling advice for these times, almost a retreat, some militant feminists would say, as would many of the nearly seventy percent of women who comprise today's workforce. Still, many women are beginning to feel that early maternal connection with babies empowers those children. The optimum, says Dr. Galenson, is to have the mother in the home almost full-time during the first year and the better part of the second. The next best thing is to have a very loving and experienced caretaker in the familiar home. If this caretaker has to leave, as often happens, the situation is not the same as the child deserted by two women in the unfamiliar atmosphere of a large day care center. The third best thing is to leave an infant in a smaller caregiving atmosphere, perhaps a neighbor's home, where, preferably, the mother can pop in and out.

How about a father nurturer in those first two years, as some child care experts advise? It has surely been a much-talked-about option these days. Personally, I must admit, I *wish* Dr. Galenson's opinion on this were different.

"In all my years of observing and working at it, I've never really seen an effective venture of this kind, because we get into the whole problem of gender confusion," she says. "Little girls, at the end of the second year, naturally and normally get somewhat angry at their mothers and turn, more erotically, toward their fathers. If you have a father who's been there all the time, confusion occurs; if he's been there all the time, as her mother, how's he supposed to be her 'sexual' person? It just never works. Little girls often stay in the infantile mode if their fathers have acted as mothers. And if the child is a boy, it's no easier. Boy babies ideally become very close to their mothers, connecting strongly in the first sixteen or seventeen months. Then, they have to disengage in a natural way and identify with their dads, becoming more masculine people. If they've never had those first eighteen months of attachment to a female, they're going to have trouble later in life, attaching to grown-up females. It's often a no-win situation when a mother leaves during that first year or so."

Betsy Jablow, an administrator at the Museum of Modern Art in New York, has found what for her is the ideal (*nothing* is ideal) situation. She has managed to convince her bosses to allow her to work part-time, giving her three full days in a row at home with her baby, who otherwise remains in the care of a sitter.

"I'm a woman who would have hated spending full time at home, *especially* during the first one or two years," she says. "I'm more involved with Simon as he becomes a person—more than in his infant stage. Still, although I like working part-time, I don't mind telling you that it breaks my heart when I occasionally come home and he prefers the sitter to me.

"Real jealousy. If I have another child, though, that's when the real crunch will come. I can't see working even part-time in the beginning, with two children at home; the responsibilities will be just too massive to walk out on."

Marilyn Nelson, of Boston, Massachusetts, has chosen to stay home, full-time, for "—I don't know—I just can't tell yet. This is one I have to play by ear." She is an advertising copywriter with a large textile manufacturing company, and she is divorced. Money is extremely tight.

"I am working free-lance at home, for a while. I think the skills I learned on the job have given me more power to be an at-home mother," she says. "I organize better, I can stop and start if I have to (turning the typewriter off to feed or diaper the baby is no different from turning it off to take phone calls or dictation), and I've learned to focus in on the job with all the minor distractions. I'm not saying it's not hard—just, that I don't know any other way to do it. I don't have a husband to come home and daddy my baby at night, so I'll be damned if I let him miss out on mommying during the day."

Nelson feels somewhat bitter. She knows her decision means she will be missing out, has already missed an administrative job that was given to someone "not half as good, not there half as long . . ." What's more, she doesn't expect to find even the copywriter job waiting for her when she returns.

"But, you do what you have to do," she says. "I hold this child and I feel the power of parenting—and I'm not about to release that from my grasp. I know I won't be able to get these years back."

Marlene Randall of Providence, Rhode Island, is, she says, "paying a price" for motherhood, and that is a temporary lull in her career. There are, she says, "trade-offs—I wish there weren't, but there are. I'm anteing up. I'm twenty-eight, and yes, I give up work for home with my baby. You know what? I see a lot of men who would be crazed out of their minds with happiness if they felt strong enough to do the same thing. I work a few hours a day, every weekend, and that—plus the money I'd pay a nanny that I'm saving—almost makes up for my salary. I won't be promoted, and I've dropped off the fast track, but it's what I want. Don't worry: I figure that I'll work with demonic skill when Melissa's in school, and get back on. It's better than waiting till I'm forty to have kids when I'll be in line for a vice presidency and have to give *that* up."

Women like Marlene and Betsy, who have loving, supportive spouses, have a somewhat easier time of it when they opt to stay home in the early months or years of their children's lives. It is, of course, far more difficult for women like Marilyn, who must go it alone; and, with the current divorce rate in the United States at almost fifty percent, the numbers of women who parent alone are enormous. Somewhere along the line, it would seem imperative for big business and government to know that it is to their advantage to work out some compromises with women who opt for time out, temporarily.

The women's movement is about choice, after all; and if financial necessity precludes real choice, surely every parent should at least know that there are two schools of thought about leaving very young children to substitute mother care. It is no choice at all if we have to ignore new information that indicates problems, no matter how unpopular or uneasy we feel if we heed what we learn. Whether the primary nurturing role is to be played by mothers, fathers, or surrogate parents, the solution to the problem will never be to deny there is a problem. Further to the point, researchers don't mean to imply that infant day care *necessarily* augurs anxious children. What they clearly say is that women who feel the need to be present during their infant's earliest months should be encouraged by industry, government, and public opinion to do so.

Psychiatrist Willard Gaylin calls for continuing inquiries. He says, "the women's movement, struggling to free women from the indignity of a gender stereotype that has placed them in a constant state of dependency, must not view this argument about the crucial bind of parent and child as deterrent to its aspirations. . . . I am stating the unavoidable fact that all achievement and all pride, all confidence, rests on certain inviolable loving contacts early in life. If a woman then wants to have a child she should be free to have one without the impediment of sacrificing other creative drives and needs. How this is to be done, I do not know."

Opting Out and Cashing In

One of the most beloved women in the world is one who opted for time out permanently. She stayed home, raised her kids, and then became a multimillionaire telling everybody about it. Erma Bombeck is a national legend, and because she embodies, along with power, so many of the gentle tender traits, like the one of empowering others, she made room in the midst of her pressured schedule for a talk that would help me. The way that Erma expresses her femininity is through, what else?, humor and playfulness, long a tool of women but in the past claimed by men as their own property.

"Humor has always been thought of as masculine," she says. "Male stand-up comics and male sit-down comedy writers once dominated the field. It was considered very unfeminine to be funny," says Erma, "so we stifled the wit.

"When women like me entered the field, we looked for more balanced humor," she notes. "At least, I did. I can write about my husband being cheap (if you really wanted to see old dad lose it, you should have seen him walk into the kitchen and discover three kids with both doors of the refrigerator flung wide open while the hair in their noses froze up) if I let readers know that the same woman can write about parents of handicapped children. People will forgive even the most acerbic humor if I remind them that we can laugh at ourselves and then cry, in the same paragraph."

It was those women who stayed at home to nurture families, says Erma, who were the ones the world had the most trouble understanding. "It was because when we finally fought for our dues, people were not used to mothers who thought of themselves, once in a while. It was we who always took the bent fork and the egg with the broken yolk. We were *supposed* to do that, thought everyone. Later, when we began to march, one of the strongest criticisms of the women's movement was that we were too 'tough.' *Tough?* If men acted the same way they were called forceful and decisive."

Bombeck proved that any ground, including home ground, was fertile ground. "Someone once asked me, 'How can you write with small children around?'

" 'Easy,'I answered. I'd just say to any kid who interrupted, 'Unless you're on fire, I'll take care of you later because now, *I'm busy.'* "

Bombeck talks about the six years in which she actively fought for the women's movement, and the ambivalent feelings most women had—even while marching.

"It was Liz Carpenter who muttered, one day, 'All these women going out to work and equality and all that is great; but if I'm lucky enough to have a daughter-in-law, I want her to stay home a while and raise my grandchildren.' When it comes right down to it," says Erma, "it's how I feel. I just don't want my own daughter to miss all this stuff, if she can possibly help it. In retrospect, I was far from Betty Crocker when I was home raising kids. In fact, I was downright surly. But, by God, I was there, and I probably shouldn't have been anywhere else, at that point in life. You never can recapture it. Look," she says earnestly, "if you desperately need the paycheck, or you really hate the idea of home, even for a while, well, of course, you've got to get out into the workplace. But, my son, who is a teacher, talks to me about the latchkey kids, and he makes comparisons with his own life: Imperfect as I was, I was there. It's not for everyone, but women should not be made to feel less powerful if they choose to stay home."

How can we teach little boys the traits that we used to save for little girls—warmth, sharing, and the expression of compassion?

"We sure can't do it by ourselves," Erma says. "A child wants to be like everyone else, to copy those he admires. If he sees a world of tough-macho and tender-female, he's not going to go for the tender. But," she continues, "let his teachers keep Tender Power in mind every day. Let the sports figures that he idolizes display connection and gentleness, let all of us, all across the board pave the way for this little boy, and he's got it made."

You Don't Have to Have Kids to Stay Home

"Do I have to have a baby to drop out for a while?," asks one fast-track young attorney. She's only half kidding. There are a growing number of young women out there who want more free time so desperately, they'd take any excuse to get it.

A brand new study by the Decision Research Corporation in Lexington, Massachusetts, found that people, especially women, may be wearing themselves out with chores. Indeed, stated the study, because women who work also assume more household responsibilities than husbands, they have a full twenty-five percent less leisure time than men have. Most of those women, you couldn't pry from their jobs with a metal pole—that's how much they love their work—reduced leisure time or not. But, some of them, maybe not so very few of them if you really counted, want out. If the women's movement is about choice, these women need to be able to choose other life-styles without feeling they've failed anyone—least of all themselves.

Sue Alstedt was a middle manager at AT&T. She quit her job because, "well—it took all of my life. I needed time for *me*."

She felt very guilty, she says, about leaving work she loved. "People usually leave because they had babies. I had no such excuse. But, I never had any control over my own time; I also had no confidence that I *could* control my own time. I never had a break—went to work right from college. Finally, *'enough,'* I said. 'Seize the moment.'"

What turned out to be a permanent leave from her job first started as a two-week vacation that grew to three, then four weeks. When the telephone company changed its monolithic system, one of the incentives toward reducing staff was to offer various money options, which Sue accepted.

Her husband, some years older, decided to retire, and the two took off for a couple of years of travel and self-appraisement.

"It was four years on New Year's Eve, that I left my work," says Sue. "I thought about how I'd changed my life—and was it for the better?"

First of all, she says, on the down side, having "enough time" still represented a problem. Her day, for example, continued to "fritter away" before she even had a chance to taste it. "I still had no time, for instance, to send Christmas cards this year!" But, she remembers, "in the corporate world, I could work on a project for a year, and also fritter my life away on that."

The "up" side of the decision, for Sue, is infinitely better. "I pay more attention to my *self*," she says. "What do *I* really want?" She's gone back to graduate school for a Master's degree in psychology, something she had always dreamed of doing.

Most important, the skills she had learned at work proved invaluable to her chosen second life, as many who opt out have discovered.

"For the first time in my life, I had to manage my own money," she says. "At the telephone company, it got saved for me, and it also came in every month, but the business tools I learned at work made it possible to develop investment and money management skills at home. Another thing," says Alstedt, "my work required a great deal of interpersonal social skills: I traveled a lot, and I had to learn to relate to others, had to learn to draw people out. Well, in my personal travels, these skills made all the difference in enjoyment."

On a more technical level, Alstedt bought computer equipment to do her banking and manage other personal affairs at home. She soon became impatient with the computer because it was not as advanced or as fast as the one she had learned on at work. "I couldn't stand to wait for it, even though it was coming out at the rate of speech," she wryly says, which proves you can take the person out of the office, but you can't completely take the office out of the person.

Permanent Time-Out: Volunteerism

Most everyone's mom and sister early in the century stayed at home. It was these women who constituted the full force of the volunteers who worked with no pay and for whatever hours they might spare, at making the country's hospitals, old-age homes, and various charitable institutions run smoothly. Naturally, these women were taken advantage of, and their loving hearts were imposed upon ruthlessly, time and time again, usually by men who made splendid money doing precisely the same things the women were doing for free.

Along came liberation, and women were encouraged to get paid for their hard work, surely an honorable stance. What happened, which was not so honorable, was that women came to be *dishonored* by many for giving away that which could now be done for a salary. By acting in so old-fashioned a manner, these women were said to be undercutting other women who worked so hard for women's rights. And so, women who chose not to work for money, either because they didn't need it or because they hated the marketplace, were traitors of a sort at worst, and at best they were now considered as idle, foolish, and lazy dilettantes—thorns in the side of feminism. Financially solvent women who opt out of the marketplace in favor of donating time are increasingly rare. They've been made to seem, well—frivolous. Because the kindness of strangers has been taken advantage of, abused, and devalued in recent female history, many vocal women's advocates speak strongly against volunteering one's time.

"As a general rule," cautions Betty Lehan Harragan, in her book *Games Mother Never Taught You*, "women must be extremely cautious at 'volunteering' to do anything in the business milieu because of the stereotype that women love to be volunteers just 'to help other people.' All your volunteering must be accompanied by an ulterior motive: What it will accomplish for *you*. . . . Collecting dolls for orphans at Christmas or taking handicapped children to the circus are typical. These smack too much of 'women's work.' . . . donate to and support such activities, but don't offer to help with the nitty-gritty details; they don't need you anyway; lots of employees enjoy doing these things, so let them."

While Harragan's remarks are directed at women in business who might consider implementing feelings of caring and support, they surely act as a barometer of current feelings toward volunteerism in general.

Women who feel drawn to "give of themselves," as my grandmother used to say, must learn to defy such overreactions. It is a sign of a civilization's decline when its needy institutions are ignored by powerful people. Women who give away their time and energies are exercising the right of the advantaged to aid the disadvantaged. It is a powerful right.

An interesting aside to this issue comes from Margaret Hennig and Anne Jardim who write about the volunteer woman in their book *The Managerial Woman*. It is their contention that women who succeed in business all have readily identifiable traits in common, and this applies strongly to the woman whose entire work experience has been with volunteer organizations. She, who all her working life has been a "giver"; she, who is "tender" in its purest sense; she turns out to be powerful in managerial and leadership skills. The authors cite an example of a midwest housewife who had held leadership positions at the local and national level in a number of volunteer organizations. Over the course of twenty years she had managed seven-figure budgets, raised huge funds, and chaired policy committees. She had, as well, managed organizations of both paid and voluntary personnel.

Then, her husband got sick, and for the first time in her life the woman was forced to find work that paid—cash. The only job she could think of that she was qualified for was driving a taxi, because she knew every street in the city. Lucky for her, a fund-raising acquaintance happened to be president of the local bank. He was appalled at her decision to drive a cab and told her she had more *useful* and brilliant business experience than most bank vice presidents. Purely from what he knew of her volunteering skills, he offered her a job (she was then fifty years old) in the bank's management training program, and in eight months she was vice president of the bank.

Never, ever, devalue the intelligence, skills, and business sense—in addition to heart—that are required in most volunteer efforts. Never, ever, devalue the society matron, the "just a housewife," or any woman at all, who chooses to give away tenderness. In that, she derives the power of immense satisfaction. She is a life force of humanized society. She is an endangered species.

Are We All Coming Home?

Naturally not. Finding power by staying home is just for those who choose it. There is no question that most women will not return to the home permanently in the manner of Jane Austen. Raised consciousnesses, the exhilaration of the well-made deal, the surging economy that depends on women's skills and energies would never countenance a mass return to tender without workplace power. For that, most of us are grateful.

According to pollster Lou Harris, seventy percent of women under thirty want marriage, children, *and* a career. When working mothers were asked what they would do if finances were not an issue, an overwhelming eighty-two percent of them declared that they would work anyway. And, among nonworking women, fully seventy-one percent, says Harris, say they would prefer to be working. In every likelihood, by the 1990s, most will be dual-career households; by the turn of the century, the number of such households will be eight in ten. Women in the workplace are not going to go away. The men who used to say to us, "Be grateful you're not out here in the cold, cold world—it's no fun at all," were lying. Although it surely is not *all* fun, the dignity and spur of good work is a treasure.

What is going to change, what *must* change in the timetable of the woman of the nineties? Early in the feminist movement Betty Friedan talked frequently about the fact that women do not have to choose between marriage and career at all. What they have to do is rethink their blueprint of success; and rethink the notion that men and women must adhere to the same blueprint. Dropping out temporarily to have and raise children for a few years may indeed temporarily "punish" women, may indeed slow down our meteoric rise to the top. On the other hand, by making the painful choice of sequencing, one can certainly come closer to the "have-it-all" ethic. Moreover, while realistically it does slow us down, it doesn't preclude our eventually reaching the top—witness the tortoise and the hare.

Jeane Kirkpatrick, former ambassador to the United Nations and United States cabinet member, made sure her entry in *Who's Who in America* reads:

> My experience demonstrates to my satisfaction that it is both possible and feasible for women in our times to successfully combine traditional and professional roles, that it is not necessary to ape men's career patterns—starting early and keeping one's nose to the grindstone, but that, instead, one can do quite different things at different stages of life. All that is required is a little luck and a lot of hard work.

Sure, there are trade-offs, but the trade-offs aren't a matter of choose one, lose the other, a women's syndrome of our own making. Sequencing, in fact, is such a good idea that it might (and certainly should) become part of the male agenda as soon as men, no dummies they, begin to observe that the quality of human life and love is vastly improved when one has a little of everything.

Still, there is no one way, no right way, to make a life. Women who choose to build the traditional traits of affiliation, connection, nurturing, empathy, and cooperation based on something other than the workplace must know that very strong women can operate from home. They must understand that the skills they have picked up in even a short work tenure can serve them in a temporary, at-home hiatus from work. There are always business options to be found away from the traditional places of business. Finally, an emotional climate that will honor a choice of home, along with an economic climate that will aid and abet it, will be well served if we publicize the benefits to be derived from a more humanized marketplace—one that gives credence to home-based power.

Lashing Out

I remember hearing of an angry woman, an opponent of the Equal Rights Amendment, who said she feared for the very state of home and marriage if the amendment were passed. Questioned by a reporter, she drew herself up and said to him, "I don't care to be a person, thank you. I am a wife."

How is it that such a misunderstanding of the ERA could happen? How is it that one woman and probably uncountable others think that to be a wife and have a home and family is incompatible with equal rights? How is it that we feminists have somehow gotten the wrong message to many—the message that tenderness and power are enemies—when the opposite is true. And finally, how is it that so many women never learned, or forgot, that Tender Power can operate at home as well as in business in *myriad* different ways . . .

Sadly enough, it is women who most often lash out at each other, and it is women who have the most trouble understanding why others want to go back home to nurture, for a while at least. It is a frail self-image that causes such lashing out.

The lashing is lessening. Experts who are adept at reading the pulse of the country are finding that women in power are listening harder to other women and understanding better that power is sometimes to be found in unlikely places—one of them being the place from which we have been trying to escape—Home Sweet Home.

11

Relationships:
Complicated Connections

Relationships are complicated animals.

The one constant in all good relationships, complicated as they may be, is intimacy. The closest relationships are the most intimate ones. Intimacy figures in not only sexual but also friendly relationships, and new patterns of progress insist that we cut and alter our relationship patterns so that intimacy is a snug fit.

A new, national study, the largest investigation to date on the need for intimacy, was recently reported on in the *Journal of Personality*. Dr. Dan P. McAdams, a psychologist at Loyola University in Chicago, reports that although women seem to have a slightly higher need for intimacy, men feel the need for this tender trait almost as much. The differences lie in the way men and women experience intimacy and in what it does for them. Women, says Dr. McAdams, find that emotional intimacy leads directly to satisfying roles like wife, mother, or friend. Men, on the other hand, find that emotional intimacy and a sense of closeness is not as directly related to personal relationships as it is to their sense of resilience and confidence in the world around them—the same confidence and resilience that makes for achievement in work.

How exactly do men and women differ in expressing intimacy? According to research done at Yale and the University of Washington, women share their feelings much more easily than men, and this self-disclosure gives them a satisfying sense of intimacy. For many men, simply sharing activities, rather than discussing and disclosing feelings, creates the closeness.

The importance of this study is underscored by Dr. McAdams's further study indicating that men who value intimacy tend to have happier marriages. Women do seem to know this instinctively; if we had to choose the one trait above all others that is traditionally most important to the female psyche, it is that of being able to engage with others.

More than ever, says writer Daniel Goleman in the *New York Times*, therapists are reporting that they're seeing far more patients who say they have immense difficulties in their relationships. They don't have a clue as to how to build intimacy. And the books that tell us how to achieve vitality in our relationships just keep on coming.

Every week there's another book by another expert telling women where they went wrong and why their relationships soured. Every week there's another thousand women trying to do better, trying to be tougher, trying not to be so sensitive, so self-destructive, so vulnerable, so . . .

The theory is that women should act like men in order to succeed in the marketplace (and find books in the business section of the bookstore that tell them how to accomplish it). The same women who buy this wend their way over to the psychology section to find there the same self-berating theme.

Hand-wringing, self-blaming, head-banging—women have spent, according to the latest estimates, a cool forty million dollars on books that tell them how to love a difficult man, why they love too much, how foolish are their choices, how masochistic are their personalities, and how to love men who hate women. Whatever goes wrong with marriage, the kids, her career, *his* career, the conversation over the morning coffee, the nonconversation after the love-making, the entire relationship—is her fault, they both agree. Sad. Sad and wrong.

Make no mistake: there's plenty wrong with the state of relationships today. Recently the advertising agency of D'Arcy Masius Benton & Bowles released the results of a national survey of 1550 men and women. One question asked was, "Which of the following items gives you a great deal of pleasure and satisfaction?" The possible responses included professional activities, marriage, making money, friendships, sports—thirty different options.

Of all the choices, do you know which item won hands down? Television. *Sixty-eight percent of 1550 people rated* television *as the number one source for "a great deal of pleasure" in their lives.* Terrific.

Most people reported that children gave them more pleasure than their marriages, and twenty-one percent rated hobbies over either children or marriage. Even reading lorded it over sexual relationships. And "just taking it easy" rated higher than home, marriage, or sex.

Whatever we're reading in those how-to books, it doesn't seem to be working. Our relationships are not as satisfactory as is blaming ourselves for their failure.

If there's any blame to place (and the activity of blame-placing is notoriously unhelpful), place it not on women—but on the moment in time when women were encouraged to act like men, not only in the workplace, but in the arena of personal attachments. The baffling question is this: We *invented* personal attachments, so why should we do it their way, the wrong way? Why do we listen, when the books tell us we are too needy of commitments, too sensitive, too eager to explore feelings? Commitments, sensitivity, feelings-exploration—that's *the heart* of relationships.

The news is really grim when it comes to legal relationships, and it's been grim for a while. As soon as the baby boom generation came of age, divorce statistics "went through the roof," says Cheryl Russell, editor-in-chief of *American Demographics* and author of *100 Predictions for the Baby Boom*. These baby boomers are really the first to reap the benefits of a more liberated society—as well as the disasters. The number of divorces rose from about 400,000 a year in 1962 to 1.2 million in 1981. In 1982 and 1983 when the economic recession forced people to stay together (two can live cheaper than one and one), divorces dropped. By 1985, with the economy improving, divorces were up again. The threat of AIDS may well bring the divorce statistics down once again; still, it all bodes ill for the state of relationships between men and women today.

Ambivalent Men and Fantasy Women

In view of the divorce statistics, perhaps it isn't surprising that many young men (13.8 percent of thirty- to forty-four-year-olds—well up from a decade ago) have never married. Trip Gabriel, a contributing editor of *Rolling Stone Magazine*, writes about this new phenomenon in "Why Wed? The Ambivalent American Bachelor," a November 1987 article in the *New York Times*. "Grown-up American men in the full swim of life," says the author, "are scared stiff of getting married." He notes that this is a demographic group largely "characterized not by its own members, but by its opposite: the army of single women in their thirties who are increasingly perplexed by the unwillingness of men their age to marry and get on with life."

Gabriel concludes that many of the "ambivalent bachelors" he interviewed had an adolescent attitude about connections, a yearning for "fantasies of feminine perfection." Thinking of a commitment to a mate, they didn't consider the richness or the emotional depths possible, but only of the unobtainable dream. They preferred to wait indefinitely, thinking, "What if the right girl walks into my life? Shouldn't I be free to go after her?"

Many of these bachelors, says the author, began to develop an obsession for "working out"—a substitute for a relationship.

After Gabriel's article appeared, "Letters" buff that I am, I eagerly awaited the "Letters to the Editor" column the next week. I was not surprised by what I read.

"I find it appalling," wrote Janice Fouks Blum from California, "that men who can risk the ups and downs of Wall Street, climbing Mount Everest and racing in the Grand Prix, are 'scared' of taking on the greatest challenge that life has to offer—the ability to commit to caring about another human being."

Carla Nordstrom wrote from New York, "There is a joke circulating among singles in New York City: 'How does the single woman get rid of roaches? She asks them for a commitment.' "

And, finally, a letter from Dr. Jeffrey Kahn from New York that sent me to the telephone book to find him.

Dr. Kahn wrote, "Many of those interviewed seem to be afraid of intimate relationships, with several expressing a fear of being trapped. The men in the story (and women with similar concerns) are faced with quite a dilemma. Intimacy is frightening, but career success and athletics alone will leave many unfulfilled in the long run."

Assistant clinical professor of psychiatry at Columbia University School of Medicine, Dr. Kahn says, "There are a great many men who have trouble with intimacy, and these difficulties are not specific to getting married but are applicable to difficulties with intimacy at work. If they go into treatment, it even applies to the way they deal with their analysts. One very successful businessman who began therapy last week had an initial reaction of great trepidation that he was now expected to enter a relationship with me that might appear to be intimate. Given such men's fear of connections, if the 'right' woman should, indeed, ever come around, most would probably head in the opposite direction."

Although the words intimacy and commitment are often used in the same breath, they usually mean different things to men than they do to women. To many men, an intimate commitment is more serious sex, maybe even monogamous sex, or a shared hour at a ball game or movie. To most women, intimate relationships consist of sharing their deepest hopes, dreams, and fears, and maybe, a promise of forever.

In a 1987 issue of *New Woman* magazine, for example, one cartoon has an earnest young woman patiently explaining to a puzzled young man, "But I don't want a deeper commitment, Lionel. I want to get married."

Why is intimacy, a willingness to commit, so important to women? According to Dr. Jean Baker Miller, author of the landmark *Toward a New Psychology of Women*, a woman's very sense of self is likened to her ability to make, then maintain, relationships. It is crucial to her identity to feel related and to be close to others.

Dr. Sheila Jackman, the director of the Division of Human Sexuality in the Albert Einstein College of Medicine in New York, and a therapist specializing in couples' relationships, agrees. She says, "I have heard the analogy 'up on stilts' or 'suspended in mid-air' more than once from young women I am treating who complain they don't have a sense of intimate connectedness with someone. The earth's foundation seems kicked out from under them—and, I'm speaking of heavy-duty career women as well as those who choose not to work. If these women are intimately linked to someone, their work as well as their self-image improves."

It didn't just happen that women feel more comfortable with connections than men. Modern society has applauded the men who are able to make early breaks from their mothers to stand alone.

Freudian theory, for example, teaches that one of women's strongest assets, the ability to connect, can be destructive. Kids, particularly male children, have to separate from parents if they want to be healthy, said Dr. Freud. The ideal is to become autonomous, dependent on only self. Independence, not interdependence, is the way to go.

Letty Cottin Pogrebin, editor of *MS.* magazine, along with many other feminists, questions this pattern of thought.

"Freud's test of a successful, mature male is someone who has turned his back on everything feminine," says Pogrebin. "Turning your back on your mother is the first step. We reared our sons, in the past, to turn their backs on us in order that they may become 'real men' and in the process we created an equation of masculinity with dominance and lack of emotional expression. A man defines his strength by his ability to stand alone."

New research shows that standing alone creates unbearable distances between men and women. Most women, in fact, have powerful needs to connect; indeed, one of the enduring and endearing behavioral traits they have perfected over centuries is the building of excellent affiliations. Women's best work comes as a result of making connections and maintaining relationships. But Freud, a most respected man in matters of the mind, says one must emotionally separate from one's parents. Many women feel, as author Carol Gilligan does, that war and the very act of "aggression is tied . . . to the fracture of human connections." Indeed, many women also feel that it is this male lack of an ability to make connections that dooms so many couples in their sexual and emotional lives.

"He's afraid to make a commitment," complain thousands of women over thousands of coffee cups. Dr. Karen Hopenwasser claims there is a Freudian middle ground.

"Yes," she says, "in order to develop a sense of autonomy, it *is* necessary to get enough distance from one's parents so as not to feel overwhelmed by them—to feel one can take care of one's self. But, I kind of see Freud's theory as a first effort to understand connectedness, and I certainly feel he missed a lot of it. The need to put space between parents and children doesn't mean it's healthy to separate to the extent that the model for male psychology suggests."

The model for male psychology often includes the retention of give-away emotions. It is probably this propensity of the male model that causes the most grief in adult relationships. Perhaps the kindest *and* most powerful present a mother can offer a small son is the power to show vulnerability. The lucky little boy whose parents impart the message that it's okay to display pain, sorrow, and fear grows into the mature adult man who connects well with women.

I remember my own son running toward me one day, biting his lip in an effort to control his tears. His knee was skinned from a bad bicycle fall, and it wasn't until he was inside the house that he began to cry. When his knee was cleaned and bandaged, I asked him why he didn't cry until he reached the house.

"Big boys don't cry." It was a message his teacher had given him.

It took a whole lot of talking to convince him that his dad cried, his basketball coach cried, and, indeed, he too could show the hurting parts of himself and, in doing so, attain even greater strength.

Ambivalent Women

There's a new kind of woman out there, one who is as ambivalent about showing her vulnerability and need for intimacy and connection as is the American bachelor about weddings. This woman, making her mark in the workplace and fully conscious of the effort it took and the effort it still takes to avoid being ignored there, seems to be muddying the waters of traditional relationships. She, who for generations has thrived on intimacy, now fears in addition to loss of intimacy, a loss of self; she fears becoming engulfed—by home, love, and family.

This same woman, once defined as a nurturing caretaker, is now using the same energy it took to excel as homemaker to excel in the work arena, which doesn't come easily. It takes, says one woman, "supreme concentration" to develop those parts of ourselves that have been lying fallow for generations. Perhaps, for the first time in eons, women are not working so hard at intimate relationships in order to conserve their stamina for autonomy. Of course, they still yearn for affiliation and connectedness—but, maybe, not quite so much. Of course, they still wish for intimacy—but are questioning the cost to limits of strength. Many women, in short, are trying to become, if not impervious to the demands of lovers, spouses, and children, at least not so painfully vulnerable.

"I'm not as willing to knock myself out, as before," says Margie, who at forty has gone back to work as a department head in a chain of stores. "Let him keep the football game on; if he wants to live that way, I give up. I don't have the time anymore to dig for his anxieties. So, we don't talk. So be it."

Result? A tenuous straining of relationships. With the advent of power, the old tenderness sometimes seems just too difficult to sustain. Where once her very breath of life depended on it, now, if her work is satisfying, she may just find the confidence to say, "Look—I don't have the patience to pull tenderness out of you any more, and I don't have the time to deal with your aloofness. I think that I am attractive and skilled enough to make it myself, and although that's not what I want, I know now it won't kill me to be alone."

Or, as one woman put it, "Enough already with the empathy. I just want to put my feet up."

The practical mind will soon see that for many couples there isn't *time* for a whole lot of intimacy. Dual-career couples, in particular, sometimes pass each other like ships in the night. "It gets so out of hand," says Dorothy Weiss, editor at *Glamour* magazine, who is married to a young doctor. "Sometimes, one or the other of us will say, 'Oh, how much I miss you.' Think how insane it sounds to say you miss someone when you sleep in the same bed every night."

Some experts on relationships fear the worst. They say that the relentless dual-career drive and the concurrent result of separateness in many new-age relationships will stretch them too thin for survival.

"You don't join your resources, you don't join your names, you don't call yourself husband and wife—one might wonder why you got married," says Maggie Scarf, a behavioral science writer whose book *Intimate Partners* examines modern marriage patterns. "It sounds as if these are marriages where they have to struggle to maintain their intimacy . . . and when sexual lives suffer, I promise you, other aspects of the relationship do get affected."

This then, is the bottom line: Is the new power women have gained in the marketplace the death knell for intimacy as we have known it? As women become more powerful, will their sex lives suffer? No! It doesn't have to happen, at all.

The opposite is possible, says Dr. Sheila Jackman, who knows about such things. Power can be an aphrodisiac, as women have known forever, providing that we don't sustain amnesia abut the forcefulness of tender.

Outrageous Lovers

It will take constant remembering, as a matter of fact, to assert and then to teach to men, the female traits.

"When women describe to me the men they consider to be the most outrageous lovers," says Dr. Jackman, "they unfailingly describe a man who is both tender and powerful. They have in mind men who don't fear gentleness, who touch with exquisite lightness but with sure, strong intent. Most women call such a person a 'real' man. What they mean is that he's man enough to claim all the traits we classically call female along with the traits we classically call male. When men describe a total woman to me, the entire range is there as well. The greatest woman lover is one, say men, who can enjoy a man's body with some assertion, explore it, play with it, ask for the pleasure it can provide and still derive great pleasure from being more passive. This woman moves with her lover in a graceful, strong dance that doesn't insist on either leading or following all the time, but on taking turns in control."

Don't mislead yourself, Jackman cautions. Control is part of the dance. Control is about survival. Women have learned about control in the business world and they're not about to leave it there; they *will* take it into the bedroom. But, here's where women's age-old instinct for cooperation comes in. "Good sex has an extraordinarily cooperative nature," says Jackman. "First me, then you, then me, then you. . . . The best business is not a win/lose situation—it's a win/win situation. Men and women who excel in business can also excel in sexual relationships if they think of it as win/win."

In a recent article for *Glamour* magazine I researched and wrote about the reasons for "Men's New Sexual Fears." It was an eye-opener. Talk about win/lose. The very same men who for ages, it seems, have been complaining that they had to do all the work, that women weren't aggressive enough in bed, are now feeling more stress as women feel less inhibition. In the wake of sexual emancipation comes much performance pressure, loss of interest, anxiety about rejection, and confusion about the male sex role.

I know that for many female readers the tendency here to make a sarcastic comment of the "poor baby" genre is irresistible. After all, haven't we been the repositories for anxiety, rejection, and confusion for so very long? Sarcasm might be in order if we were not, once again, to be the losers by so doing. The sad truth is that women, feeling our oats for the first time in centuries, insisting on equal orgasms, and double control, are experiencing a new kind of victimhood for our efforts.

While there's no epidemic of male impotence, says Howard Weiner, a psychiatrist at New York's Lenox Hill Hospital, "there seems to be a new *fear* of impotence—which in the end may result in the same thing."

Does this mean that women have to feel guilt for their newfound, hard-won self-confidence? Emphatically no. That we should revert to the way it was? No. That women should be less assertive, less clear about their needs? No, no, and again, no.

It does mean that women ought to get those old intuition antennae polished up again. It means that the old empathy that allowed women to read men was a useful tool, and not one to be discarded. Who are we kidding? If either men or women have sexual anxieties, their partners suffer as well.

If women's intuition had been working as well as it could these last few years, it would have hinted to women that men, for one thing, were going to have trouble "performing" on cue. It would have been clear to most women that men would start to suffer from what has been known lately as the "ready teddy" syndrome—having always to say yes. Men ought to be able to say no, just as women have been so allowed. Saying no doesn't make a man a wimp, gay, or uninterested in you; it just means he's tired, or the World Series is claiming his attention. Perhaps it's your breath.

Years ago, women might have used their intuition to sense this, but they didn't have the courage to talk about it and bring this and other male and female sexual fears out into the open. Today, women have found the courage to ask for sex, to talk about anything. Ironically, though, they're not calling on the old empathic tools to help them understand the new sexual problems that may be inhibiting their partners. In the battle for sexual equality, a very dear kind of female sensitivity is often shunted aside. Instincts count for too little. What should count are connection into the other's psyche, caring, and a your-turn/my-turn mentality, as Dr. Jackman phrases it. That, says the therapist, is what cooperative sex is all about.

Cooperation is the operative word. A trait that women have fine-tuned for years, cooperation works as well in the bedroom as it could work in the boardroom. When sex is an "always-me" affair instead of a "you-then-me" affair, the result is win/lose. One wins, the other loses.

The following story is a perfect illustration. W.W. Meade, a writer for *Working Woman* magazine, tells of his chemist friend who had always been very proud of his architect wife, very much in love with her, and very "steamy, lets-get-physical." When the architect wife became locally famous, says Meade, his friend "folded his tent." Sex ceased.

Anguished, the wife asked their good friend Meade to speak with her husband. In an emotional meeting, he told Meade that he couldn't make love to his own wife any longer because "there's tension where the woman used to be."

Meade asked what he thought the woman did when "there was tension where the man used to be."

And, earnestly, sadly, the chemist responded that he didn't believe this was ever a problem for women, because "tension makes men sexy."

Possibly, just possibly, women, now gaining in men's business footsteps, are putting hexes on relationships with that same brand of arrogance and ignorance.

We tend to see our problems as unique; we tend to think our mates don't bleed in the same places. Worse, we tend lately to solve the problems with the same male responses.

* "Don't bother me, I've had a hard day at the office."

* "I just need to relax, I don't feel like talking."

* "How can I tell you what I did, when you wouldn't understand?"

Despite the fact that for eons women have been pleading, "Try me—I *can* understand," most men have remained silent. Compounding the problem has been the human propensity of women to offer advice instead of mere listening, which made men clam up even tighter. Relationships withered.

Now, ironically, women follow the same script, pull the same "don't bother me" lines, says Dr. Jackman. Men feel deprived and devalued.

When we do open up and our men offer solutions instead of attention, suspecting paternalism, we shut down. Both men and women fail to guess how easy it is to satisfy a need for intimacy, says Jackman. Just listening, just making a few sympathetic sounds, is all that's necessary.

Today, both men and women are either clamming up or being wise-guy experts on the other's career, with very little in between. Relationships face double jeopardy.

Communicate, Don't Explicate

There is a workable solution. Just as attentive listening is a power tool for managers in business, it is equally a great resource in shoring up relationships. "True listening is an art," says Dr. Jackman. "Since most men and women now have work and home selves, perhaps we're really ready to embark on new levels of improved communication through shared experiences. *Listen:* don't explain what the other means to say. If one is able to listen without opening the mouth, there's hope," says the counselor. "Learn the difference between your own opinion and merely muttering soothing words that tell your partner you're hearing."

True listening is a creative act, says Dr. I. Ralph Hyatt, author of *Before You Love Again.* "It means reading the unspoken language of the eyes, the stance of the body, the slumped shoulder, and the expression that belies the words. It means hearing 'I'm low right now and need some stroking' behind the hearty, 'I'm fine.' It means sensing the hurt or pride of accomplishment behind the casual recounting of some event."

Real listening?

- It's not selective hearing, paying attention to just what's nice and not threatening.

- It's not finishing other people's sentences.

- It's not figuring out your answers before you hear the other person's entire comment.

- It's not thinking you have to solve the other person's problems; sometimes people want just an audience, not a panacea.

- It's certainly not reading, writing, or doing anything else while the speaker speaks.

When it's your turn to talk, disclose, don't lecture. Tell the secrets of your honest heart. Hope your partner is listening. That's communication.

Women are not going to give up their newfound economic or any other kind of power to salve men's egos anymore, says Jackman. That era is dead and gone. Still, say most experts, women don't have to come on as gangbusters either. And what if a man *sees* gangbusters, when only love is there? Talk, talk, talk—soothe each other's inner devils. It's a nurturing and caring thing to do, when a mate is clearly experiencing angst from the new rules.

Break Through the Crust of Habit

Expressing a real interest in each other, asking questions that are not everyday, going to the heart of the other's psyche sometimes establishes intimacy, say some therapists. Dr. Aaron Beck, a psychiatrist at the University of Pennsylvania, says that many women he sees often turn to female friends who know how to ask the right questions and transcend the usual, boring conversations. "The wife needs to try again," says Dr. Beck, "and the husband needs to make more effort to persist in asking questions that will break through the crust of habit to the real feelings."

Relationships are often so baffling and contradictory in nature; Tender Power accepts contradictions.

For example, here's a contradiction in terms: As women, we have learned how strong and self-reliant we can be. But think, and answer honestly: Don't many of us still like to feel our men are stronger and wiser in those dark, three o'clock in the morning times when we need nurturing?

And another contradiction in terms: How many of those strong, wise men have turned to us, three o'clock in the morning style, with the tiny, petulant word, the baby pouts?

It's okay.

To be fair, couples also have to take turns on the trivial things—not so much on the momentous things. You saw the war movie this week, we get to see the science fiction one next week; Indian food last week, Chinese tonight; fishing this Saturday, the museum next Saturday.

And we should stick up for each other. It should always be Us versus The Kids (when the match is called), Us versus Our Parents, Us versus The Rest of the World. Everyone needs a champion or a partner when a throat feels filled with close-to-the-surface frustration or tears.

Complicated Connections

Dr. Willard Gaylin, psychoanalyst, clinical professor of psychiatry at Columbia University Medical School, and director of the Hastings Institute in New York, says that another psychoanalyst, Harry Stack Sullivan, was one of the very few doctors "who adequately appreciated the complexity of contact. He used the simple word "tenderness," says Gaylin, to describe this complex amalgam of caring contact in relationships and social living.

Humans need strong relationships. Relationships depend, in great part, on the ancient, greatly female skill of connecting. "We are not," says Dr. Gaylin, "and never can be, 'individual.' The paradoxical lesson of identification is that we achieve our unique selves via our fusion with others. Whatever individualism means, it is something we can only gain through early attachments to later identifications with, and finally, loving of other people. To find ourselves we must embrace others. It is a peculiar creature that is so constructed."

I believe, as does Dr. Gaylin, that one of the truest measures of love between lovers and friends is when one's own pleasures and pains are so connected to the pleasures and pains of the loved one they can seem indistinguishable from the other's. While, of course, there are differences, as Dr. Gaylin points out, "between one's self and the person loved, we find ourselves, at least on an unconscious level, continuously confused as to where they begin and we end."

It is this blurring of boundaries, this empathy, this complicated connection that has been women's special province forever. If, on a tunnel-vision path to career success, women lose or forbear to teach to men these traits of nurturant attachment, we will have gained little and lost too much.

One of the finest spurs to a marvelous man/woman relationship is teasing and playfulness. If a relationship is humorless, polemic, perfectionist—it's doomed to failure. Laughing at yourself, seeing yourself in absurd exaggerations, tends to release the build-up of tensions and resentments. Learning to love the silly imperfections in each other actually makes the imperfections endearing. What's more, such love allows each to ply one's unchangeable imperfections in an unself-conscious manner. When someone makes you repress your true nature, you hate it.

I am fast, fast, slap-dash, get-it-done, careless, but—it's done!

My husband Larry is precise, careful, maddening, do-it-right (it'll never get done, I think!).

Our imitations of each other painting the bookcase are relentless, overpolished caricatures, but they clear the air for the actual painting. Instead of killing each other, we laugh.

What's your secret?, many have asked me. What's your clue to a great relationship?

There is a major secret, but I'm afraid I can't claim credit. Larry taught it to me the first time I ever said to him, "that was a really dumb thing to do."

Listen carefully: Don't be a judge.

A good relationship is mutually nonjudgmental. You can't be fearful of each other; if you have to worry about your mate's poor opinion of you, your spirit can dissolve.

Comments like:

• That's the dumbest thing I ever heard.

• You're too fat (or thin or naive . . .).

• You can't understand this.

are never helpful. That's *my* experience, anyway.

Friendships and Lost Friends

I was young, I was engaged to be married, and I was having a bridal shower to which I invited my closest and dearest friends. I knew that I was making memories, and the planning for the shower was *heavy*. In those days, though, when we said heavy we meant fat.

At 10:00 P.M. the night before the phone rang. It was my college roommate Sybil. She loved me and I loved her and we would share everything eternally except, apparently, the next day's bridal shower.

"I met this incredible guy," she told me, fully expecting I'd understand. "And he asked me out for tomorrow. So, I feel awful, but of course I can't come to the party." She didn't.

Funny thing was, I did understand. Guys came first, surely before girlfriends. Anybody would understand that. I understood, but deep inside, I never, ever forgave her. I never got over the sense of betrayal until three years ago when, still friends, we finally discussed it. In retrospect, she was as horrified at the memory as I was.

The women's movement accomplished so much for so many, but one of the things it best accomplished was the understanding that women's friendships with each other were unique relationships. The movement taught us to value such friends, cherish them with respect and wonder, almost above all things. The women's movement taught us never to take each other for granted. It was sisterhood through the eons that helped us to refine and sustain our nurturing, caretaker roles. It was our sisters with whom we whispered, celebrated, mourned, shared, planned, and confirmed our importance, a fact of life that was often lost on men. How could we have gotten through our days and nights without friends?

The trouble was that we knew all that in our heart of hearts, but we still bought into the male joke that girlfriends buzzed on interminably about nothing and mostly spent their togetherness exploring the virtues of clothes, men, and hair. If you didn't have a man with you, you were invisible. This was the era that Lily Tomlin remembers when she tells of the man who approached a woman having cocktails with three women friends. "Hey, baby," he said, "what are you doing here alone?"

This was the era when, even as we empowered each other, built each other's egos and strengths, we undervalued, repressed, failed to mention, failed to notice how truly indispensable we were to each other.

The traditional manner of dealing with women's friendships was to disparage them as inferior to men's relationships, a habit no doubt tied to the more general notion of female inferiority. Ideals of male bonding, such as Dameon and Pythias and Achilles and Patroclus, have been much glorified for their macho love, but when females bond tenderly, it's not power that's lauded. Historically, such friendships have been disparaged or relegated to the limbo of lesbianism. Some years ago, a cache of loving letters between Eleanor Roosevelt and her dear friend were discovered. The letters, written in the manner of the time, employed affectionate nicknames and emotional confidences. Eleanor and her friend were instantly labeled homosexual by an inordinate number of readers who should have known better.

Females were even taught by many of their respected own to devalue friendly relationships; Simone de Beauvoir, for example, maintained that men's friendly communications were on a high level; they spoke of important ideas and projects. Women, on the other hand, were more limited by their natures to exchanges of mostly trivia, confidences, and recipes.

And then came the movement. Hey—we've got something incredible here. We stopped to notice. Men don't have it. We reveal ourselves, we connect—men just swat each other on the back in the locker room. Intimacy was powerful. It transformed us.

Self-congratulations grew. The art of friendship, out of the closet, honed through milleniums, became both anodyne and energizer to our new-age selves.

Lately, the friendship batteries are wearing down. If the marketplace mentality has encouraged us to wear male armor, it is also beginning to erode the deep female knowledge of the goodness of friends. Instead of polishing up our skills as a model for men who often wistfully admit they would love to know what we know, we're letting those skills rust.

Lack of time is only one reason why the power of tender friendships among women lately is being ignored. A sense of competitiveness among some women is another. Yet another is a polarization from each other, because of an insidious and often unconscious devaluation of women who choose to stay home to nurture in lieu of joining the marketplace. It's almost as if we have blocked off our emotions to counter the old way of thinking that had women unable to do—just feel.

Hundreds of women were asked a question in a recent national survey: How do you best deal with stress? The answers were not surprising. Ranking number one, higher than vacations, television, and psychotherapy, was this response: "Talking to a friend or family member." There's no question that women know how valuable intimacy in friendship remains. And yet some recent findings are troubling.

- Dr. Anne Bernstein, psychoanalyst and professor of clinical psychiatry at Columbia University College of Physicians and Surgeons, reports that "many women, particularly never-married women, tend to get caught in a vicious cycle. They so neglect friendships in their zeal to succeed that they finally have nowhere to turn except to work for their gratification."

- The American Management Association says that women at work ranked *lowest* in priority, one-on-one work friendships.

- Nine out of ten women, reports another national survey, have almost no time for friends. "I'm out five nights a week on business," says one. "The other two nights I want to be with my husband and kids."

- In a new study conducted by the Decision Research Company, 600 people with household incomes of $25,000 or more were asked how they spent leisure time. From a choice of eight leisure activities, spending time with friends was third from last (twenty-four percent of the sampling); only playing cards, sewing, and gardening came after friendship. What does that say for the old, companionable ways?

- In a survey taken by Edith Gilson for her book *Unnecessary Choices*, women listed in Dun and Bradstreet's *Million Dollar Directory* were asked about "very important" aspects of their lives. Eighty percent rated "doing the best job I can" as *very important*. They were in the majority. "Being the best I can be" was rated as very important by seventy-seven percent of the women. "Developing close personal friendships" was rated far, far below—only thirteen percent of all women thought that was very important.

- In *Women vs. Women*, author Tara Roth Madden says that "female office friendships interfere with business and interfere with business decorum. Qualities that make fine friendships can directly interfere in the frenetic pace of the work day. Enjoying the warmth of good friends at work is an indulgence women can ill afford when they're deeply engaged in all-out business competition."

I, for one, am tired of books that promise dire trouble if we don't act in the male mode. Friendships are kinships that can direct the way a society behaves. Our present society, the one that neglects child and elder care, the one that has to be browbeaten into accepting the needs of some adults to personally nurture their very young, the very society that had to be shamed into even a semblance of equal rights for women—this society's marketplace is predicated on the male mode of friendship. It hasn't been so great for human rights. Why should women emulate it?

His Kind of Pal

Is there really a difference in the way men and women have traditionally expressed friendship? There surely is. Some experts are pretty glum about male friendships. Daniel J. Levinson, professor of psychology at Yale, suggests in his seminal work, *The Seasons of a Man's Life*, that, with males, "friendship was largely noticeable by its absence. As a tentative generalization we would say that close friendship with a man or woman is rarely experienced by American men. . . . [even though] a man may have a wide social network in which he has amicable, 'friendly' relationships with many men and perhaps a few women. . . . We need to understand," says Levinson, "why friendship is so rare, and what consequences this deprivation has for adult life."

Even researchers who find it uncomfortable to admit to male and female traits, preferring to claim only human traits, see differences in male and female friendships. Men have fewer intimate friendships than women. Letty Cottin Pogrebin, for example, claims that this is not just a stereotype. In her extraordinarily rich book, *Among Friends*, she quotes a ten-year study on male intimacy conducted by Michael McGill, chairman and professor of the Organizational Behavior Department at Southern Methodist University in Dallas, Texas. Men, compared to women, don't value friendship, says Dr. McGill, and they sustain "superficial, even shallow" relationships with far less inclination than women to offer affection, intimate talking, or nurturing.

Donald Bell, author of *Being a Man: The Paradox of Masculinity*, found that most women communicate on three levels—topical (work, politics), relational (the friendship itself), and personal (thoughts and feelings). Men were generally limited to topical. Fascinating to note was the point that many men *perceived* their topical conversations as intimate, saying they were very close, even intimate, with their pals because, didn't they discuss business, sex, *even* salaries?

In an article entitled "Men," Linda Perlin Alperstein, former co-director of clinical training in the Human Sexuality Program at the University of California at San Francisco, says that one can see the obstacles to men becoming loving friends when they spend most of their childhood learning *not* to be feminine—with an almost total omission of tender feelings and acceptance of responsibility toward those who may be weaker emotionally or physically. "One wonders," says Alperstein, "if the difficulty for men to nurture and protect each other is linked to a rejection of weakness."

The real question, says Alperstein, is who should be men's teachers? Is this just one more burden for women to shoulder—teaching men how to employ the tender traits toward each other?

Maybe not, she speculates, and suggests that poet Robert Bly may have the right answers. Men, feels Bly, need initiation into friendship and the rites and rituals of manhood by a community of other men—most notably, their fathers. These fathers, he claims, should take responsible leadership for the good of the community and not for personal aggrandizement, thereby setting a model for goodwill friendship.

The trouble, think many, is that men simply don't know what to do with honest emotion. "We deal with the cosmic questions—what to do with the war in Southeast Asia, is there a God, what's the real difference between Good and Evil," says a husband of a friend, "but when it come to telling the other guy his breath is bad—and maybe that's why he's having trouble getting girls—forget it!"

San Francisco psychologist Stuart Miller interviewed a thousand men to determine the boundaries of male friendship. He finally found "most men clearly admitting they had no real male friends and most of the rest pretending or thinking they did when they did not." Heterosexual men in male relationships are often fraught with worry that they will be thought homosexual, or indeed even *are* a bit homosexual; it is heterosexual man's rabid fear of homosexuality that crimps the lovelight out of many potentially fine friendships. Miller himself explores his own "rosy good feeling" toward a friend, worrying whether or not it bears hidden homosexual yearnings.

No, he answers himself, it does not. "My true problem, rather, is what to do with my *tenderness* toward him," says Miller.

"I sit in my chair and feel what I feel. But I do not caress that tired head. And he probably could use it."

Miller quotes a male friend who helped him to learn the niceties of friendship. Men, says the friend, want to keep the expression of feelings superficial to avoid confrontations. They want to stay rational, protected, and important. In analytic terms, continued the friend who is also a psychiatrist, "They are afraid of the unconscious—the things that are never said, barely thought, shadows that haunt, the jealousies, the yearnings for depth."

Don't Let Anyone Know I'm Nervous

For many American men, it is the competitive nature of their work that both prompts and encourages their friendship patterns. The typical male must be careful not to reveal too much about his secret self—the self that may be acting, he feels, as an imposter. If anyone found out how tentative he felt, how untough, it would spell ruin for his career—or so he thinks.

Because of this deeply inbred insecurity, many men are accustomed to live with isolation and loneliness, which they feel is tolerable as long as success is the result.

Probably, says one expert, Robert R. Bell, sociologist and author of *Worlds of Friendship*, many males in America *want* to become more tender, expressive, and open in their friendships. It has not been lost upon them that the incidence of ulcers, high blood pressure, heart attacks, and other twentieth-century plagues seem to center upon more males than females. To change, though, says Dr. Bell, "means giving up many of the value commitments to notions of traditional masculinity. And it is difficult to give up what has been a fact of your life for so many years."

There really is only one time in the lives of men when they feel free to value intimacy in friendship beyond all other qualities, and that is in the military. Ever notice the way men speak of their foxhole experiences? With reverence. In times of horror and extreme tension, when their lives are on the line, men tend to share their deepest worries, their most intimate expressions of love and other feelings. It's a familiar theme: When men are thrown together in a common danger, the walls they build come tumbling down. They empathize, cooperate, talk about hidden desires—in short, experience friendships that they will not allow in moments of less mortal danger.

When the fighting is over, men remember the wartime years and their foxhole buddies with a poignancy they do not find in civilian life. The ball, as it were, is in the other court. Friendship is women's middle name. Women have always exchanged with friends important information that enables us to deal with men, partners, parents, stress, love, and death—not to mention sex.

But now, with so many changes marking our days and our place in society and the work world, it is inevitable that we take a larger look at the place friendships will have in our lives, already overcrowded with priorities. This one thing most of us know: It doesn't feel good to lose the tender from the power of female connections. Nor do we have to.

In a fascinating new study *Between Women: Love, Envy and Competition in Women's Friendships*, authors Luise Eichenbaum and Susie Orbach, both psychotherapists, say that in friendships most women unconsciously play out unresolved mother-daughter issues that rest in their most subconscious levels. Since girls grow up in a state of "merged attachment" to other women—their mothers, their very identity is rooted in connectedness. As they move normally to degrees of autonomy and separate identities, they often feel little pulls of guilt and even confusion. When these girls are grown up, say the authors, they carry these conflicting feelings into grown-up friendships. Should I be proud of my friend or envious? Are we tied together or individuals? Inevitable questions like these arise from their need to connect *and* their need to separate. Thus, we new women revel in women's groups, disclose our secrets, and help each other to succeed. At the same time, particularly in these work-aggressive times, we also play for high visibility, great prominence, and individuality. Do the two needs war with each other?

The authors think not. They never suggest we fall into the "ready-made masculine ideology" of cutthroat competition. Women have always struggled, successfully they say, to find ways of competing that don't require vanquishing others. Women who are conscious of tenderness can learn to develop their new-age strengths and individuality without losing empathy for the struggle of friends. In fact, the ideal, say the authors, is "separated attachments and connected autonomy"—a complicated way of saying Tender Power, if you ask me.

Friendship and Empathy: No Boundaries

Nancy and her husband are both in their mid-fifties. Married thirty years, they had, she thought, a truly excellent marriage. All in the course of four scant months Sam became progressively moody, progressively despairing. "Is this all there is, is this all there's going to be?" he asked her.

"What's wrong with this?" Nancy remembers saying. "To me it feels great."

But Sam wanted to look for his lost youth, he told Nancy. Stunning her and the children, he took an apartment and just moved out.

Just like that? a friend asked Nancy. Did he discuss it with his friends, do you think?

"He has no friends," she answered. "It was just *our* friends—couples we play tennis with and have dinner with."

But Nancy had friends. And, "you ought to see," she mentioned in a moment of wry observation seized from her monumental grief, "how the women's networking ethic really comes to the fore in times like these. Joyce's husband left five months ago, and she called to commiserate. With all the male put-downs of women's vanity, and so-called weaknesses, with all our dieting, hair-coloring, and face-lifting, neither of us knew of even one woman who opted out of a marriage to search for lost youth—while you heard about men doing just that all the time."

Women, mused Nancy, seem to leave for a better future, perhaps, but don't think much about the possibility of reclaiming the past.

"Sarah called, even though I'd never told her we were having problems," says Nancy. "She'd heard the news at work. It wasn't easy to pick up the phone, but she wanted to comfort me by disclosing her own marital break and subsequent reconciliation."

Calls came in to Nancy from over twenty women. Friends, even those who had been friends from a distance, gathered around her to disclose their own secrets, to nurture her in a time of terrible fear and self-doubt. Empathy flowed like water.

"Catch men making those hard phone calls," said one of the friends. "They'd worry about interfering, being thought nosy, overstepping boundaries."

Sometimes, women's friendships are not on such solid ground. During a marriage, it is traditionally the woman who usually makes a couple's friendships. When marriages break up, often it is *not* the woman who retains their mutual friends. It all depends on the basis for the friendship in the first place.

In an article I recently wrote for *Glamour* magazine, called "Who Gets Custody of the Friends After the Divorce?," experts told me that very subtle circumstances determine the distribution of friends. For instance, Cese MacDonald, a New York psychotherapist, said that many women "unconsciously buy into the myth that their husbands are the better and more powerful half. If the better half is gone, the worse half is left," says MacDonald, "and who in the world wants to stay friends with the worse half?" These women don't feel worthy enough to keep the friends, and, a self-fulfilling prophecy, they usually don't.

Relationships based on business power, says MacDonald, will remain the custody of the person who wields the most business or power—usually, the male.

It is the friendships that are based on the sharing of true feelings, say the experts, rather than on power bases, that tend to stay whole, loving, and available long after a divorce; these usually end up in the custody of the female. It is, after all, women who make the dates, keep the loving connections, write the notes of empathy, and encourage the vulnerability, and they inherit the loyalties.

The New Careless Woman

In trying to be a clone of the male competitive model, what kind of woman is lately forgetting about the good there is in feminine friendship? Your kind of woman, my kind of woman. In short, many of us don't *mean* to devalue intimacy, because intellectually, of course, we are aware of its value. We're not terrible people either. What we are, is careless, and our inattention to our instincts may truly harm us.

So, we juggle our deadlines, and balance our priorities, and our old friends come last on the list—somewhere just before sleep. We make friends at work in new ways, keeping a quite "appropriate" distance, as men do. We don't seem to trust our new colleagues. We don't even try to touch in the old ways—call someone up at home when we know she's having trouble; offer to talk over coffee when someone has red, teary eyes; take over one another's responsibilities, temporarily, when the other has nurturing emergencies at home; offer to stay late to help another meet a late-breaking deadline.

Carolyn Tremont, a financial analyst at a large brokerage firm in Los Angeles, says "Sometimes, I have to pretend my hands are tied to my side—that's how much I feel like 'interfering' or what I think might be perceived as interfering with my colleagues at work. Last month, a woman who occupies the desk next to me came in white-faced, literally trembling. I'd gotten to know her fairly well—we had dinner on several occasions and even slept in the same room once at a conference—but I simply could not bring myself to ask her what was wrong. I mean, I had to say to myself ten times—'mind your own business'—before I was able to mind my own business.

"The crisis seemed to pass," said Carolyn, "and the next day she was in control. Later, I found out that her husband had left her. I was a little ashamed of myself that I didn't do *something* to ease her over that miserable day, but in a way, I felt more professional for staying out of it."

It is so wrong that we begin to equate professionalism with control and insularity. Perhaps, the new trend toward "mind your own business" friendships won't last—that's the best that can be said. Some experts believe this is so.

Dr. Sheila Jackman says, "I don't believe strong women will continue devaluing female friendship behavior—the kind we grew up with. It's more a matter of getting used to our new work roles, and finding ways to fit the old behaviors comfortably in with the new. Both men and women, when they're trying on new behaviors for size, start at zero and race immediately up to ten. We're wearing the whole suit of male clothing now, in terms of relationships. As we begin to understand that we can strike balances, we'll begin to discard the accessories that don't fit, figuratively and literally—look how we've already thrown out the ties and the pinstripes."

In the end, it is women who must become teachers to men, not by polemic but simply by exhibiting the connecting traits that have always nourished women's friendships. If the new woman is too busy, as many lately are, too afraid of giving a competitive edge, by showing vulnerability, too self-protective and wearing male armor, then we are closer to something Alvin Toffler, the famous seer of *Future Shock*, calls Schedule-A-Friend in his new book *The Third Wave*. There are, he says, social consequences of the dual-career couple, and new work/time constraints can intensify loneliness and social isolation. "If friends, lovers, and families all work different hours and new services are not laid in place to help them coordinate their personal schedules, it becomes increasingly difficult for them to arrange face-to-face social contact." Toffler then opines that the traditional friend-making social centers—the pub, the clambake, the church—are losing face in the new rush to achieve in the marketplace. He suggests a not-such-tongue-in-cheek solution: A personalized, computerized service—call it, he suggest, "Per-Sched" or "Friend-Sched"—can be pressed into service to remind you of appointments, schedule friends' schedules, and offer appropriate possibilities for friendship. By pressing a button, you can call up a likely pal to lend an ear, or heart, or even, God forbid, money.

I think, perhaps, there is a middle ground.

New Approaches to Friendship

New York psychoanalyst Anne Bernstein says that "the new woman" has the capacity to blend the traditional, nurturing, and noncompetitive style of friendship with a more time-condensed, somewhat less needy modern approach without losing tender or power. Business friendships will incorporate some of the old-boy, networking strengths, and overall, a self-revealing sense of cooperation that could change the very nature of business. This more balanced style of friendship will be adaptive and more appropriate than strictly male or strictly female approaches. Business friendships do require some modifications, says Dr. Bernstein.

"In our rush to succeed," she says, "empowering of others and caring have slid somewhat down the drain." Some women have had good reason to be careful about trusting business colleagues in the traditional no-holds-barred approach to friendship, because some women have indeed, in the name of competition, undermined others, grabbed undeserved credit, gone behind their sisters' backs. Suspicion of other women was quite common in the workplace for a while.

Is there a simple prescriptive? How do we modify our style, when the need arises, to create more balanced friendships, particularly among working women? It's never simple, but this is what Dr. Bernstein suggests:

- If we are to teach men to be more open with friends in the marketplace, we must also teach women to learn about those male qualities that work well in business—a certain pragmatism, a refined ability to tap into mutual outside interests. Combining pragmatism with intimacy could have an enlightening effect.

- If we are to teach men the good of intimacy, we must teach women not to overdo intimacy—as is sometimes our wont. "Dumping emotional garbage, 'spilling it all' on inappropriate people, is not appreciated in the work arena."

Business, certainly the new competitiveness that has been responsible for women's rise in occupational status, has sometimes caused the model of friendship for many women to change for the worse. Letty Cottin Pogrebin says she sees competition between women as a real "blot" on friendships, as "disfiguring in its way as male competition is to male friendships." In *Among Friends*, she writes:

> The higher we rise in occupational status, the greater our stresses. The greater our stresses, the more we need the support of friends—but the more barriers we erect against revealing any vulnerability that might contradict a strong, confident image. So we're conned into "winning by intimidation" and "looking out for Number One." Cool detachment frees us to shaft the next person.

A hard shell protects us when we are the one being shafted, and social distance keeps us from an elbow in the ribs when a "friend" passes us in the fast track.

It would be a pity to succumb completely to the male model of "keep your distance" when it comes to affiliation in business. Nevertheless, realism dictates that, as Dr. Bernstein suggests, some changes, some accommodations in the totally intimate female model of friendship, may be necessary for balance.

If the nature of friendships at work often requires some modifications to fit the circumstances, personal friendships may also have to change to achieve balance with women's new lives.

As women juggle work, husbands, children, parents, and the proverbial "room of one's own," the nature of their personal relationships can't possibly remain intact. If, however, friendships must change, quality can hold. Pogrebin suggests that one change that may be made in the old-style friendships is the realization that at home, as well as at work, too much intimacy can be too much of a good thing.

"Little girls," she says, "overtrained in the art of affiliation grow up to be 'relationship junkies,' women who need to be needed before they can feel worthwhile or alive." Pogrebin suggests a model of a friend "who gives enough to establish intimacy but does not set herself impossible standards of altruism and devotion to others. . . . there is nothing admirable," says Pogrebin, "about always being there for one's friends, if it makes a woman increasingly absent from herself."

This, then, is the reality.

Time constraints alone require women to modify some of the old-fashioned concepts of friendship, even as we retain their connective qualities. We simply don't have the hours to chat while the soup simmers anymore. It's also true that with our new business interests, we no longer rely exclusively on friends for inspiration and succor. Finally, in the workplace itself, new proprieties demand we cut down on the amount of intimacy we display and the amount of neediness we disclose.

But a new art form is emerging, a unique possibility for friendship. Along with sharing intimacies about successes and failures in the area of men, parents, children, love, death, and sex, many of us now have business in common as well. Where spouses and old pals may be bored witless listening to intimacies about business, our new colleagues are as entranced as we with the subject. Instead of treating our business friendships as bloodless and superficial, we can find new depths of closeness with work peers. We can empower each other, in short, in the new, modern work world as well as in the tried-and-true old ways. Business friends are a new animal, to be stroked and cherished.

The experience of many successful American businesswomen will set an example for their sisters and for men. As author Francine Klagsbrun suggests, "If women bring their skills in sharing and caring to the office, workplace relationships can produce really big business."

"In my husband's office, the closest anyone comes to friendship is discussion of the week's sports scores," says Maria Falala of Phoenix, Arizona. "In my office we have a real women's network, and it operates with what I like to call Quiet Power. Conversation on any given day can revolve around the dental appliances we manufacture, the stock market, the au pair student one of us hired to take care of her child, as well as the best way to get the boss to give us raises. At least twice a week, I come away with something someone told me that's helpful for work. And at least four times a week, I come away with a personal insight. I have little time for friendship outside the office, but it's alright; I don't feel cheated, I have my office pals."

Friendships made through mutual work experiences can enrich days like no others. When one shares both play and work—the positive fallout is of legendary proportions. Before entering the workplace, women were restricted to only one level of friendship. Now, retaining what we know of that, and "mixing it up" with the challenges of work, we attain new complexities of relationship.

A friend who is also a colleague is a double blessing.

The lessons to be learned are these: First, women have a genius for friendship. They should fight, fight until the dying of the light before they weaken it by imitating the masculine model. This doesn't preclude improvements on the feminine model. It is through intense connections that we find sustenance, inspiration, and strength to face new conflicts. It is women's ability to combine power with empowerment of others that defies loneliness.

Second, "real" men ought to rise to the challenge and learn to do it better—this making of friends. Their teachers can be a combination of their analysts and the men and women in their lives. Real men *do* eat quiche, tell secrets, and share failures. Tough men—and women—cry.

Connection

Billions of words have been written about the relationships between parents and children. I only want to write a few more.

Her name is Martha Bridges, she lives in Nashville, Tennessee, and when she was fifty-three her world collapsed. Her husband wanted out—out and away from Martha, their three daughters, and a marriage that seemed happy to everyone but him.

The walls closed in. Martha looked at her recently divorced cousin and saw, she says, "a basket case." She was terrified that she would become one also. She looked at a male-directed work world and despaired of ever entering. She could never compete with the young women who had learned to do things just like those men. She looked at her children, who looked back with questions in their eyes.

One day, Martha remembers, she stood helplessly near the sink in her own kitchen filled with tears and fear, surrounded by her daughters and her own eighty-seven-year-old mother.

The old woman planted her hands on her frail hips and confronted Martha.

"I am of pioneer stock," said the eighty-seven-year-old, "and so are you. You *will* pull yourself together. These girls and I will not let you fall, or fail. We are connected."

The old woman radiated pure power, says Martha. She was the essence of invincibility. And from all that strength poured a healing tenderness, a nourishment, an energy that defied terror.

"She willed me to survive and make a new life. I hadn't any other choice," said Martha. "The connection was too strong."

We are all of pioneer stock, of strength tempered by nurturing.

12

Are You Man Enough
for Tender Power?

Lynne is *off* men, maybe permanently she says. I hate to hear it. How can you be off men, off half the population?

"Simple," says Lynne. "The whole gender stinks. They're not in touch with their feelings, they take advantage of women and have for years, they're infantile, they're secretive, they're selfish, they're terrified of commitment."

You cannot make harsh generalizations about thirty million people, I tell Lynne.

"Okay," she concedes. "How about if I just make generalizations about American men. Or men between thirty and sixty?"

She's not kidding. It makes me crazy with sadness. I can't stand it when women lump all men into neat boxes of macho.

Granted, I've been seeing more and more friends *felled* by their husbands' inexplicable desertions or irresponsible refusals to share the burdens *or* the power, no matter how much they're supposed to have read about the New Man. Granted, I see, we all see, some pretty unfinished humans out there who think they're manly—either meat-and-potatoes manly or that cold, taciturn kind of manly.

But then, I look at my son in his mid-twenties and his friends and I think, they sure are cute, they're pretty whole. Even as they struggle with what sociologist Daniel Levinson calls *the Novice Phase*, which begins around age seventeen and continues till around thirty-three (a young man, says Levinson, needs about fifteen years to come out of adolescence and commit to his place in adult society and make a more stable life), they seem to embrace many of the nurturing, affiliating, tender traits that some of their dads never trusted.

I think there's a great deal of hope precisely because of these young men.

Family Conference

I sit down with my son Adam during his law school vacation, and I talk to him about men and Tender Power. It's *hard* to interview your own son as the New Man when mostly what you see, as you begin to speak, are endless dribblings of basketballs, unacknowledged (to this day) scribblings of crayon on lampshades, and the time he got lost.

But look at a person in a new way, and he becomes a new person. What I want to find out is why he and his crowd, Alan and Mike and Mark and John and Ted and the rest of the guys, beloved friends since childhood, are so nice, caring, and noncompetitive with each other. What I also want to find out is why he and his pals, despite their displayed warmth, still don't seem a whole lot advanced in the intimacy department.

What do you talk about? I ask my son, hoping to finally discover as an interviewer what I couldn't as a mother.

"We talk about our relationships with others," he says. "Why we are frustrated by our teachers or our bosses, why this or that woman doesn't seem to think we're great; if one of us seems to be in trouble, another will mention it—we're not afraid to ask—or tell. But, if you're talking deep confidences, well, I don't really understand what you mean by that."

I am talking about in-depth stuff, I tell him. Really getting down to confessing worst fears. Do you relate them as I do to my friends?

He says no. He understands very well what I'm talking about, what we've always accused him of—this, well, *taciturnity*. This stand-off quality of his and of many of his friends. This keep-your-distance-please stance, as sweet as they are.

"Yes, I guess I do know what you mean," he says slowly. "And I know you want me to say that my generation is very different from the one before, but I'm not sure it's so.

"We just don't have the vocabulary for this intimacy thing. Or, if we have it, we haven't used it. It's like knowing a foreign language, but feeling dumb speaking it, not knowing it to the point of fluency. We sort of dance around the pronunciation."

Adam's conversations with his friends are intellectual banter for the most part, he tells me. Yes, he would like to be able to express deeper parts of himself, he guesses. Maybe when he gets married, it'll happen, although he's not sure.

While Adam isn't sure his ability to be intimate is much different from his father's generation, there are things about my son and his friends that *are* different from the men of my generation:

1. There is almost no competitiveness between friends, even though all are highly motivated. "I believe," says Adam, "that although disagreements on issues are welcome fodder for discussion, topping the other

guy is not. In fact, we all tend to stay on safe middle ground when it comes to who's done what lately. I want to succeed but I see peer competition, at work and in my personal life, as counterproductive. And I tell you, very honestly, if a friend of mine fails at something, I hurt."

2. He cannot conceive of working in an atmosphere that didn't value bonding and cooperation. "No amount of money could have me stay in a place where others are so status-hungry, they'd step on you to get there. If people can't fall into other people's offices to break the work tension, I don't want to be there. I don't want to work anyplace where a sense of humanity doesn't prevail."

3. He and most of his friends are most attracted to strong, productive women. "I've never met anyone, with a raised consciousness, male or female, who intimidated me, and I think most of us thoroughly identify with movements like the women's movement, where people try to free themselves of social and economic shackles."

4. He expects to take full responsibility with his wife (if he has one) in raising and nurturing children (if he has them). "Dad is my absolute role model. I don't necessarily want to lead the same life he's led, but I hope I can conduct my business, my life, my personal attachments as he has conducted his own. He's an absolutely tender person. He did everything you did—and more. He never cared for himself whether I scored the point or aced the exam—only for me. Other fathers never admitted that their kids' scores were a reflection on them, but they did feel that. Dad is so affectionate, always touching one of us. He relates to his family with great emotion as he does to families in the largest sense; for instance, I always knew my dad had great love for the soulfulness and sanctity of Irish literature and the people of Ireland, and it was that that made me want to study and live there for a while. I want to be able to influence my kids in the same nonjudgmental, loving way." Do role models count? "More than anything I can think of," says Adam.

5. Given his excellent education and opportunities to make it big in the workplace, Adam and his cronies value their personal time with friends and family too much to sacrifice, if that's what it takes to make it big in the workplace. "I expect to do well, but I will always resist being enslaved by work. There are human connections in life I won't give up for money or position. I mean that. Money is not the most telling measurement for success. Kids get screwed up with rich and poor parents."

6. The word *masculine* doesn't set off too many signals for Adam. Neither does the word *feminine*. "Those word just don't have a lot of meaning.

My identification is wrapped up in ethical and moral considerations, which have little to do with either gender."

Adam's generation, if he, his friends, and all the students with whom I've spoken are representative, is less fearful of women on women's terms. They have grown up, for the most part, more respectful of bonding, cooperation, caring, nurturing, and the power of women. They should accept, indeed they probably will expect, the application of these traits in their workplaces.

Most of Adam's male peers will be unwilling to sacrifice the sharing of nurturing and the warmth of good marriages for the chair of the chief executive officer. They have seen the turmoil and the tumult in their parents' lives, and they want something different in terms of quantity as well as quality time. They've grown up with working mothers and sisters, and they have heard, until it has come out of their ears, that real men are expected to do their share of nurturing and household responsibilities. Most of these young men are enthusiastic about sharing the nurturing part, although they're frank to say they're not so sure about the dusting and waxing. Still, I suspect they won't put up quite the battle their dads waged, on even this.

The majority of Adam's friends will marry: Although they will marry later than their parents, the specter of AIDS and loneliness will probably spur a return to the marriage patterns of the early part of the century.

If the young men of the late-eighties understand far more about being equal partners, sharing love, tenderness, empathy, and nurturing, one traditional dichotomy of the sexes in history holds; females still experience a much stronger capacity for intimacy; and for males, a sense of separateness still prevails. Is it because males are afraid of entrapment, wary of a loss of individuality, as Carol Gilligan suggests?

I ask Adam.

"Oh *Ma*," he says with irritation.

The Threat

The generation just coming up gives hope that many men will come to understand just *how* powerful is tenderness. The generation just behind gives even greater hope. Some men are learning to rework their relationships so they include the empowering, caring, reaching-out traits. This is not an easy thing to do. Men who care to change are national heroes.

Peter is the husband of Diana Harris, a participant in the focus group of Chapter 2. She began to talk about him when Kathy, the young cerebral palsied woman, said, "When is it my turn? When do I get to be taken care of?"

"I empathize with what Kathy says," Diana had quietly noted. "I always had that same feeling with Peter. It was not even acceptable for me to get sick. So, I never got sick. In the pit of my stomach, I worried that someday, I'd need him to take care of me—and then where would I be?

"Even worse," she continued, "when I went back to school, there was another big problem and it was mine. I had identified myself as the Taker-Carer of everyone. Frankly, it was very hard for me to give up that role, that control. The day finally came that I heard myself say loudly, 'I don't care if dinner's on the table or not; there's food in the refrigerator— you figure it out!' All of a sudden it was amazing to see how a husband and three kids started taking care of themselves. Up until that point, I'd been saying 'do it—do it,' but deep inside I felt it was really my job, so no one did a blessed thing. When my own head changed, everyone else was able to change. I had to take a solid stand; same thing with my marriage."

At this point in the focus group Lois said to Diana, "People can change, but we have to communicate our wishes to them."

"It was more than communication," answered Diana. "I had to threaten."

She wasn't kidding. Married for twenty-five years, she was prepared to leave the man she had loved almost all her life for yet another reason. Beyond making his own dinner, there was a deeper problem.

Since she had met him, Peter had been a strong, cheerful, companionable man. He had never, however, been able to share his thoughts, dreams, and fears. It was not his way, and Diana had accepted it. Theirs had been a marriage of great love, but little intimacy. If business was scary, Peter didn't talk. If he worried about death and dying at middle age, he wasn't talking, even though Diana suspected it was very much on his mind.

When their son was eleven, Peter renounced kissing kids. It wasn't manly, he thought, and so he began to shake hands instead of hugging and kissing. It would give the boys a sense of masculinity, he thought.

"That was almost the saddest thing I ever saw," remembers Diana. "A father shaking the hand of his eleven-year-old. My heart hurt for all of us."

Time went on. The women's movement raised consciousnesses. Diana began to know she was right. Disclosure, vulnerability, sensitivity—these were good things. She tried to convince Peter, but he was having none of it. Old lessons died hard.

So, the veiled threat. Diana implied she would leave if Peter didn't share in family counseling with her and their children. Their friends, for the most part, secretly thought she had no hope of reconstituting the psyche of a fifty-year-old man. She was stubborn. It was their only hope. Peter knew she was dead serious.

He tried therapy and hated it, just as he knew he would. The process was anathema to his carefully constructed walls.

But Diana was rock-hard adamant.

Peter knew Diana's threat was real. "I recognized that most clearly," Peter says. "You have an investment of twenty-five years of your life in one person—you know when they're bluffing. There is no doubt in my mind that there would have been a split, and probably a divorce if I didn't make an attempt at this unpleasant thing she was so insistent I try."

So he tried.

"It was seven years of torture, the therapy," Peter remembers. "Look, you go to a restaurant and you pay a lot of money, but you go back because you like the place, you felt good there. With therapy, we're talking about paying thousands of dollars, great deprivations of time, terrible pain while you're there. You go out of your way to go into this room, get beat up, pay the guy for beating you up, leave and come back two days later and do the same thing. Seven years! Maybe ten percent of your life."

When Peter started therapy, he owned a house, a car, a boat, a very angry wife, and kids he held at arm's length. When he completed therapy, he had retrieved his children, his wife, and his life. Therapy, he says, taught him how to *tell* about things that hurt. It taught him to share and to connect. It taught him that niceness and generosity weren't enough to give a family. You had to give deep parts of yourself, as well.

Peter Harris was four when his father, an overweight, fun-loving man of forty-four, died. Peter, tending toward the poundage as well, always secretly feared a similar early death. Raised by his elder brother and his wife, Peter thrived in an atmosphere of love, but learned to keep his counsel. In the army at twenty-two, he was taught that keeping secrets was commendable behavior; he was the one most often given top-secret clearance on many projects, because the army soon learned that he understood the seriousness of keeping his mouth shut.

So, he kept his mouth shut, even long after the army.

Peter was a good provider. That was, he thought, a husband's job. For many years in the family furniture business, he eventually split from that safety net and went out on his own.

"Some years were good, some not so good. Occasionally, sure I was scared, but I kept it to myself. It was not a husband's job to burden his wife with insecurities. Men were strong and sure," recalls Harris.

"Men didn't hug their sons. I associated that type of touching with homosexuality. I wanted my boys to be strong, manly, and tough. I kissed my daughter, but felt quite constrained from kissing her brothers," says Peter.

He placed a heavy burden on himself. No wonder, hardly a day passed when Peter didn't rely on a few drinks for relaxation. That was another thing. Peter never got drunk. Still, Diana sensed he used alcohol as a crutch of avoidance. She felt it was one more thing that came between their communication.

The therapist agreed; rest assured, that did not further endear the therapist to his prospective patient. Peter had to stop drinking completely—

or else he would not be accepted as a candidate for therapy. If Peter was tough, the doctor was his match.

And so, the long battle began. Initially Peter thought it would be a little bit like "asking this man to give me a prescription which I could bring to a pharmacist, take home, swallow with water—and I'd be finished with it. But, instead, the process was murder. I stuck with it, though, because I felt I'd lose not only my marriage, but my kids, and I really couldn't afford to let all that slip down the drain; I didn't have enough time left to make another family as good as the one I had. So I went through the strangest seven years of my life—but what I've gained!"

What *has* he gained?

"This thing you women have, this telling, sharing, connecting. It's worth everything," he smiles. "Communication in our family had become a convoluted animal. The whole family, not just me, was full of secrets we were dying to share, but couldn't. I would have a secret with one child but not with another. I could talk to Diana about some subjects, but she wasn't privy to my thoughts on others. Walls, walls, walls. It took me years before I tore down even one tiny one. It took so long. That was the most frustrating thing.

"Today—? I'm closer to my wife than I have ever been at any other time in our entire lives. Do we disagree? You bet. Do we have some parts of our lives that are still somewhat private? You bet. But, we talk, talk, talk, talk. I used to avoid all confrontations. Today, I'm still not in love with anger, but I'm not terrified of expressing it. I don't run from intimacy. I listen, she listens, the whole family talks.

"My business has never been better. I've never made more money in my entire life. Do I attribute it to my personal catharsis? I do, in great part."

Recently, I attended the wedding of Peter's older son. When his younger son stood at the dais to toast his brother, Peter, moved beyond words, went up and in view of hundreds of friends and relatives, held and kissed his two sons with joyful and tearful love.

"That's another thing," says Peter. "I'm no longer afraid to express sadness as well as happiness. It is such a relief. My good friend recently died. I was shaken with grief but held myself together at the funeral, as was my habit. A few days after the service, I had to make a telephone call to his son from a public booth on Madison Avenue in the middle of New York City. I came away from the telephone sobbing, tears streaming down my face and *I was not one bit ashamed*—I'd never done that before in my life."

Peter Harris has discovered the power of tender. His relationship with his family, his sense of self-worth, even his business productivity has increased a millionfold. He is able to disclose emotion as well as his dreams, his fears, his hopes. He is able to bond deeply. He shares. He is a new man. He did it. He really did. He *changed*. They said it couldn't be done. But Peter B. Harris was man enough, at last, for Tender Power.

Man Enough to Cook Quiche

Ken Brett of Woodstock says "Real men can change diapers, and real men can not only eat quiche, but they can cook quiche also."

He is part of a new generation of dads who take time off from work to nurture their children. Although no one would suggest that his way is the only way, certainly his daughter Rebecca would vote for Daddy's time off, as would Brett's wife, who wished to return to work after Rebecca's birth.

The jokes, in the beginning, were as stereotyped as the attitudes from others that belittled Brett's choice. "I think a lot of people assumed that because I'm a man, I'd be kind of helpless with this baby," says Brett. "All those 'Mr. Mom' jokes; all I could do was to respond by saying it was really a lot of fun, but the nursing was kind of hard."

The jokes are becoming boring and redundant, especially for fathers who take their nurturing skills seriously. Jim Levine, a director of "The Fatherhood Project" at New York's Bank Street College of Education, says "It's becoming an increasingly tired joke."

This is not about revolution, but evolution, says Levine. Evolution takes time as does any change in fundamental behavior. The result will be a closeness in family never before seen in American society, and the children of these new men will find it utterly natural to nurture their own young, in turn.

Levine feels that women can take the credit for getting men to take a bigger part in the baby business. "The more women do out of the home, the more men are doing within the home."

In the final analysis, men who are man enough for Tender Power will change their mind sets about the fathering role. Day-to-day nurturing will provide enduring closeness and pleasure. "The key issue is not just who does the diapering," says Levine. "It's not who carries the baby in the frontpack or the backpack. It's who carries the baby in their heart and in their mind, day to day, minute by minute. It's who does the worrying; what the kid's schedule is with the pediatrician; who knows what cereal he or she likes; who knows when new socks have to be bought; who is attentive to the fact that Johnny or Susie is having a hard time because they've just been rejected by their friend Jennifer or Brian. . . . it's those little things. It's not just the mechanics of getting the kids clothed and fed, it's all the stuff in between."

Steal This Technique

Those who are in earnest about developing a new kind of power that is based on tender may like to explore new therapy approaches that aim toward developing neglected aspects of human identity. These formal and informal therapies (usually short term) concentrate on increasing flexibility in thinking, feeling, and acting. Among many approaches, one method gaining popularity is Neuro-Linguistic Programming (NLP). Says David Fitelson, a psychotherapist and associate director of the New York Training Institute for NLP, the technique actually teaches one to "steal behaviors." Theoretically, says Dr. Fitelson, a man who wishes to learn how to be more nurturing, more self-disclosing, can find a "good example" mentor and observe him for the purpose of checking out his behavior, stealing it and incorporating it in his own repertory. The good part about NLP, says Dr. Fitelson, is that people are never left feeling defenseless. If a man feels that by "expressing certain feelings or sharing certain secrets it will reduce his viability as a macho-mover, we won't push him into expression until we can offer him another technique for protection that will do him at least as good as his old nonexpression."

Dr. Fitelson calls this approach a concern for "personal ecology."

Daniel Levinson, in *The Seasons of a Man's Life*, also suggests that:

"When the work world is hypermasculine—when women are absent or highly subordinated, and many qualities in men are devaluated as 'feminine'—a man will find it harder to integrate the Masculine/Feminine polarity. The freer participation of women in the work world is an important step toward the liberation of men from their one-sided masculinity and their anxiety about the feminine. Men need women as colleagues, bosses, and mentors. These relationships enable them to form richer identities, to live out more aspects of the self, and to reduce the burdens created by the excessive masculinization of work."

It's a fine idea to seek out strong, tender women friends and mentors, either alone or with your significant other, to develop a new way of looking at women. If you are in a hiring position, consciously attempt to include women in your workplace who seem to speak in authentic voices. Remember: Power does not preclude kindness, compassion, and caring. Power does not preclude empowering.

Share the Wealth—Share the Taxation

The development of male Tender Power is not purely a male responsibility. Women must share some of the problems, pitfalls, and pratfalls as men learn new behaviors, just as men must begin to consider multiple roles as women gain the marketplace. If we are to share the wealth of reconstituted male psyches, we must also plan to share some of the taxing hard work of getting there.

The realities of the situations were different. We gave plenty of lip service to wanting our men tender, but at the first sign of their doubts, inexplicably many of us began to panic. It was one thing to call for poetic sensitivity, quite another to have them scare us to death with their fear. The double messages we sometimes fed our husbands and lovers annihilated each other.

Also, we got pretty picky and therefore somewhat intransigent.

Our more vocal leaders told us never to put up with brutishness—and they were right. Some of us, though, developed positively Olympian standards and had little patience for even normal falls from grace. Men who displayed callousness even for a second were on their way out the door before they could reconsider.

Divorce rates soared. Although this surely wasn't all our fault, too many of us refused commitment to anyone less than spiritually, humanistically, poetically, nurturingly perfect—and dreamy cute, besides. Middle grounds were unacceptable. Men would have to get their act together completely—or forget the whole thing. We'd buy, or even write books called *Love for One*.

As we searched for these perfect men with machismo and tenderness, those biological clocks out-ticked the Fax machines, tick, tick, tick.

Today, we seem to be at a crossroads. Without giving up one smidgeon of power, we need to be reasonable about adjusting some unreasonable demands of men (like asking them to show doubts, then fleeing in terror when they do), and we also need to help them locate, then learn to value, the caring traits in themselves.

Rita Freedman, author of *Beauty Bound* and *Bodylove* is a clinical psychologist who specializes in behavior. She has some stellar ideas on how to do it. There are two ways to react, she says, instrumentally or affectively.

"Men have always been encouraged to act as instruments," says Dr. Freedman, "almost as pieces of machinery. What does a machine do? It conquers, plows through, gets things done, knocks things over.

"But," she continues, "it is as potentially valuable for men to display emotion, like tenderness, as it is for women. Human traits displayed humanize us further. They indicate that we're people who can interact with the world, not only instrumentally, but also emotionally or *affectively*. Affective actions are the other side of the coin from instrument actions," says Dr. Freedman. "When we react affectively, with emotion, we bond, we cooperate, we share and display intimacy. We don't plow through."

Men tend to concentrate on instrumental rather than affective methods of sustaining relationships. It's harder for men to display emotion because they haven't been rewarded for doing so in the past.

On the contrary, when, as children, they tried to display qualities of nurture and caring, they were probably excoriated and called sissies. Further, it is difficult for men to display tenderness and think of it as power to gird relationships because they have had few tender male role models to emulate, says Dr. Freedman.

One way, she says, for society to help men achieve Tender Power is not to reward them so heavily for instrumental powers and to reward them more heavily for emotional traits. If we were able to pay more financial attention to men who opt for cooperation instead of competition, it would provide strong messages of the worth of tenderness.

Women, however, can't wait for the big changes, the society transformation. In small, everyday ways, they can encourage tenderness in their men, says Freedman.

"Instead of asking them to open jars, shovel walks, and drive the cars in which we ride, perhaps we can tell them that we desperately need them more for other things—like staying up at night with us when a kid gets sick. We might also encourage men to develop personal interests outside of money-making activities," notes Dr. Freedman. "This develops the person inside the person. Another approach is to relieve a mate of some of the instrumental responsibilities, which is *exactly* what a working woman does; she takes away the necessity for earning quite so much by giving him the freedom and time to cultivate other parts of his life.

"The best thing you can do," says Dr. Freedman, not entirely in jest, "is to put Mr. Rogers into your husbands' lives as well as into the lives of your sons. We need sweet and gentle role models for our men. We need shy role models, quiet role models, maybe even timid role models. All of these qualities can mesh with and humanize power."

In short, says Dr. Freedman, women have got to put their actions where their mouths are. It's not enough just to laud empathic men. If we hope to convince men that power is in part tender, we have to start "marrying such men, in greater numbers, rather than their macho-but-rich counterparts; we have to start asking our daughters as they return from dates, not 'what does he do?' but 'is he a kind, caring person?' "

The importance of this last point is dramatically underscored by recent polls that indicate that, even among the youngest females eighteen to twenty-five, about half feel that a man's ability to generate income is as important to them as it was to their mothers. This is quite surprising, because one might expect young, liberated women to say it's less important, now that the woman may likely be a breadwinner as well. Dr. Freedman's suggestion that we reorient our daughters into searching for male humanity as well as male earning power is well taken.

Finally, says Dr. Freedman, it all comes back to balance. Women, in the rush to attain more instrumental power, may themselves have gotten out of balance by shunning the emotional and affective traits. Men, who may never have had balanced behavior because Tender Power was not properly rewarded, have now to learn that it is of precious value.

Feminist leaders like Gloria Steinem, Betty Friedan, and Letty Cottin Pogrebin have long maintained that males stood to gain as much as females by equal power and equal nurture. "You have nothing to lose but your coronaries," says Steinem to males.

Multiple Roles

Along with psychologist Dan Levinson, many of us believe that there are several distinct stages to men's lives. Their childhood, adolescence, and creating-a-career stages, for example, are well defined and markedly different from each other.

But, a woman's life is not so easily staged. From young adulthood on, the boundaries of women's stages are blended and smeared into one another, because there are a profusion of tasks we must attack in unison—not in any reasonable order. Because we are bound in one degree by our biological clocks, these stages and tasks revolve around the clocks—but usually by a self-determined order of importance.

Once women are grown, so many extra responsibilities fall to even those who work full-time that they must forever be involved in balancing acts. In the same year, week, even day, a woman is asked to passionately devote herself to being wife, mother, daughter, housekeeper, and careerist. Depending on where the most energy is needed, she builds one tower, takes down another, builds two more.

This makes for a complex, sometimes harried existence, but not necessarily a terrible one. The only time it gets terrible is if there is no one at all with whom to share.

Dr. David Hellerstein, psychiatrist at Beth Israel Medical Center in New York and assistant professor of psychiatry at the Mount Sinai Medical School, sees the building and dismantling of many towers as "multiple roles." Multiple roles, he says, is the direction of intelligence for modern men. In fact, one of the most significant ways men will learn to combine tender with power is for them to identify, then share, the multiplicity of roles that women have been juggling for decades. Multiple roles, says Dr. Hellerstein, can lead not to unending frustration, but to multiple satisfactions.

Traditionally, says the doctor, society's tyranny dictated that men and women would be limited to one role each. More recently it was decided that while men still had one role—oh, maybe a role and a quarter—women could own at least five, if they were going to be so adamant about joining this work force.

And now? Now, says Dr. Hellerstein, perhaps equitable distribution means sharing the whole shebang, if not equally, at least with tender equity—otherwise known as fairness.

"People who do many things are far more interesting," says Hellerstein, "than people who do just one thing. Just as women have traditionally been told it was impossible to be a wife *and* a career woman, so men have gotten the message that they couldn't be a doctor, perhaps also a writer, and a nurturing, *active* father. It seems to me that those who have solved, through need or desire, the basic problems of combining life-styles and chores have a far richer understanding of life."

Man Enough to Break from the Tribe?

Are you man enough for Tender Power? asks the title of this chapter and I did not choose those words lightly. It takes a great deal of courage to change one's behavior, look for rewards in "all the wrong places," buck the establishment that is firmly rooted in macho manners. Opening to tenderness may imply that men have to give up some of the old turf with affectionate good humor, as many did when they saw Gayle Sierens become the first woman ever to occupy a stadium broadcast booth. She gave a play-by-play description of a National Football League game, and some male fans were heard to bitterly complain. "These diehards," noted *Newsweek* magazine, "needed a macho-ectomy."

Daniel Levinson says that as men become more attuned to asking themselves "how do I feel about my life and my behavior and how shall I live in the future?"; as they become more individual and more in touch with their own feelings; a process of "detribalization" sets in. A man trying to partially separate from the mores of the business or social tribe to which he's always belonged becomes, says Levinson, more critical of the institutions and traditions that in the past held the greatest meanings and satisfactions. "Having less need to idealize certain individuals and groups, he is less inclined to condemn others," says Dr. Levinson.

He may indeed begin to cherish warmth and affiliation instead of disparaging it; he may indeed begin to reorder his priorities, keeping relationships and family in the forefront, where in the past they were relegated to somewhere after the promotion to CEO.

This "new man," putting the business tribe in an appropriate place to allow time for family and other intimate connections, moves along on a more horizontal plane, rather than on a stepladder to corporate heaven— but, he gets there.

Maury Nardell is a case in point: In a training program for executives he was "man enough" to turn down a promotion that meant working weekends and traveling heavily. He doesn't lack ambition, says D. Quinn Mills, teacher at the Harvard Business School and author of *The New Competitors*, but may be "defining another kind of ambition to advance in the company but also to balance other responsibilities."

And pleasures. Don't forget pleasures. Men who opt for people-connection seem to enjoy their lives substantially more than those on a crash track to the top. One recent Yankelovich survey indicated that the men with people priorities may be multiplying: A growing number of them seem to be refusing corporate transfers in favor of more time with families. The pleasures of home seem to be competing for the first time, among men, with the pleasures of the workplace.

Market researcher Judith Langer also has identified a new attitude among people in their thirties and forties that she calls "backing off workaholism."

Some ambitious men, she says, are opting for less demanding jobs and flexible work schedules in order to have more time for pursuits that value warmth and commitment.

A Kick in the Pants

Dr. Willard Gaylin, psychiatrist and president of the Institute of Society, Ethics, and the Life Sciences at Hastings-on-Hudson, New York, says "Let me tell you how hard it is for a man, when he's not yet reached the top, to operate with Tender Power—and why it's essential that he keep trying.

"Take three people who apply for a job in a major law firm. The first, a man, says he's first in his class at Harvard, is not married, has little social life, and is prepared to work eighty hours a week.

"The second, a woman, says she's first in her class at Columbia. She has a husband and kids who, she says, are an important part of her life, so she can't give eighty hours, but she would give her incredibly best work for the hours she does put in.

"The third, a man, says he's first in his class at Stanford, feels a strong attachment to his wife and family, and wouldn't want to put in eighty hours—but, like the woman applicant before, would give his stellar best,

"Do you know what would happen?" asks Gaylin. "Number one would get the job. Number two would get the job, because the firm has to hire a certain amount of women. Number three would get a kick in the pants.

"Freud said," smiles Gaylin, "that work and love are the basis of life. It is terrible to be disempowered in work, but to be unfamiliar with the most fundamental thing in life—attachment to others—is equally as terrible. Men truly have to be manly to insist on tenderness in life."

If You Are Man Enough to Claim Tender Power, Remind Her That She Wanted It

Women mustn't forget. We are quite capable of asking for warmth and disclosure, and then running a mile when we sense doubt in our men. Warren Farrell, author of *Why Men Are the Way They Are*, says "When and if men ever get in touch with their feelings on a mass level, they will be venting anger and hurt . . . at women who go for heroes while saying they want vulnerability. They will be asking, 'Why are women threatened by unsuccessful men?' "

Women must take care not to forget that intimacy, in part, is expressing neediness; we must get past the societal brainwashing that has taught us that neediness is somewhat suspect, somewhat unmanly. Thus, it is not only appropriate, it is necessary for men to remind us of inconsistency when we claim we value feelings and disclosure but act as if we value security more.

Fear of Tender

We've said in these pages that men need role models who display tenderness in the corporate life. Find a guy who is respected for his tough decisions and his productivity, watch him display caring, cooperation, and emotion in his work—and whammo—tender is in.

John B. Evans is that man.

President of Murdoch Magazines, a division of Rupert Murdoch's vast communications empire, Evans, before this corporate position, previously served as publisher of *The Village Voice*, the angry, idol-smashing, iconoclastic newspaper of Manhattan's Greenwich Village.

I first heard Evans speak at a heavy-duty women's business seminar. He was addressing the American Woman's Economic Development Corporation and, when I listened to his thoughts on managing with compassion and love, I knew I had to interview him for *Tender Power*. Welsh-born, British raised, Evans is a wry observer of contemporary life.

Most men, says Evans, are not particularly giving or empowering in business situations because the "Citizen Kane" tough-guy image prevails in America. "Most men are fearful about what effect an appearance of being compassionate will have on their reputations. Fear transforms. Fear throws tenderness out of the office," he says.

If men feel fearful of showing tenderness, what does this attitude do to a woman bent on success in a male-run corporation? If she chooses to employ traditionally humanistic values, she's punished because she "thinks like a woman," and that translates into weak or frivolous thinking. If she ignores the tender side of herself, both sexes call her cold. If she tries to respond in a basically androgynous fashion, free of gender differences, she's got to fail, because who can deny gender?

No one, says John Evans. "Even though it's a controversial issue, I absolutely believe in some gender difference, although both men and women do have aggressive and nurturing aspects. Many women in business today are the commandos of the women's movement who have had to charge in and slash their way to power. We can't blame them, but denying their gender and copying their male counterparts creates the same results men evoke when they deny the nurturing part of themselves; they operate on only fifty percent of capacity.

"Men can easily be divided in half," explains Evans. "One half houses Aggression, Assertiveness, the Old-Boy Network, and Madison Avenue. The other half houses Painting Pictures on the Weekend, Writing Poetry, Being Reasonably Kind to Children and Animals, Helping Others, Weeping in the Movies. Women, like men, have two sides as well. When they're being corporate executives, only one side, fifty percent of their personalities, the tough side, is at work."

If both men and women are aggressive and sensitive, where are the differences in gender?

"I would suspect it's even harder for women than for men to vanquish the more sensitive side," he answers. "Throughout history, they've been steeped in the expression of compassion. In broad and sweeping terms, women are also longer-sighted, more immediate, more reactive to danger signals. When dinosaurs came to the cave, men defended the cave and women defended the children. I think we're learning now that that kind of history, over millions of years, builds a genetic case for women being more protective and nurturant of children and one for men being more aggressive. If you can add nurturing and teaching to aggression skills— think what a great coup for management that would be. Economically, it is a sound investment for business to encourage men and women to tap as many facets of their personalities as possible."

Many middle managers would take issue with Evans. One executive with American Express in Nashville, Tennessee, says she hesitates to deal in obvious gestures of compassion for fear she'll be misunderstood. "If I reach out to touch someone to show I understand, I'll be less popular with other executives who prefer a show of solitary strength in management. If I admit to doubt, people could easily misunderstand and take that for weakness."

Evans reacts strongly to this statement. Being misunderstood is not the end of the world, he says. Neither is being unpopular. "Management often has to forego Popularity and settle for Respect," he says. "For example, it's not exactly a popular image to be a football hero in tears. I remember Staubach, the quarterback for the Dallas Cowboys, he was so red, white, and blue, unbelievable, so All-American, rough and tumble. When he retired Staubach made this speech—and utterly lost it in front of all those two hundred-pound boys. He was weeping, gulping for air, absolutely speechless for thirty seconds, and then he said, 'I wasn't going to do this.'"

The issue of tears is a very controversial one. Macho management tends to feel that tears diminish authority. Tender Power management tends to feel that an occasional show of tears is a human response.

Evans, agreeing, says that if it's appropriate to show emotion, it will be accepted. "I myself have become completely unraveled on several occasions, notably farewell speeches to people who move on. Compassion and expressing emotion in business is important for men to learn and for women to keep. Maybe it inspires fear of failure, but people have to learn to live with fear. People who are fearless are very dangerous."

I ask Evans how he supposes both men and women can learn to live so that fear doesn't inhibit tenderness on the job.

"Sometimes it's a question of developing something very close to the spiritual in life—and when I say spiritual, I don't necessarily mean religion," he answers. "To be a rounded and superb business leader, one must be able to reach out, step on an edge, and put a hand out to someone in a corporation who everyone else thinks is a leper. To do that you need inner peace, and to get inner peace, you have to be a bit spiritual."

It is an interesting thought. To display the humanistic values takes bravery, Evans implies. When people are comfortable with themselves, they can afford to act without fear of judgment from jump-on-the-bandwagon types. To act warmly, to display emotion, and to give others some of your own power is humanity in action.

Evans has yet another theory, a parting shot.

"The real reason why men are so freaked out about women entering the workplace with all their compassionate qualities intact is because men instinctively know women are superior beings. I mean that with all the spirit I have! Men have traditionally been marauders, as in prides of lions: They invade the female merely to fertilize them. The building of homes was woman's creation, actually, and men have conned women into believing that male power is an inviolable legacy from history; they want to be like cats, come in and sit by the fire in the house without doing any of the work. What men really fear is that when good and caring women knock down the last bastions into the business world, they'll be out on the street— because women will own the house, the fire, *and* the business!"

Other men in quiet ways, through all their days, are living proof that tender, properly taught, is genderless. George Lusk in White Plains, New York, is such a man.

Hey—I'm Not in the Financing Business!

But, sometimes, it seems as if he is. Compassion and connection become a reality when men, on every level, exhibit it in their business lives, as well as in their personal lives. George Lusk doesn't lead a mammoth corporation, like Murdoch Magazines, but Westmail Press, the printing company of which he's president, is responsible for the livelihoods of the thirty-five or so workers it employs. George is a tall, handsome man in his sixties who serves on his local hospital board, as well as on the local Board of Education. A modest and kind person, he is not given to self-promotion, and indeed, was notably reticent to talk about the way he employs Tender Power at work.

"A business day isn't made up of virtuous cosmic issues, of good and bad," he says. "I believe the making of money is a good goal to set in business and don't for a minute think that altruism is at the bottom of every decision. Still, different people arrive at making money in different ways, and I happen to think that we all do better if I develop friendly relationships with those who work for me."

One of the ways Lusk does this is by putting his money where his mouth is. At any one time, he tells me, the company always seems to have three to four outstanding loans to employees who run into money problems. Lusk's habit is to lend varying sums interest-free, against an employee's paycheck; the worker takes as long as he or she needs to pay an outstanding debt.

"It's terrible to run short," Lusk says, "and if someone is in trouble, how can you *not* respond with empathy and compassion?"

In many small ways, Westmail Press operates as a connective family. If an employee gets an urgent call telling him to come home to take care of a frozen pipe, Lusk lends his own car to deal with the emergency. If business is slow, Lusk avoids layoffs like the plague, offering vacation time to the workers until things pick up. "We'd try part time, but that interferes with a worker's ability to collect unemployment, so, if push comes to shove, we lay off for just a few weeks—and then hire the guy right back, the moment we can."

When it comes to going to bat for his employees, George Lusk has no peer.

Some months ago, a young man applied for work as a labeling machine operator, and Lusk quickly realized he was overqualified for the job. Bringing the young man along, Lusk trained him in a very short time to be "a trusted and reliable employee with vast responsibilities. But, suddenly, he wasn't so reliable," Lusk remembers with a grimace. "We wouldn't see him for days, and then he'd reappear with little explanation. Finally, the morning came when he very skillfully signed my name to a large check and cashed it."

Lusk felt used, betrayed, and angry. Still, talking it over with his partner, another gentle man, they both decided to discuss the issue with the employee, rather than fire or prosecute him. The problem was drugs, the young man confessed; he felt terrible and promised it would not happen again. It didn't—until the next month, when, despite the fact that the office keys had been taken away from him, the employee stole and forged two more checks.

Lusk, horrified, still didn't prosecute.

"This kid was in real trouble. I took him by the hand down to a rehabilitation organization; if he would promise to go through a drug abuse program, and report his progress to me, I'd consider taking him back. I called his dad to discuss the problem with him—it was terrible for the old man. I just felt so sorry for the kid—he had unlimited potential and was throwing it away!"

The story does not have a happy ending. The employee dropped out of the program and out of sight. Lusk, sighing, considers it somewhat of a personal failure.

But, it is not Lusk's failure. It is not he who failed at tender.
"It's no big deal," George Lusk says, impatient at what seems like blowing his own horn. "It's no big deal being human at business. If we're responsive, we expect and usually get a fair return for our efforts from our employees. That's not being saintly—that's good business. Look," says Lusk, "I'm the first one to notice if an employee turns off the presses earlier than he should. But I don't see how anyone can run a profitable concern without looking at employees' problems as his own."

The New Man

In the past, tender was suspect in manliness, except for a rare few influential men in whom caring and compassion surfaced dramatically. Walt Whitman, for instance, described Abraham Lincoln as having the "purest, heartiest tenderness." He and Franklin Delano Roosevelt, whose New Deal reached out to the depressed of spirit and purse, are two examples of compassionate power.

But, what of the new man? It is tricky, but more and more possible to find traces of this guy who is man enough for Tender Power. Although he makes concerted efforts to work caring connection into his business and personal life, the new man is just now beginning to surface publicly. Every now and then one reads a headlined story of a man who, in a small or largely tender way, noticeably influenced the economy or political climate of the country. Politicians, who may not even mean it, are playing homage to the concept of Tender Power, because the shrewdest see that the notion is catching on. The Reverend Jesse Jackson recently was quoted as saying, "You're not a man if you can make a baby; you're only a man if you can *raise* a baby." In Windsor, Connecticut, officials at Bradley International Airport have decided to install diaper-changing tables in men's restrooms. They noted "a lot more men traveling with children."

The new man who is really man enough for Tender Power has become more than a shadowy figure in his own home, appearing for dinner then vanishing into a den. The new man gives more than rare glimpses of his persona to his family and friends. Could we make a composite profile of this new man who reflects increasingly greater "feminine" values?

Anthropologist Barbara Meyerhoff and educator Elinor Lenz think so. In their book *The Feminization of America*, they maintain that the more caring man has changed his life-style in important ways—one of which is the manner of play he chooses. He tends to prefer, they say, tennis, skiing, jogging, and swimming to the traditional basketball game and other team sports of yesteryear. A man who opts for tender generally has liberal leanings and "wholeheartedly supports environmental and anti-war causes," says Meyerhoff and Lenz. He's physically fit, believes in mind-body unity, and takes a "creative interest" in his home and its furnishings, his clothing, his low-cal, low cholesterol meals. Conversations with his male and female friends often center around unusual recipes and new restaurant finds.

Decisions about toilet training, school, and day care are as much on his mind as his wife's, say other experts. Conversations about kids' prowess is no longer confined to women on park benches. In fact, the new more tender man is as comfortable about subjects that focus on their mutual home and kids as he is with subjects that focus on both their business worlds.

The man who is man enough for Tender Power has a deep distrust of political follies (like Watergate) and of the traditionally masculine values that appear to be responsible for such travesties of justice and government. Most political pundits note that male (as well as female) members of the baby boom generation are increasingly uncomfortable with the abyss that separates their new values and their practical life-styles. These political seers suggest that coming elections will favor candidates who go less heavy on military concerns in favor of humanistic values.

The new man takes off the boxing gloves at home and work. Traditionally, he might have lusted for power *over* people, particularly lower ranking people like wives, children, and employees. Today, he knows better and opts for power *to* rather than power over—the power to convince, the power to empower others, the power to connect. A man who sees the power in tender, negotiates instead of rules. This new man values that fine place in himself that encourages cooperation and reason. He's given up on threatening as a poor substitute for examining, because he's found that people run from threats. No one ever runs from empathy—just runs with it.

In sum, the man who is man enough for Tender Power is a keeper.

The Challenge: Dare to Change

Every day another strong woman casts off another macho trait, and her newly liberated feminine muscles ripple with grace, beauty, and power. Every day another strong woman reclaims a forgotten feminine trait: When she meshes these traits with newly achieved economic power, her influence surges, her voice rings sure and true.

One woman reaches out to empower another person and she herself grows.

One woman relies on her intuition as well as the computer, and now, with two powerful tools, soars ahead of the competition.

One woman manager tells a painful secret and revels in the network of colleagues that springs to her support.

One woman decides to cooperate instead of compete with an office rival; the company is stunned by new profits. The two women find out they like each other.

One woman at the helm of a great organization insists that family and relationship count as much as dollars. She puts her money where her mouth is. The great organization becomes greater.

One powerful businesswoman looks closely at another woman who has decided to stay home and raise her children. The powerful businesswoman honors her sister's right to choose. At that moment, the women's movement is at its most potent.

One moxie politician lobbies for people ethics instead of profit ethics. America gets nicer.

One woman and one man vow to really listen to each other, creep into each other's moccasins. Their relationship becomes vital.

One parent teaches a child to connect rather than separate, and the child becomes self-reliant.

One woman senses that there is no place for tenderness in her workplace and chooses to leave and start her own business.

One woman senses that there is no place for tenderness in her workplace and chooses to stick it out, bide her time, and certainly not feel guilty for playing by men's rules—for a while.

One woman bucks the corporate mentality and against all precedent shares, empowers, cooperates, connects, and is emotionally responsive as she does her job. The corporation relaxes. Many follow her lead.

One man, then another man, then thousands of men choose, along with their wives, to help nurture their children, care for their sick and aged, and with such tenderness, strengthen the balance of power between men and women. Thousands of men for the first time feel wholly masculine and wholly human.

Epilogue

Power tends to corrupt. Absolute power corrupts absolutely.

Lord John Acton (1834–1902)

There is only one remedy. Tender power.

"I have trouble with your title," said Cathleen Black, publisher of *USA TODAY*. "I think the word *tender* gives a very mixed message. It's not an attribute for a man or woman in the executive suite. It's well—very *pink*."

Well, then, if tenderness is pink, pink's terrific and pink's powerful.

Novel Prize winner Toni Morrison, the prescient, eloquent writer, in her eulogy of James Baldwin on December 8, 1987, at the Cathedral of St. John the Divine in New York City, said the following: Baldwin gave gifts to his friends, declared Morrison, the first of which was his friendship and art of language, "as it was meant to be: neither bloodless nor bloody, and yet alive."

The second gift Baldwin gave, said Morrison, was his courage that "transformed distances between people into intimacy with the whole world."

The third gift was "hard to fathom," said Morrison, "and even harder to accept. It was your tenderness—yours was a tenderness of vulnerability that asked everything, expected everything, and like the world's own Merlin, provided us with the means to deliver. . . . I suppose that was why I was always a bit better behaved around you, smarter, more capable, wanting to be worth the love you lavished."

Tenderness, pink? Then go for it, Pink! Tender is the human bearer of Power.

Bibliography

Ash, Mary Kay. *Mary Kay*. New York: Harper & Row, 1986.

Ash, Mary Kay. *On People Management*. New York: Warner Books, 1984.

Astrachan, Anthony. *How Men Feel*. New York: Anchor Press/Doubleday, 1986.

Becker, Carol. *The Invisible Drama*. New York: Macmillan, 1987.

Bell, Robert R. *Worlds of Friendship*. Beverly Hills, Calif.: Sage Publications, 1981.

Bern, Paula. *How to Work for a Woman Boss*. New York: Dodd, Mead, 1987.

Blumstein, Philip, and Schwartz, Pepper. *American Couples*. New York: William Morrow, 1983.

Breakwell, Glynis M. *The Quiet Rebel*. New York: Grove Press, 1985.

Caplan, Paula J. *The Myth of Women's Masochism*. New York: E.P. Dutton, 1985.

Casale, Anthony M., with Lerman, Phillip. *USA TODAY: Tracking Tomorrow's Trends*. Kansas City, Mo.: Andrews, McMeel & Parker, 1986.

Chernin, Eve. *Reinventing Eve*. New York: Times Books, 1987.

Chernin, Kim. *The Hungry Self*. New York: Times Books, 1985.

D'Arcy Masius Benton & Bowles, Inc. *Fears and Fantasies of the American Consumer*. New York. May, 1986.

Dimen, Muriel. *Surviving Sexual Contradictions*. New York: Macmillan, 1986.

Dolan, Mary Anne. "When Feminism Failed." *New York Times Magazine*, June 26, 1988.

Eichenbaum, Luise, and Orbach, Susie. *Between Women*. New York: Viking Penguin, 1988.

Eisler, Riane. *The Chalice and the Blade*. San Francisco: Harper & Row, 1987.

Fausto-Sterling, Anne. *Myths of Gender*. New York: Basic Books, 1985.

Friedan, Betty, *The Feminine Mystique*, New York: Dell, 1963.

Friedan, Betty. *The Second Stage*. New York: Summit Books, 1981.

Gilligan, Carol. *In a Different Voice*. Cambridge, Mass.: Harvard University Press, 1982.

Gilson, Edith, with Kane, Susan. *Unnecessary Choices*. New York: William Morrow, 1987.

Gochros, Harvey L., Gochros, Jean S., and Fischer, Joel, eds. *Helping the Sexually Oppressed*. Englewood Cliffs, N.J.: Prentice-Hall, 1986.

Hardesty, Sarah, and Jacobs, Nehama. *Success and Betrayal*. New York: Simon and Schuster, 1986.

Harragan, Betty. *Games Mother Never Taught You*. New York: Rawson, 1977.

Harris, Louis. *Inside America*. New York: Vintage Books/Random House, 1987.

Heilbrun, Carolyn G. *Reinventing Womanhood*. New York: W.W. Norton, 1979.

Hennig, Margaret, and Jardim, Anne. *The Managerial Woman*. New York: Pocket Books, 1976.

Hewlett, Sylvia Ann. *A Lesser Life*. New York: William Morrow, 1986.

Jennings, Diane. *Self-Made Women*. Dallas, Tex.: Taylor, 1987.

Jensen, Marlene. *Women Who Want to Be Boss*. New York: Doubleday, 1987.

Kline, Linda, and Feinstein, Lloyd L. *Career Changing*. Boston: Little, Brown, 1982.

LaRouche, Janice, and Ryan, Regina. *Janice LaRouche's Strategies for Women at Work*. New York: Avon Books, 1984.

Lenz, Elinor, and Myerhoff, Barbara. *The Feminization of America*. Los Angeles: Jeremy P. Tarcher, Inc., 1985.

Levinson, Daniel J. *The Seasons of a Man's Life*. New York: Ballantine Books, 1978.

Madden, Tara Roth. *Women vs. Women*. New York: AMACOM, 1987.

Margulies, Eva. *The Best of Friends, The Worst of Enemies*. New York: Doubleday, 1985.

McBroom, Patricia A. *The Third Sex*. New York: William Morrow, 1986.

McCormack, Mark H. *What They Don't Teach You at Harvard Business School*. New York: Bantam Books, 1984.

Melia, Jinx. *Breaking into the Boardroom*. New York: G.P. Putnam's Sons, 1986.

Miller, Jean Baker. *Towards a New Psychology of Women*. Boston: Beacon Press, 1986.

Mitchell, Juliet. *The Longest Revolution*. New York: Pantheon Books, 1984.

Montagu, Ashley. *The Natural Superiority of Women*. New York: Macmillan, 1974.

Peters, Tom. *Thriving on Chaos*. New York: Alfred A. Knopf, 1988.

Pogrebin, Letty Cottin. *Among Friends*. New York: McGraw-Hill, 1987.

Russell, Cheryl. *100 Predictions for the Baby Boom*. New York: Plenum, 1987.

Scarf, Maggie. *Intimate Partners*. New York: Random House, 1987.

Schneir, Miriam, Ed. *Feminism: The Essential Historical Writings*. New York: Random House, 1972.

Stechert, Kathryn. *On Your Own Terms*. New York: Random House, 1986.

Taylor, Charlotte. *Women and the Business Game*. New York: Times Books, 1985.

Taylor, John. "Nervous About the Nineties." *New York Magazine*, June 20, 1988.

Toffler, Alvin. *The Third Wave*. New York: William Morrow, 1980.

Waterman, Robert H., Jr. *The Renewal Factor*. New York: Bantam Books, 1987.

Woman's Day. 50th Anniversary Issue, October 27, 1987.

Working Woman. 10th Anniversary Issue, November, 1986.

Wyse, Lois. *The Six-Figure Woman*. New York: Fawcett Crest, 1983.